# Lost Lands, Forgotten Stories

ALEXANDRA
PRATT

# Lost Lands, Forgotten Stories

*A Woman's Journey
to the Heart of Labrador*

Harper*Flamingo*Canada

First edition

"Little Gidding" (extract of 4 lines) from *Four
Quartets, Collected Poems 1909–1962* by
T.S. Eliot/"The Whitsun Weddings" (extract of
2 lines) from *Collected Poems* by Philip Larkin.
By permission of Faber and Faber.

"The Listeners" (extract of 4 lines) by Walter de la
Mare. By permission of the Literary Trustees of
Walter de la Mare and their representative, the
Society of Authors.

Photos pp 1–4 of photo insert: Centre for
Newfoundland Studies, Queen Elizabeth II
Library, Memorial University of Newfoundland.
Reprinted with permission of Betty Ellis.

National Library of Canada Cataloguing in
Publication

Pratt, Alexandra
Lost lands, forgotten stories : a woman's journey
to the heart of Labrador / Alexandra Pratt.

ISBN 0-00-225515-4

1. Hubbard, Leonidas, Mrs.—Journeys—
Newfoundland and Labrador—Labrador.
2. Canoes and canoeing—Newfoundland and
Labrador—Labrador. 3. Labrador (Nfld.)—
Discovery and exploration. I. Title.

FC2193.4.P72 2002     917.18'2042'092
C2002-902405-6
F1136.P72 2002

HC 9 8 7 6 5 4 3 2 1

Printed and bound in the United States
Set in Sabon

This book is for all the kind
and generous people of Labrador
who went out of their way to help
me along mine.

*We shall not cease from exploration*
*And the end of all our exploring*
*Will be to arrive where we started*
*And know the place for the first time.*

T.S. Eliot, "Little Gidding" from *Four Quartets*

# Contents

# Prologue

*I am not suffering. The acute pangs of hunger have given way to indifference. I am sleepy. I think death from starvation is not so bad. But let no one suppose that I expect it. I am prepared that is all. I think the boys, with the Lord's help, will be able to save me.*

Leonidas Hubbard's diary, Labrador, 1903

That night, I dreamed of the last camp of Leonidas Hubbard. I dreamed of the small silk tent and its occupant, alone in the centre of a wild and empty landscape. Beyond my hotel window lay that land which had sapped his energy in a skein of unnavigable lakes and rivers, then smudged out the last flickers of life in a drift of snow. Buried in the snug warmth of my bed, I felt the sharp tang of spruce-scented air at the back of my throat and the cool rushing of mountain waters against my cheek, rushing endlessly into the distance. It was a dreamland of beauty and death, where caribou graze and wolves pad silently through the night.

When I awake in a Newfoundland hotel, I feel as if I have lived here forever, but only my belongings, scattered around the bare room, are familiar to me. A magazine lies open on the floor. It's an old *National Geographic* from 1993, and the heavily thumbed pages lie as they slipped from my grasp a few hours before. They tell the story of another woman entranced by the beauty of this place called Labrador, a land that took the life of her young husband almost one hundred years ago. It is her story that has brought me here—a tale of defiance in the face of social convention and a determination to live a dream that was never meant to be hers, but which would come to consume her.

Leonidas Hubbard was a young journalist working for the New York outdoor magazine *Outing*. Recently married, he had a boyish love of adventure that his new responsibilities had not quashed. He had enjoyed the idyll of a rural childhood, spent in the woods fighting imaginary battles and conquering new kingdoms, poring over maps and plotting daring journeys into the perilous unknown. This had given way, in time, to an adult life that had taken him to newspaper offices in Detroit and later New York City, but still allowed for the indulgence of an occasional trip to the edge of the wilderness at Hudson Bay.

As the nineteenth century became the twentieth, a public fever of excitement began to surround expeditions such as those of American Robert E. Peary, who made several pioneering journeys to polar regions during that period. It was a time of expansion, development, and exploration, and perhaps it was this fervour that inspired Leonidas to consider that his own fate may indeed have lain in those great barren wastes of the North. So when he heard of a place that remained one of North America's last truly unexplored areas, he was enthralled. At that time, the Labrador interior was still unmapped and exploring that region would bring not only adventure, but also fortune, as the trip and his written record of it would carry him straight into the history books.

The romance of the idea quickly caught Leonidas' imagination, and before long, he was planning to fulfill his boyhood dreams by embarking on his own expedition to Labrador. He realized, however, that he could not go alone, so it seemed natural to invite his old friend Dillon Wallace, a lawyer from New York City, to accompany him. As they sat beside a campfire one night while tramping in the Shawangunk Mountains of New York state, Leonidas spoke of those plans, his childlike enthusiasm once more rising to the surface: *"Think of it!"* Wallace later records him saying. *"A great unknown land right near home, as wild and primitive today as it always has been!"*

Wild it certainly was. When the sixteenth-century explorer Jacques Cartier stumbled onto Labrador's rough southern shores in 1534, he called it "the land God gave to Cain," referring to the fate of Adam's murderous son in the Bible's Book of Genesis. At the turn of the twentieth century, Labrador remained desolate and inhospitable, largely a pristine wilderness of forests and mountains and, in the North, tundra. It was inhabited by the largest caribou herd in the world and was home to Native peoples who remained largely unknown to Europeans. The winters were cruel and the summers a torture of mosquito swarms and blackflies.

By the time of Leonidas' journey, the extreme coastal and southern parts of the province had, it was true, been charted and settled for over three hundred years. The population consisted mostly of fishermen who flocked to the rich fishing grounds of Newfoundland's Grand Banks in the summer season, with only the most hardy remaining during the long, bitter winters. An ocean inlet called Lake Melville extends westwards across the southern part of Labrador for about a hundred and fifty miles, and this had allowed some settlement deep in the heart of the land. By the mid-eighteenth century, the shores of Lake Melville were home to immigrants from Europe, scraping a hard living from fur trapping and salmon fishing, and subsisting partly on hunting, in the manner of their Native neighbours.

The central and northern parts of Labrador, however, remained largely unexplored by Europeans and no reliable maps existed of its many rivers, valleys, and hills. Once the idea came to him, Leonidas must have regarded it as his destiny to be the adventurer who travelled across the uncharted interior. *"It will be a big thing,"* he told Wallace. *"It ought to make my reputation."*

Despite extensive preparation in New York, it was not until they reached the settlement at the western head of Lake Melville called North West River that Hubbard and Wallace were able to gain any detailed information about the route they planned to follow. This route was to take them across the length of Labrador, to its northernmost shore on Ungava Bay. In their questioning of local people, the two friends learned only that the Naskaupi River, their chosen route up into the interior, could be found over forty miles away at the far end of Grand Lake. Its waters feed into Lake Melville through a set of narrows, on the shores of which North West River is built.

The two men and their Native guide, George Elson, a part Cree man from James Bay, departed North West River on July 15, 1903. When they reached the western end of the lake, however, a sandbank obscured the mouth of the mighty Naskaupi on the northern shore and they mistakenly paddled onwards to the shallow Susan River, which feeds Grand Lake from the northwest. One can only guess at the lack of communication in the settlement that resulted in the three men mistakenly following the Susan River, believing it to be the Naskaupi.

The Susan soon dissolved into a network of small rivers and long portages, yet the men never realized their error and continued in their attempt to reach the interior. The heavy work involved soon sapped their energy, which, in turn, put pressure on their supplies, as they had decided to travel with only the minimum of food, taking what game they could from the country. Labrador was soon to live up to Cartier's pronouncement. When the winter set in, their food ran out, the uncertain game supply failed, and the three men were reduced to boiling moccasins for broth.

The inevitable decision to return to base at North West River was delayed too long. The party did eventually turn around, but only thirty-three miles from the western end of Grand Lake, Hubbard, suffering from the lack of food and harsh conditions, could walk no farther. Wallace, too, was soon unable to continue the struggle, so Elson, the most experienced of the three men, was the only member of the group with the strength to go for help.

For seven days, he travelled on alone through deep snow. Partly snow-blind, he nevertheless managed to shoot partridges with his pistol, and by eating them raw, stayed alive. All their equipment, even the axes and extra clothing, had been left along the trail as the men became weaker. Elson found himself walking on in his socks, often wading waist deep across icy streams. As he recalled later, *"The bush [was] so thick to go through and at last it began to rain. I was soaked to the skin and the snow very deep. My hands were always so cold without mits and travelling in such rough country and falling down often into the snow and rocks, and cutting my hands on the rocks."*

When he finally reached Grand Lake, Elson was still forty miles from North West River, and he discovered several sizeable rivers cutting across the lake's southern shoreline. All were too wide and cold to swim, so he built a series of rafts and propelled himself along using a pole, dodging chunks of newly formed ice. It was to be his lowest moment, as he recorded later in his diary: *"My raft was breaking up. Piece of piece would float away. So I got down my knees and tried to keep the pieces together and the sea would just cover me. For about two hours I stayed on the raft and sure it was my finish."*

Luckily, long before he reached North West River, Elson came across a remote cabin belonging to a fur trapper called Donald Blake and his family. Despite his poor condition, Elson was still carrying a pound of flour and six partridges he'd shot along the way. The next day, Blake and three friends, Allan Goudy, Gilbert Blake, and Duncan McLean, set off in a canoe to retrace Elson's route. It was not long before they found Wallace half frozen in the snow. He was suffering from snow blindness, frostbite, and exposure, but he was still alive. Hubbard was found wrapped in blankets next to his diary inside a tent. He was dead.

In June 1905, Mina Hubbard set off from North West River as her husband had done two years previously. Just two months later she'd completed the journey northwest up the Naskaupi River to its source at the height of land, across Lake Michikamau, and north down the George River to Ungava Bay by canoe—a distance of 576 miles. She was accompanied by, among others, George Elson, Leonidas' former guide. He was to become a dear friend, and many regarded him as being largely responsible for the success of her expedition.

Dillon Wallace also attempted the route again and this time he, too, succeeded. Unbelievably, he departed North West River on the same day as Mina, but he arrived in Ungava Bay sixty days after her. When both ended up at the trading post on Ungava Bay, the atmosphere between Mina's party and Dillon's was so bad that he chose to return by dogsled across the winter snows, rather than enjoying the relative comforts of the supply boat *Pelican*, in the company of his archrival.

There is no record of anyone having travelled this entire route, the cause of so much hope, despair, faith, and jealousy, since 1905.

# Part 1

## WHISPERS

# CHAPTER 1

I was twenty-three when, in 1997, I read the story of Leonidas' death and his wife's valiant journey in that old copy of *National Geographic*. I, too, became seduced by the dream of that wild yet beautiful land and now, two years later, their stories continue to haunt me. Yet it is Mina's strangely less famous tale that alone has the power to draw me across the Atlantic from my home in England's West Country to a cold basement archive at Memorial University, Newfoundland.

I take a deep breath and open the door, unannounced.

"You must be the lady from England. We've been expecting you." The archivist springs out of her seat and beams at me. It seems the local grapevine has been working overtime.

Minutes later, I am holding something I can barely believe exists: Mina's diary. It was rescued from an attic trunk in Scarborough, England, and brought to the university in Newfoundland only a few years ago. It had proved extremely difficult to find a copy of Mina's book *A Woman's Way Through Unknown Labrador* in England, and I had no idea her original diary was here in Newfoundland. The harsh fluorescent glare makes the faint pencil copperplate difficult to read, but suddenly Mina is in the room with me: *"Today,"* she wrote, *"I feel something of what I think must be an approach to the right thrill as we come up to the hilltops and prepare to leave our river to cross Seal Lake. Before the situation has not seemed extraordinary. Now I begin to feel just a little like an explorer."*

I can barely believe my luck as the archivist returns again with a small package, wrapped in tissue. Trembling, I unravel the paper, and into my palm falls Mina's pocket compass and a locket, small and slightly rusted. I turn them over, trying to glean some sense of Mina and the wilderness from their smooth, cold surfaces. Has anyone used this compass since she tucked it safely away in her pouch on that last triumphant day in 1905?

A pile of photographs distracts me and there, staring back at me, is the young Mina Benson, a Victorian child with wide eyes, standing between a stern father and sister whose image is slightly cracked. Mina was the sixth of eight children born of Irish immigrant parents, all of whom were raised on a farm near Bewdley, Ontario. We know very little about this young Mina. Did she revel in her pastoral playground of well-tended farmland and kindly woods as Leonidas had in Michigan? Did she, too, fish the rivers and climb the trees of this new world into which she had been born?

Despite their new Canadian status, the Benson family was not poor, and whatever adventures her childhood had held, Mina was educated well enough to become a teacher, working throughout her twenties in her hometown. This settling of her fate so early in life obviously failed to satisfy her, because at the point when many parents of the period would expect a good daughter to be marrying and raising a family of her own, Mina instead left her Ontario home and travelled south to New York to train as a nurse.

I pick up another photograph and see a much different Mina's, starched and proper in her nurse's uniform. Her gaze is slightly nervous, perhaps anticipating the extraordinary life to come, as it was this decision to go to the United States that ultimately led to Mina's paddling her way into the pages of Canadian history and the pantheon of great pre-war women explorers.

Her first position was as nurse to Leonidas Hubbard, who was recovering from typhoid fever. The pair married soon afterward, in

1901. It was to be a short, but happy union. They stayed in Congers, New York, while Leonidas pursued both his writing career and his love of the outdoors. In the preface to the book about her expedition, Mina wrote a great deal about the fine, noble man her husband was and about his passion for adventure, felt at such a young age. It is clear that this was a passion the couple had shared, so when the opportunity arrived (in the form of an inheritance), Mina, it seems, was as enthusiastic as Leonidas about using the money to fund an expedition to Labrador.

They sailed to Newfoundland together, accompanied by Dillon Wallace and George Elson, who had travelled to New York City to meet his employers. Then, as now, the ferry from Newfoundland to Labrador stopped at the numerous small fishing settlements that cling to the rocks, stoically facing the Atlantic. It was at one of these, known as Battle Harbour, that Mina said goodbye to her husband for the last time, a moment they would both come to think of often in the days that lay ahead. Mina stayed in a small wooden house on the shore of Labrador for a few days, waiting for the ferry to arrive on its return journey to Newfoundland, perhaps bringing news of Leonidas' departure from North West River.

The news, when it did arrive two months later in New York, was everything Mina must have dreaded in the small hours of many lonely nights. Her beloved husband was dead, killed by a dream that had sunk into nightmare. Dillon Wallace returned Leonidas' body to New York, yet he kept the photographs, maps, and field notes Leonidas had produced during the expedition. As he was effectively second-in-command on that expedition, Dillon now clearly regarded them as his property and he would, in time, need them for his attempt to make his own reputation in the cold wastes of Labrador.

Meanwhile, those notes also became a bestselling book called *The Lure of the Labrador Wild*, in which Wallace portrayed Leonidas as, at best, inexperienced and, at worst, partially culpable for the dramatic failure of the expedition. Mina was outraged at the sacrilege she felt had been wreaked on her husband's memory and wrote darkly of suspicions that Dillon had kept the last of the food for himself. She had begun to feel suspicious after talking with Elson about what he'd found when he returned with help to rescue Hubbard and Dillon.

*"He* [Wallace] *had a good fire and a good bed of boughs and was quite able to walk. They tracked him to within two hundred yards of the tent, there was no trace of his having wandered about . . . Allen said that he and Donald thought it just looked as if he did not want to get to the tent. He still had some of the flour."*

Dillon himself records that he lay exhausted in the snow and believed that *"I was entering upon my final sleep."*

It is perhaps no surprise that a strong-minded, passionate woman such as Mina decided to take matters into her own hands. In proving that her husband's attempted journey was feasible, she hoped to restore Leonidas' reputation and demonstrate that his fate was due more to bad luck than bad judgement. So it was that against all social expectations, Mina showed a spirit that must have caught Dillon, a middle-aged lawyer, by surprise. She decided to make Leonidas' dream a reality and paddle across Labrador.

I look in vain for some hint in all those photos lying on the table in front of me, for some aspect of Mina's character that led her to such extraordinary feats. The pictures taken during her expedition interest me most. One shows Mina sitting on a log next to a smoking fire in a rough forest camp, looking steadily into the camera. It appears to be a bizarre photographic hoax: a genteel lady picnicking in the park, transposed onto an entirely unlikely scene in the backwoods. Sunday hat in place, hair neatly pinned, the only hint of anything untoward an embroidered ammunition pouch and knife at the waist of her heavy tweed skirt. Yet I know it is no optical trick.

Perhaps it was no surprise that, as a woman of twenty-three, my imagination had been so caught by my first discovery of Mina's tale, for the seeds of romantic illusion were sown long before then. As a nine-year-old, I started to write a novel. Fingers stained with ink from a cheap blue pen, I laboured alone in my room. My brave heroes built an open canoe, panned for gold in the icy rushes of a mountain stream, and paddled for hundreds of miles through wilderness and rapids.

Whatever influenced me to put that flight of imaginative fancy on the page stayed with me until I read of another wild land of mountains and rapids called Labrador. A childish fancy, perhaps, but something awoke inside me when I read that article, starting a process which has now brought me almost unconsciously to this point. The more I learn about Mina and her journey through one of the last genuine wildernesses in the Western world, the closer I feel to her and the more my fascination grows. What kind of Edwardian lady would decide to live out her husband's plan to make a name for himself by completing his eccentric and ultimately fatal journey?

Sitting in the Memorial University archive surrounded by the dry whispers of Mina's life, I know my quest must take me that last stage from Newfoundland to Labrador. The need to see this land so central to the Hubbards' story overwhelms me. I close my eyes in that basement room and hear the siren song of a lonely wind on desolate tundra.

I long to cross the great silent solitude of Labrador as Mina did. A small thrill twists in my stomach at the thought. Perhaps I'm already beginning to understand why she did it. Yet I know I must start with finding the place where Mina first put her canoe into the cold waters almost a hundred years ago. I decide to go to the settlement known as North West River.

The bus pulls out onto the highway, a long, dispiriting strip of discount stores and fast-food joints on the outskirts of St. John's. In the background, country music is playing just loudly enough to be irritating and I gaze, distracted, out the window. Huge intercontinental trucks roll by, their steel fenders set in menacing grimaces, some amputated of their loads. All that power and nothing to pull. Gradually, pine trees take over from the neon-lit forecourts and the sun comes up over low forested hills rising endlessly into the mist. I settle back. Only two more days to Labrador.

The *Sir Robert Bond* is one of two ferries that connect the island of Newfoundland to mainland Labrador. These are two very different places yoked together under the banner of a single provincial name—

a place which until 1949 was governed from London and flew the flag of Great Britain. Labrador is larger than the UK, but with a population of only 30,000—about the size of a small English town—it has rarely been able to exert significant influence on its rulers, regardless of whether they have been in London or St. John's.

The ferry leaves from the shelter of a former timber town called Lewisporte on the north coast and arrives two days later in the town of Happy Valley–Goose Bay, now home to an airbase used by members of NATO. Twice a week, the *Sir Robert Bond* dodges along Labrador's inhospitable coastline littered with chunks of ice bigger than the one that sank the *Titanic*. I eye my new home, tied to a tiny wharf on the edge of the great, grey ocean. It doesn't look unsinkable to me.

The ferry leaves Lewisporte at sunset, which, during late summer, is about 10 P.M. Although the sun has disappeared by the time we set out into the maze of small islands that protect the harbour, the sky is still a bright teacup blue, with a weal of red low on the horizon. Islands loom black out of the still, reflecting water, the lines of spruce on their hills biting into the delicate sky like rows of juvenile teeth. Occasionally, a light glimmers on the dark mass of land, indicating that we have yet to cross into real wilderness.

The following morning, I climb on deck under a low, grey sky. I'm the only one out in the open air. My fellow passengers are all Labradoreans for whom the excitement of seeing icebergs has long since palled. Far to my left, a brown smudge stretches across the horizon—the Labrador coast. So far north in the Atlantic, it is encased in ice for almost nine months of the year, reducing access at those times to a frighteningly expensive plane ride. But this sea route has its drawbacks, too. Open for just two and a half months each year, it's known as "iceberg alley" due to the thousands of 'bergs that float down from Greenland every summer, some occasionally carrying stray polar bears.

Before long, I am joined on deck by a short, round man in a boiler suit who introduces himself as the bo'sun. I'm beginning to realize that everything I've heard about Newfoundland hospitality is an understatement. On discovering my country of origin, my new friend

quickly assesses my standpoint on the Royal Family. Then, before I
know where I am, he's introducing me to the captain in that lilting
mixture of Canadian and Irish that so distinguishes the Newfoundland accent. The *Sir Robert Bond* takes her time, and life on the
bridge continues at a pleasant amble. Icebergs flicker unthreateningly
on the radar, small bright dots that are outclassed by broad swaths of
light indicating rain closing in on us from the southeast.

Our captain is a portly, stately man, who has served twenty-five
years on this sea and tells its story with a kind of solid resignation.

"This ship, her sister the *Northern Ranger* and those before them
have serviced all the communities along this coast for generations,"
he says. "It's all changing now—coming to an end. They closed the
codfish industry seven years ago and the salmon went three years
ago."

In the warmth of the cabin, I'm beginning to wilt in my outdoor
clothing, but I dare not move as the captain is putting his full force
into the tale, slapping an empty coffee mug down on defenceless navi-
gation charts.

"A third of the men who lived by the ocean have left altogether,
while the rest stay and live off the government. The lucky ones fish for
crab. Their families have been here for two hundred years—what else
are they supposed to do? The young go off to the big cities and won't
come back and now it's decided the coast needs a road." He sighs, a
little melancholic. "It's all changed now." He shakes a silvered head
and pushes himself away from the support of the table.

There doesn't seem to be much else to say, so I leave the cozy
warmth of the bridge and consider the irony of what is happening
here. The end of the commercial salmon catch is the final death knell
for these communities and a way of life whose rhythm has remained
largely unchanged since the first European fishermen arrived from the
Basque Country in northern Spain five hundred years ago. Just as the
young and the dispossessed leave their homes for work in the cities,
the opening up of these communities to the rest of the world comes
that much closer. Where once the people of these settlements were
almost completely isolated by winter for nine months of the year, they

now face the twin challenges of losing their traditional livelihoods and gaining easy access by road, something which will bring with it a steady stream of curious tourists like me, armed with cameras and an open invitation to an entirely new kind of life.

Standing on the deck once more, I have the majestic sight of a chunk of ice five storeys high all to myself. The opaque whiteness is riven in two by a streak of translucent turquoise. Dazzling purity in a grey world. I take pictures and feel slightly ashamed, as though this were somehow a voyeuristic thing to do.

The strong wind carrying a spatter of rain suggests a hot chocolate in the cafeteria and I struggle back toward the door. Down in the warm fug of the café, the chef tells me humpbacked whales have been sighted off the coast during the morning, but, of course, not by me! Wildlife seems to have an uncanny ability to hide itself in my presence. I take a sip from my mug and gaze out a porthole. The cold sea below washes away from the bow with a seductive monotony.

What did Mina feel, looking out the porthole of the *Harlow* as she crossed these same waters in 1905? The ten-day journey from Halifax must have given the young widow plenty of opportunity for self-doubt and spells of melancholy. Her diary records little of such feelings, however—only a determined capability, almost a relishing of the task ahead. Mina's grief was channelled into vindicating her husband's name and completing the journey he had so fatefully begun.

Travelling in this part of Canada is still an adventure, but when Mina came here, much of Labrador, in the eyes of many white people, remained little more than a blank space on maps. Those who did venture to these stark shores were either hardy or desperate, but despite the tenuous nature of life in the region, there is a thrill to existing on the boundaries of the known world. I feel it, standing alone on the icy deck of a supply ferry. The thread that ties me to home has been cut. Here, I feel, is true freedom. Could it be that Mina also felt something of this? Was she also seduced by the heady escapism of the wilderness, yet forced by the drawing-room worlds of New York and London to present her journey in the frame of her husband's ambition alone?

The next morning, under a light drizzle, I step off the ferry at the town of Happy Valley–Goose Bay and congratulate myself on reaching the only waiting taxi before any of my fellow passengers. But I need not have hurried; they all stroll over eventually, and clapping the driver with handshakes that speak of abiding friendships since childhood, they throw their bags on top of mine and squeeze into the old Pontiac next to me.

"Who're you visitin' then?" the driver asks. He doesn't take his eyes off the cigarette he's lighting, but I know he's talking to me. I realize he wants a name, not an address, so I say, "Dave and Ann Raeburn—do you—"

"Oh, aye." He nods briefly and turns his attention to my travelling companions: two large men who look as though they've spent their lives in the backwoods, a thin woman with shopping bags in tow, and a boy of sixteen or so all settle into the armchair-like seats, making the stuffing pop out in odd places. We make the short journey into town in a state of enforced intimacy, and the trip takes the form of an impromptu get-together, as everyone is updated on the local gossip.

". . . They reckon old Bill got bit by a rabid fox out Mud Lake way," the driver tells our little company, to a chorus of sharply drawn breaths and low whistles.

". . . Five bears seen up on the airbase again last week . . . ," adds someone else, not to be outdone.

I listen in fascinated silence to the lilt of local news. My fellow travellers regard me with a polite interest which is far from intrusive, despite the fact that I'm the only "foreigner" to arrive on the first ferry in nine months. I'm made welcome by the pretence that I'm no stranger at all, so I'm included like everyone else.

I look keenly at my surroundings. Through the drizzle, I see pretty wooden houses painted white, blue, or occasionally brown. They are spaced apart as though placed haphazardly on a recently cleared plain. Flimsy-looking fences mark off areas usually known as gardens but which seem strangely inappropriate here, where the houses look vulnerable against the immense backdrop of Labrador. Always, a line of spruce hovers at the edges, as though waiting to return to its rightful place when all the people have gone.

Happy Valley–Goose Bay is built on a delta at the westerly end of the Lake Melville ocean inlet, about a half-hour drive from North West River. Unlike in the rest of Labrador, the land is flat, the earth sandy and poor. Goose Bay is little more than the military base and commercial airport that spawned the town of Happy Valley at the beginning of World War II, in 1939. Passing the gates to the airfield, I stare at the acres of tarmac through a rain-washed window. A distant hangar and concrete barracks complete the bleak scene. Dave and Ann live at this end of town, near the airport, where Ann works in administration, and it is not long before the taxi pulls up in a small cul-de-sac.

I am disgorged—amid a chorus of goodbyes—outside a wooden, gabled house painted a pretty pale blue. I ring the bell and hope these friends-of-a-friend are indeed friendly.

"You must be Alex." The door opens to reveal Ann, a small, attractive woman in her middle years, whose round face is bright and full of interest. Her dark eyes flicker over me, grubby after two days on a boat, with a weary rucksack by my feet. She allows me to step inside and makes me welcome, but I sense her trepidation at the sight of this strange woman on the doorstep of her pristine home—more fear than I have of suddenly appearing in their lives.

"So, do you often have travelling strangers to stay?" I say with a smile, trying to break the ice. I'm perched on the edge of a dusky pink armchair, praying my boots haven't left muddy prints in the hall. Ann smiles and shakes her head 'no.' A few minutes later, her husband arrives. He's wearing a uniform that, I later learn, is that of a prison warden. Dave is an Englishman, brought by military demands to a place far from home, but like so many other immigrants, he has stayed and started a new life.

After a warm handshake in welcome, he comes straight to the point.

"What are you doing all the way out here, then?"

It's rather a long story and by the end of it, I realize they must regard me as slightly unhinged, but evidently harmless. I will find time and time again that Dave and Ann typify initial reactions to me in Labrador, which are invariably characterized by a strong generosity of spirit, pleasure at my interest in the place, and an unhesitating willingness to help me with my unusual plans.

Ann takes me upstairs and I throw my gear onto a huge comfy double bed in a room that could be the set of a lifestyle magazine photo shoot. After two nights in a room the size of a broom closet, I look on my new quarters with delight.

By the evening, I'm completely at home. I stroke the dog and put my feet up. Dave and Ann are both familiar with the stories of the Hubbard expeditions, and Dave shakes his head partly in disbelief, partly in thought when I ask about people who might be able to tell me about conditions along Mina's route today.

"That's gonna be pretty rough going out there."

"The flies in the summer—have you ever experienced the kind of flies we have here?" Ann adds. I assure them I don't expect it to be easy. A little reluctant to be complicit by encouraging such folly, they think for a moment, then Dave says, "Well, there's always Joe Goudie. There's not much Joe doesn't know about this part of Labrador. He was a local journalist for a while, back in the sixties—"

"And then he was an MP, over in St. John's," breaks in Ann. "Isn't he related to one of Mina's guides? Yes, call Joe."

So I make a call to someone who will bring me that much closer to Mina.

Mina took four guides with her on the journey across Labrador. At sixteen, Gilbert Blake was the youngest in the group. Manhood arrived early in the trapping communities of the North. Gilbert's skills with canoe and shotgun made him the equal of any of the older men. None of them knew the whole route, however, as no one ever travelled that far into the northern interior for trapping or hunting—and only Gilbert, from one of the oldest trapping families in the region, called this part of Labrador home. The other men had come from Ontario, travelling out to Labrador with Mina on the *Harlow*.

The Goudie family has also long called this inhospitable land home, hunting, fishing, and trapping here since the eighteenth century. Family prominence has not diminished with the passing of generations, as Gilbert Blake's great-nephew, Joe Goudie is something of a local legend in Labrador society today.

Joe and I meet in a coffee house on the only main intersection in town. It is full of working men taking their morning break and mulling over the local gossip.

"If you want to know what's going on in this town, you just need to turn up here at the right time," Joe jokes as we take the last table in the smoking section. I'm nervous and feel out of place. A girl in a man's world. The first thing I notice about Joe is the size of his hands—at least twice as large as mine, tanned and strong. The rest of him dwarfs the small plastic table, and underneath the peak of his baseball cap, I can distinguish the lines of his ancestry: Scottish, Innu, Cree, French.

I fiddle with the string attached to my teabag while Joe looks at me calmly, a small smile lurking under the shadow cast by his cap. I don't really know where to start. Suddenly the tale of my discovery of Mina, my desire to follow her footsteps across Labrador, the way her story so easily crossed ninety-five years of history to touch me, seems impossible to articulate. I stammer a quick summary, eyes fixed on the now nuclear-strength tea. Joe leans back thoughtfully and takes a long draught on his coffee before firing off a few questions. I'm beginning to wish I'd never heard of Mina Hubbard and my gums have that funny tingling sensation which, in me, always signifies extreme nervousness. Finally, Joe rocks forward on his chair and looks me straight in the eye.

"It will be hard—very hard—but it is possible to retrace the journey. No one has done it since 1905. In fact, it needs to be done and there is no reason why you shouldn't be the one to do it."

A river of relief runs through me like the nicotine of a morning's first cigarette, leaving me slightly giddy and a little high. We start talking canoes, bears, supplies, maps, and I realize that by believing in me, Joe has made me believe in myself. For the first time, someone agrees that my crazy idea *might just work*.

I'm a little surprised to find that the stories of Leonidas and Mina Hubbard are still so well known here. It is soon evident that the people of Labrador—even its newest residents—are fiercely proud of their history and heritage. Justifiably so, I feel, given the inhospitable environment. In a place where every individual's story seems remarkable and is remembered as such by everyone else, the Hubbards stand out. They are two of the best-known people associated with Labrador outside the region itself, and even though they only "passed through," their memory is ingrained in the fabric of the local identity.

At the end of our conversation, Joe promises to take me the next evening to the place where Mina's journey began—where one day my journey will begin. He promises to take me the few short miles to North West River.

I have not yet seen all that Happy Valley has to offer, however. The same day, Dave and Ann decide to take me out for a jaunt after dinner. As I climb into the pick-up, I ask where we are going.

"Oh—just up to the town dump," they say airily and smile at each other. I raise my eyebrows. Is there some bizarre local ritual I am not aware of? I wonder.

The journey up to the dump takes us quickly past the town limits and onto the road to North West River. After about ten minutes, however, we turn off onto a dirt track, travelling through anonymous spruce trees scattered across the unremarkable, undulating landscape. We could be half a mile from Happy Valley or a thousand miles away; Labrador has a way of closing in around you, while opening up perpetually new vistas to the eye. The result is disorientation and confusion. Only the pick-up seems solid and real.

Turning a corner, we see the end results of a consumer culture laid out in all their dubious glory—piles of rubbish, the earth stained by branded packaging, bright colours leaching into the ground. The edges are well defined by a thick line of trees, and in the centre is some trash-free but chewed-up ground, where vehicles obviously stop and turn around.

To my amazement, we are not alone. About half a dozen other

vehicles are stopped—parked, I realize—and their occupants are either hanging out of the windows or walking stealthily around. Most are carrying cameras. I look questioningly at Dave and Ann.

"There!" Ann points and I squint at a corner, then wind down the window for a better view. A strong scent of spruce tickles the back of my throat, bringing with it all the allure and romance of the wilderness. Then the wind changes direction and a smell of rotting vegetables fills the cab. The evening light is starting to fade a little, but out of the gloom, a large, shambling black shape emerges. A ripple of anticipation goes through the assembled watchers.

It is a black bear.

People jump back in their vehicles, cameras whirr and snap as one bear, then another and another, saunters past the vehicles and rummage around in the trash with their powerful noses. The bear closest to us uses a paw to pull out a particularly tasty morsel. In the last rays of a weak northern sunset, I can see a large fish hooked onto the bear's long, curved claws. Then, using its paw to hold the head of the fish down, the animal tears a strip of silvery flesh away as though standing on the banks of a salmon river in a national park.

Now, I've seen bears in Canada on earlier visits, but it's always a thrill to be this close to something so beautiful and so wild. Scenes like this happen all over the continent, and many people worry about the effects on the bears' diet and their hibernation patterns. They are also concerned about tempting such unpredictable animals into human settlements with our tasty trash and lazy ways.

One man leaves the safety of his car and inches closer to get a better picture of the scene. Dave makes a disapproving sound and shakes his head.

"Crazy guy. They just *look* tame. That bear could be on him in a second if it wanted."

Black bears seem to have a bad reputation here, despite the fact that they are less likely than a grizzly to attack. The words "just last week, a woman was killed by a bear in Quebec" were repeated like a mantra in town by anyone who thought I was listening, and in the local hardware store, a pile of black softness in a corner had attracted my touch.

Bear pelts run to only $299 in this part of the world, where hunting is both sport and a way of life. Wild meat—from caribou to porcupine—is everyone's favourite, and many pick-ups appear to have gun racks as standard.

The performance lasts for another half-hour, until it's too dark to see even the silhouetted shapes, and one by one, we all switch on our headlights and head back to town. It was a great show, but I am faintly uneasy.

"Is this a typical evening's entertainment in Happy Valley?" I ask.

"It's probably the easiest way to see the bears," Ann replies, massacring a SWAT team of mosquitoes that has responded to the invitation of an open window.

I sit back as we turn onto the highway and let the darkness drift over me. I think about a small frontier town lost in the grandeur of a vast and ancient land, where the locals spend their evenings going to the dump to watch the bears.

I have been in Happy Valley for only a few days and already I feel as though I know half the town. Seldom have I experienced a place as open to strangers. There is no public transport and I have no vehicle, yet I do not suffer from any lack of mobility as lifts are offered for wherever I want to go. The following day, in the late afternoon, Joe collects me from Dave and Ann's and we drive to North West River, to the starting point of the historic journeys made by Mina and Leonidas.

The journey takes about half an hour and consists of little more than a road travelling north through unending forest, with flashes of water from Lake Melville seen occasionally on the right through the trees. North West River lies across the bridge from the Native settlement of Sheshatshiu, yet the two villages, divided by the narrows where Lake Melville becomes the freshwater Grand Lake, appear entirely separate in every way.

More compact and much older than Happy Valley, North West River has a neat, prosperous air, with pretty wooden homes set in well-tended gardens. Mature trees border picket fences, and each driveway seems to have a shiny new pick-up parked on it. We stop on the shore of the bay, or rather, the fjord, for that is what Lake Melville is.

Behind us is the building where Mina began her expedition almost a century ago. At that time, it was the Hudson's Bay Company building, a trading post that supplied guns, ammunition, tea, sugar, flour, and a hundred other goods to the people of Labrador in return for furs trapped in the interior. Unchanged in appearance since 1905, it now houses the Labrador Heritage Museum, representing all aspects of life in Labrador since its settlement.

The first thing I notice inside is the counter in the main room, set out just as it would have been at the turn of the century, with sacks of flour on the floor, large tins on the shelves, and packs of ammunition ready to be loaded into the guns. Farther back, away from the store, is a replica of a "tilt"—one of the tiny wooden shelters that trappers built for themselves on the winter traplines.

I wander around, reading displays that tell of the first itinerant teachers who travelled to the area in the 1880s and the first school that opened in 1925, heated only by a single wood-burning stove. Health care had arrived a few years before when Welsh-born Wilfred Grenfell arrived in the province. Initially a doctor with the National Association of Deep Sea Fishermen, by 1914 Grenfell had established his own association to care for the medical, social, and educational needs of settlers. As a result, the first hospital in the Lake Melville region was built in 1915. Much is also written of a Dr. H. Paddon, who was famous for travelling by dog team to visit his disparate list of patients and who is credited with realizing that the endemic problems of rickets and scurvy could be ended if people ate the local partridgeberry. This, I later discover, is a red, sharp-tasting berry, much like a cranberry which is now used to make jam, wine, or a fine, sweet liqueur.

In the old building, I can feel and smell the history of this remote part of Canada—a past that is close enough to touch, yet so very distant to most of us in the Western world. A pile of beautiful furs hung in a corner is soft and luxurious beneath my hand, recalling the days when Sheshatshiu was a summer tented camp for the Innu, who travelled to the coast to trade their furs for flour and bullets.

The most exciting exhibit for me is tucked away in a side room—a case full of artifacts from both Hubbard expeditions. A pair of glasses lie next to dark, twisted pieces of leather that I realize with a shock are the moccasins Leonidas, Dillon, and Elson boiled for sustenance during those terrible hunger-stalked days. How were they saved? I wonder. Next to them are items from Mina's journey—a pair of gloves and the embroidered ammunition pouch, which looks strangely delicate. There are photographs, too, and I examine the images of Leonidas with interest. What strikes me first are the clothes—the gaiters, the ridiculous hat, the woollen layers. I examine his dark, time-scarred face, seeking the characteristics that inspired such devotion in Mina, or even some clue as to the origins of his wild ambition—but his gaze eludes me, cast toward a distant smudge of mountains.

Reluctantly, I tear myself away from the museum, and as day turns to evening, we stop for a quick dinner of caribou burgers in a small, crowded café. Afterward, we drive on to a place where Joe knows there is a sheltered creek. The rich taste somewhere between venison and beef lingers in my mouth. When we arrive at the water, dusk is drifting through the spruce, driving the mosquitoes into a frenzy. Joe hauls a seventeen-foot canoe off the roof rack and onto his shoulders, carrying it easily down to the creek. This is to be my introduction to canoeing in Labrador. We get in and I sit in the bow, a racing paddle in my soft, unmuscled hands.

The mackerel sky is as clear reflected in the waters below the canoe as it is in the sky above us. The air is soft and sweet with spruce. A muskrat paddles an ever-widening V across the creek, its small brown nose twitching in concentration. A bat swoops low, a welcome predator of the mosquitoes hovering around us, and a wild duck herds its offspring away from the intruders. The paddle is light in my hands as I push us through the silent, black water.

A snipe breaks the stillness and flaps away into the trees, which crowd the water like spectators to this, my first taste of what Mina experienced. After a while, it hurts as I paddle, but it also feels good; the burn in my shoulders makes me feel strong and at once part of this transitory tableau.

Like Mina, I, too, begin to feel just a little like an explorer.

# CHAPTER 2

As my train speeds west through the heavy richness of England's neatly tamed farmlands, the differences between my native country and Labrador, the land closest to us across the Atlantic, could not be underlined more clearly. It is as though the season and the weather are conspiring to warn me against my goal of retracing Mina's route: "This is what you shall be forsaking. Turn back now while you still can!" We continue to rattle west from London, more passengers leaving at every stop and fewer getting on, until the train is almost empty and I can stare out the window in silence, undisturbed.

The sun lowers to the horizon in a long, lazy summer twilight, and the landscape becomes wilder. Somerset, then Devon, flashes by, and suddenly we are hanging suspended over the tidal mud flats of the river Tamar. Birds rise in a flock from their feeding, squawking their annoyance at our intrusion. We are now in Cornwall, England's most westerly county and my home. The remoteness is marked by a noticeable and almost immediate decrease in speed. From here on, the intercity train will also be a local passenger service.

We chase the last of the light west toward a distant sea, the coconut smell of yellow flowering gorse filtering in through the open windows. After a while, the farmland falls away and Bodmin Moor rises around us, the last hurdle before the long drift down to the end of the line. Small fields cluster at the base of the tors, ancient stone walls penning in cattle, marked off from the wild ponies that haunt the poorer ground higher up. Standing black pools reflect the sunset to the sky, just as they did in Labrador, but this is a familiar place to me and the shadows hold no fear.

Not for the first time, I compare Cornwall to Labrador. Those in other, more urban parts of their countries see both as remote, peripheral, and insignificant. Both have depended on fishing in the past and share a bleak future without it. In many a Cornish fishing port foreign visitors are confused to see Canadian flags displayed with pride next to the black and white Cornish flag. "Cornish and Canadian Fishermen Unite," the logos read. Newfoundland and Labrador, originally settled by, among others, West Country fishermen and the last Canadian province to leave British rule, stands at the forefront of the relationship. The two regions are tied by the lifeblood of the seas and the blood of the people themselves.

As I settle back into life in England, I begin to realize that there is quite a difference between feeling like an explorer and actually making it happen. Specifically: money, a team, a guide, equipment, and a level of fitness I have never previously achieved, despite an active life. That gentle evening on the creek with Joe seems a whole world away, the idea of following in Mina's footsteps just a fantasy. Am I really about to try to do this?

I find the idea so daunting, I spend the first few weeks of my return home hiding behind the pleasures of the holiday season in west Cornwall during high summer. The sun shines, beach parties come and go, and I pretend I am not going to plan, fund, and lead an expedition on the other side of the world in less than twelve months. I've done just what I promised myself I would not do while lying on my bunk in the *Sir Robert Bond* on my return from Labrador: I've become absorbed in my old life; I've lost my perspective and my belief in the expedition. Two weeks at home and I've already started to lose touch with the realities of a wilderness trip into Labrador.

I sit in my study, on old fishing loft above the harbour, daydreaming and watching the life of the port ebb and flow with the tide. As night settles in from the sea, I watch the line of orange lights along the promenade glimmer ever brighter, mirrored in the bay below.

"Next summer, I will be in Labrador. . . ." The thought rolls around and around in my head, generating excitement and anticipation in equal parts. But how to make it happen?

How to make it happen, indeed. In years to come, people will often ask me how I knew how to plan and fund a trip such as mine—a question second in popularity only to "Why?" The unsatisfactory answer to both has always been, "I didn't know, not really." I do have experience of the outdoors—I have the kind of parents who considered hiking in Scotland to be a good, wholesome activity for any child old enough to walk. I am also accustomed to travelling alone, particularly in North America.

Six years previously, my love affair with Canada began, quite accidentally, with a trip that turned into a four-month stay in Vancouver. It was summer and I was unwilling to spend my first long university vacation in the north of England village I had so recently left behind. So, armed with a temporary work visa and a new rucksack, I boarded an airplane bound for Canada's west coast, with very little idea what to expect.

It turned out that I could have expected a beautiful city set in a magnificent ring of mountains and clear water, where the people were friendly and the streets safe. I made some of the best friends I've ever had that summer, fell in love, worked late into the night, drove to the Rockies in a car that should not have taken us farther than downtown, and slept on the open deck of an Alaskan ferry. All of this instilled a taste for adventure and the unexpected, teaching me a dubious lesson—that the biggest risks sometimes yield the biggest payouts.

Later on, I was to live for a year in Washington, D.C. (perhaps an unfortunate contrast to Vancouver), work in the cloud forests of Central America, and achieve my longstanding ambition to visit Hong Kong while it remained part of the British Empire. None of these experiences, or a host of others, really prepared me for what I would experience in Labrador. They merely gave me the desire to try.

As for the planning of my canoe trip, well, so much is instinctive. Far from being the woman of independent means that many assume me to be, I have, in reality, very little cash available to throw at the project. With envy, I watch wealthy and famous mountaineers and explorers mount extravagant expeditions to exotic places and try to discover their secrets. I read the equipment and sponsorship lists of recent documented trips with an avid interest. I scour my list of contacts for anyone in a business vaguely related to my needs. I talk to anyone I can about where to begin planning, and within three months I have a long, confused list of things to buy I know nothing about and things to do I cannot begin to tackle.

Somehow, though, I have developed a determination to make it happen. Once accused of being single-minded, I was greatly taken aback, assuming it to be a criticism. Yet single-minded I have truly become with regard to this trip. The stories of the Hubbards' trips have fired my imagination as they have for so many people. Something has captured my admiration, particularly of Mina. This, and my sense of adventure, has hardened into a goal that sits inside me like a stone, a heavy weight I cannot escape or unload. I no longer have any choice in the matter.

That realization strikes a chill through me, as I see the resemblance it bears to Leonidas' passion. Dillon wrote how his friend convinced him to go to Labrador that night they sat round a campfire in the mountains of New York:

> It's always the way, Wallace, when a fellow starts on a long trail, he's never willing to quit. It'll be the same with you if you go with me to Labrador. You'll say each trip will be the last, but when you come home, you'll hear the voice of the wilderness calling you to return. Thought my Lake St. John trip was something, but while I stood there at the portals of the unknown, it brought back stronger than ever the old longing to make discoveries, so that now the walls of the city seem to me a prison and I simply must get away.

Summer slides south into the ocean, and the fishing trawlers outside my window come and go, their boats' horns echoing final farewells across the waters. I find that my plans have generated a momentum of their own. The Hypatia Trust, a charity I work for as a part-time fundraiser and editor, offers me a laptop computer on loan. Toby, a friend reading postgraduate computing, offers to build a website for the expedition as part of his portfolio, and I begin to write letters to every company I can think of, asking for sponsorship. I've found a beginning.

Most important of all, however, I still need to find someone willing to go with me who knows the country. Naturally, Joe is the first person I think of, but he is soon to start a contract with National Parks Canada and has other commitments, all of which will keep him at home. Disappointed, I still cling to his words, a reassuring presence in my mind. Yet I also have a feeling that this is as it should be. The perfect person is still to enter this story, I am sure.

A call comes from Ontario.

"Is that Alexandra Pratt?" The voice is male, youngish, and definitely Canadian. I rack my brains for a corresponding face. Someone I met in Newfoundland? Labrador? No.

"We haven't met, but I'm Neville Burke. I hear you're looking for a guide?"

Bingo.

Neville (not his real name) sounds perfect. At thirty-five he's been guiding for several years and is the director of an outdoor camp in Alberta offering canoeing, camping, and wilderness trips to groups and individuals. I also learn that he has a degree in my own subject, political science. So we'd have something to talk about on those Labrador nights around the campfire. . . .

Meanwhile, the first little spurt of support I've enjoyed seems to have spent itself since, and every company or organization I approach for sponsorship turns me down. Each has a perfectly good reason, of course: "not our sphere," "the current budget has been allocated," and so on. I'm reminded of Ffyona Campbell, the woman who walked around the world, when she said in her book *On Foot through Africa* that "No one wants to see their logo on a dead body." That this might actually happen is not something I've genuinely confronted. It's not just a matter of the invincibility of youth. The single-mindedness required to make an expedition happen doesn't allow for dwelling on failure—at least not *that* kind of failure.

Through all this, I keep in mind the trials of my sister adventurer, Mina. Unlike her, I meet with very little overt disapproval or disbelief. Edwardian women were considered legitimate explorers only if they returned with scientific information. Of course, without this recognition, they discovered it was virtually impossible to find capital or institutional backing. Mina was fortunate in that she was not dependent on sponsorship or any other kind of funding for her trip, as she used the remainder of the windfall inheritance that had allowed Leonidas to follow his dream. For many Edwardian female explorers, however, the science requirement was a problem, as few women had the education to meet the demands for original work and therefore found themselves in a Catch-22 situation.

I soon discover that little has changed. I attend a weekend seminar at the Royal Geographical Society in London where I expect the majority of my fellow participants to be male, so I am not surprised to find myself in the minority. I am taken aback, however, by the degree to which the seminar is aimed at those planning expeditions for scientific purposes only. Of course, had I given the matter any prior consideration, I would have realized that the Royal Geographical Society exists for just that reason.

As I sit in the gloom under the high vaulted ceiling of the Society's historic lecture hall, I listen to speaker after speaker discuss planning for medical emergencies, the intricacies of pinpointing an exact location in remote areas, and the juicier moments of a solo attempt on the North Pole. I begin to feel very uneasy. Do I really belong here?

It seems adventure for adventure's sake is an indulgence few are prepared to support. In this goal-oriented society, I find that success is defined by the extent to which I can precisely execute my plans and has very little to do with following Mina out into the country, of staking my right to choose my own challenge, of championing her achievements. For me, the journey, not the arrival, is the point.

Gradually, however, I begin to make progress in finding financial support. Luckily, the science requirement, though apparently still in existence, is now flexible enough to admit that some journeys do not have to carry the burden of serious scientific research. This is fortunate for me, as my largely unhappy relationship with test tubes and algebraic equations ended on the day I left high school.

Neville puts me in touch with Northwoods Canoe, a company that builds traditional wooden canoes in Maine, U.S.A. They offer me a huge discount and I say yes, then remember that I need to learn *how* to canoe. The occasional paddle in Labrador or British Colombia is not going to stand up to the rigours of the country Mina travelled through, so I set about finding someone in Cornwall who knows about Canadian canoes.

It isn't easy. Most of the paddling in the U.K. is done in closed, fibreglass kayaks, and open canoes are fairly hard to find. I put the call out and eventually I meet Paul, a local headmaster with a bushy beard and a stocky frame who is, fortunately for me, accustomed to impressing ideas on slow pupils. He agrees to take me under his wing or, rather, out in his canoe on a reservoir. Paul has an experienced, almost fatherly manner that is reassuring, yet it quickly becomes obvious to both of us that my skill level will have to undergo a dramatic transformation for the better to deal adequately with the demands of Labrador.

With slowly dawning horror, I realize just how difficult it is to paddle against a stiff breeze. My knees ache from kneeling in the canoe, my hands are stiff from cold and from gripping the paddle in the winter weather, which on occasion is significantly warmer than it might be at times in Labrador in the summer. Will I have the strength for the expedition? The question taunts me for the entire year. The first section of the route is to be on the Naskaupi River to the height of land. *Upstream.*

My skinny arms don't look as if they can do it, so I add weight training to my regime of canoeing, yoga, hiking, and swimming. Already an active person, I become as fit as I have ever been, spending the long winter nights in sports halls and gyms, which smell faintly of rubber-soled shoes and men's sweat. Again, I feel out of place, but that is becoming a familiar emotion and I no longer give it any thought.

In January I win a small grant, but at the same time I have come to realize the full cost of what I have planned. The numbers are simply not adding up. I want to travel with two or three other team members and at least one, preferably two, guides, but it is becoming readily apparent that this is no longer feasible. I could travel alone with Neville, but doing so would decrease our margin of error and would mean a great deal more hard work on the trail. Mina had four guides travelling with her, all of whom were responsible for the heavy work: portaging, paddling (although she did her fair share), setting up camp, cutting trails. I will become bitterly envious of her retinue in the future. Yet, in the meantime, I have a decision to make: will I still go on, despite the greater risks and higher demands?

At each stage of my plans it seems I receive one setback, then another. The advances shine so brightly through these periods of darkness that perhaps they give me more hope than they truly bear, yet they buoy me up anyway, each defeat only strengthening my resolve still further.

One of those team members I plan to take—my partner, Stuart—is refused leave from the Royal Air Force, so fate has settled the matter. One canoe, one guide, and me. I've come this far, I reason, there's no going back.

This disappointment is soon mitigated as interest is expressed by a production company making a series of documentaries for a television channel in the U.K. The theme is wilderness experiences, and my plans fit exactly with what it has in mind. I have doubts about the extra equipment I will have to carry in just one canoe. But I am persuaded by the small yet vital funding on offer from the company and its assurances that the cameras are compact and waterproof.

Barely three months remain before my departure for Labrador at the end of June and my life has gone into overdrive. I am working at my regular job four days a week in addition to freelancing for magazines; searching for sponsors; negotiating with the TV company; researching the region, conditions, and route; and making long-distance arrangements with people in Canada by e-mail. I'm putting in eighteen-hour days and the strain is starting to show. I know I'm becoming a wild-eyed, slightly desperate creature, yet I still have to find a clothing sponsor and a satellite phone from somewhere. My previously ambitious plans for up-loading data from the field via the laptop computer are yet another idea gone by the wayside due to cost and space.

In the midst of this mêlée, I find I've won another grant from a prestigious society and am required to travel to Cardiff for a formal presentation. Then, at this bright moment of glamour in the chaos, the expedition almost dies before it even begins.

Settling into my small hotel in the city, I receive a call on my mobile. I'm busy wrestling with a broken zip on my sequined dress— a big enough disaster for any woman forty-five minutes from a seven-course dinner and champagne reception. Things, however, are soon to get much, much worse. It's June 11. I'm due to leave for Labrador at the end of the month and start the expedition on July 17. The call is from Neville, in Canada. He wants out of the trip. Things aren't going as he expected. A long, involved, and, for me, surreal conversation ensues. With one eye on the clock and another watching all my plans fade in front of me, I find that no amount of quiet reasoning or semi-hysterical pleading at my end can change his mind.

We conclude the conversation frostily and I hang up, no less stunned than if I'd been hit over the head. I can hardly breathe with the horror of what has just happened. For a while—how long, I have no idea—I alternate between pacing the room in fury and sobbing on the bed in despair. This is not merely a business transaction fallen through, it's a single-handed, deliberate extinguishing of my dreams, and I weep for the pity and the frustration of it. Then, the emotion spent, I sit up exhausted. What should I tell everyone at the dinner in . . . fifteen minutes? Can I fix this? Will I be able to find another guide? Questions whorl through my mind, but I am completely incapable of answering them. I look in the mirror and a white, stricken face with dark eyes looks back at me. I try to pin up my hair, but my hands are shaking too much. What on earth am I to do?

Without a guide, there will be no chance of attempting to follow Mina's route. And as Neville so helpfully pointed out, I now have very, very little chance of finding another guide at this late stage. They will all be engaged for the summer season and few will even want to undertake a journey of this scale even at the best of times. I think of all the money I've spent (including Neville's retainer), of the people who have supported me, sponsored me, and believed in me. Ten minutes before the taxi arrives. What can I say? Should I keep it to myself? My hands still white from the shock, I fix my zip with a safety pin and paint my face a little unsteadily.

The phone rings. It's the reception to say my taxi has arrived. I compose myself and walk down the stairs.

What follows are four of the most difficult hours of my life. On top of everything else, I am angry at being cheated out of an entertaining evening as the only woman in a room full of members of the Captain Scott Society. As roast beef follows poached salmon and I pass the port to the left, I smile, chat, and even make a short acceptance speech. After the first few hours, the cold clammy feeling of horror has been chased away by a rather fine red wine, and by the end of the evening, my old stubbornness has reasserted itself. How can I quit before I've even left English shores? Will I allow the now despised Neville to dictate my fate? No, I decide, as a poem is read to the company entitled "Quitting."

I will not give in. Not yet.

For the next week and a half, I am engaged in frantic calls to various parts of Canada, often in the middle of the night. I rather cheekily contact everyone I know who might be able to help, and finally, I receive a call from an Englishman named Jonathan who lives in Happy Valley. He's heard about my plans through the Labrador grapevine, and like many people in the area, he is enthusiastic and keen to help. He also knows someone who might be willing to be my guide. I cannot believe my luck and quickly scribble down a number. But even if the guy Jonathan knows is available, will he want to do it? Will I be able to afford him? Will my lack of experience put him off? Will he have the right qualifications? Going out into the country with someone who doesn't know what he is doing would be little better than suicide.

I am again reminded of Leonidas' expedition. He, too, had engaged a guide he had never met, a Cree from Ontario called Jerry. At the last moment, before Jerry was to arrive in New York to meet his new employers, a letter appeared, declaring that he was too afraid to come to the big, unknown city. In some haste, another man, also Cree and from the James Bay region, was engaged in his place and, as Dillon noted: *"We never have had occasion to regret Jerry's fainthearted-ness."* The guide who took his place turned out to be *"a man of intelligence, quick of perception and resourceful . . . a man of character."* That man was, of course, George Elson, and in time, Dillon would come to owe him his life. Yet only when the situation had deteriorated past redemption was George Elson allowed to come into his own. If it had not been for his strength and knowledge, Dillon Wallace would have joined his friend in the cold glory of an explorer's grave.

Fate has taken kindly to me, but I do not realize this initially, as my first conversation with Jonathan's contact is less than encouraging. Despite expressing a willingness to be involved, Jean Pierre Ashini speaks only a little and I initially find him difficult to understand. Unsure whether to interpret this as a lack of enthusiasm, as shyness, or as something worse, I am both elated to have surmounted a potentially terminal obstacle and curious to know what kind of man Jean Pierre is. Dare I hope that I, too, have lost a Jerry and found a George Elson?

Now forty, Jean Pierre tells me, he has spent almost thirty years of his life living in a traditional manner in *nutshimit*—the country—with his people, the Innu. At first I confuse the few thousand Innu of Labrador and Quebec with the better-known Inuit of the Arctic, but I am to learn that the Innu are in fact an entirely different group, with their own language, culture, and history. Anthropologists classify the Innu as part of the Algonquian group, which includes Mi'kmaq, Cree, and the now-extinct Beothuk peoples of Newfoundland. It is certain that the Innu have inhabited Labrador for at least two thousand years, and it is likely they are the descendants of the first humans to move into the area after the Ice Age—the "Maritime Archaic Indians." One Innu legend tells the story of *Tshakapesh* who killed a mammoth—an animal that has been extinct for ten thousand years. Ironically, despite the fact that Labrador was the first place to be "discovered" by Europeans, some bands of Innu were the last to have contact with the settlers. Previously known as the Montagnais-Naskaupi, they are the same people Mina met as she travelled down the George River. Those people she came across obviously impressed her, and she describes the men as being *"tall, lithe and active looking, with a certain air of self-possession and dignity almost all Indians seem to have."*

At the time, I have no way of knowing if this was a romantic view held by an awe-struck woman who had spent a long period alone with George Elson (for whom she had an unspecified affection) and her other Native guides. However, I learn that Jean Pierre lives in Sheshatshiu, the town across the bridge from North West River. I had persuaded Dave to drive me through it, after passing so briefly with Joe that evening we took the canoe out. I had been shocked by how different many of its homes were from the generally neat, prosperous residences in North West River. The bridge between the two settlements was a bridge into another world.

As Dave and I drove slowly through Sheshatshiu that first summer, I'd found it hard to believe I was still in the enlightened, developed country I had come to think of as Canada. Children stared at us, their grubby fingers pink where they pulled them out of small mouths in surprise and curiosity, and packs of dogs roamed the streets, half starved. The whole place had an air of neglect and despair, induced by poverty and alcohol abuse, which kept much of the community in a downward spiral.

Jean Pierre himself has turned away from a life ruled by alcohol and represents his people through his work with the United Nations and as a spokesperson for Survival International, a U.K.-based charity that supports Native peoples. I have little idea why Jean Pierre has agreed to join me on this adventure at such short notice, but I have a feeling I'll find out when I arrive in Labrador.

Many people assure me of Jean Pierre's boundless skills in the country, of his strength and his commitment, and I begin to realize how lucky I am. Not just in finding Jean Pierre, but in being forced to look for him. My new guide has unwittingly made me consider implications for my trip, and indeed Mina's, in a different light. I thought I would embark on my journey with similar intentions to those of my predecessor, tinged with literary and unashamedly feminist overtones. The fact that I intended to do this originally with a white guide (in contrast to Mina) did not cross my mind as significant until now. In my arrogance, it did not occur to me that my journey would take me across someone else's land. To another people, often invisible to white society, for whom Labrador was not a "blank space," but home. I will see—and hopefully understand—more of Labrador than merely the breathtaking scenery and the role the land played in the Hubbard expeditions. Mina would never have succeeded without the help she received, and without it I, too, have no chance of making my own attempt.

Mina always claimed she'd made her epic journey in memory of her late husband. Fortunately, she had the freedom to pursue her single avowed aim, which was to "*complete my husband's unfinished work . . . I hope that this may go some way towards correcting misleading accounts of Mr. Hubbard's expedition, which have appeared elsewhere.*"

I've no doubt this was true to some extent, but there must have been something else to propel her to risk her life alone with people she barely knew, in a place nobody knew anything about—the geographic "blank space" that explorers of the twenty-first century can only dream of. Neither Mina's book, nor her diaries, tell very much about the circumstances that led her to follow in Leonidas' footsteps. We have only her stated aim, which should not be underestimated. There were many points in Dillon's book that implied criticism of her husband, a man she loved dearly—and given what her expedition tells us of her character, I can see clearly how such a strong-minded woman could set herself a task that was both virtuous and daunting. Mina, I'm sure, was also driven by a sense of adventure, of curiosity, of a desire to escape, temporarily, the shackles of turn-of-the-century New York. Where she makes light of her preparations, however, I struggle on with gritted teeth. It is to become a theme of our parallel journeys.

Now that I have found a guide, I can once again turn my attention to the other thousand and one matters that are crying out for my attention. The problems of finding clothing sponsorship and a satellite telephone are both solved at the eleventh hour, as a local store gives me a generous discount on tough, breathable, lightweight clothing. Richard, the owner, also negotiates a deal with his supplier, Sprayway. As for a satellite phone, renting is my only alternative (these phones cost a prohibitive $2,500), yet it seems that almost every phone in Labrador is in use. A call from a busy public phone in Heathrow Airport, about ten minutes before I board my flight, confirms that I do indeed have a "sat phone," as one has just been returned to a store in Happy Valley.

Finally, already as exhausted as if I've paddled a hundred miles, I board the first in a series of four planes that will take me back to Labrador. Sitting back as it takes off, I look out the window onto the grey maze of London as it fades into the smog below. I am about to travel to a part of Canada I have little experience of with a man who is a total stranger to me. My only guides are the stories of a dead man and a woman whose words whisper across ninety-five years to draw me on. Cain's country lies ahead of me and my fate lies in its hands.

# CHAPTER 3

The sound of the plane's engine changes and I feel us bank to the left. We are about to land. I look out the window, excitement and anticipation starting to churn my stomach. There is nothing below us but cloud. Then, suddenly, we drop out of our cocoon and I see Labrador for the first time in a year. Bald crowns of mountains reach up to our tiny plane, the creased face of the land marked by forested crevices and river valleys. My heart sinks at the desolation. Then a shaft of light slants through the heavy grey sky and suddenly I see what sets Labrador apart: a vast land of endless hills and boundless forests. A place where the absence of a horizon creates a feeling of limitlessness.

The American gentleman explorer William Brookes Cabot spent much of his time in Canada in Labrador and travelled out on the same ship as Leonidas in that fateful year of 1903. He notes in his diary of their journey together a shared sense of anticipation: "*We looked with lingering eyes upon the far, sparsely forested hills. They were inviting to the feet and . . . no white man had traveled there. To our eyes, it was the unexplored land of our dreams.*"

What is this land, this Jekyll-and-Hyde place that induces dreams and lures the Romantic, yet can so ruthlessly destroy? I strain to discern signs of life, but I'm on the wrong side of the plane and all I can see is the flash of a river before the country retires and once again pulls the cold comfort of mist around itself.

I arrive at Goose Bay's large military airport and step off the small plane that has brought me from St. John's, Newfoundland. It was the smallest aircraft I've ever flown in commercially and the atmosphere was that of a country bus on market day. I was the only woman on a flight of middle-aged men, several of whom were reaching that paunchy stage when suits begin to show the strain and jowls give up the battle against gravity. Businessmen from Newfoundland mostly, but diluted with a dash of sports fishermen. I remember how different my arrival was last year, when I stepped unsuspecting from the *Sir Robert Bond* into the first act of this drama.

I've arranged to meet Jonathan, the Englishman who helped me so much from afar in the previous weeks. He's coming to the airport with his Inuit wife, Annette. I've been wondering how I'll find two strangers in a crowd, but I need not have worried; we see each other immediately, and they smile a curious hello.

"Welcome to Labrador."

That accent, so natural a few short hours before, now sets us apart from the rapidly disappearing crowds.

Long after the other passengers have departed the tiny civilian section of the airbase, it becomes obvious that my luggage has gone on a journey of its own. To Halifax, apparently. When quizzed, the airline official admits that this is normal, and with a truly Labradorean lack of concern, suggests that it will more than likely turn up eventually.

Too tired to argue, I climb into Jonathan's ancient VW camper van, which sits neglected among the gaggle of shiny pick-up trucks in the parking lot, and we drive to Joe's.

I have very much looked forward to meeting him again after a full year, and I am not disappointed as he comes down the wooden steps at the front of his home, then envelops me in a huge bear hug. He is just as I remembered: he still has the gruff charm, the twinkle in the eye, the concern that seems to hover somewhere between the fatherly and the flirtatious. As I am travelling light, thanks to the airline, there is no unpacking to do, and we all sit down for a cup of tea before I collapse from sheer exhaustion.

For a little while I sink back, away from the conversation, and look around the room. It is slightly familiar, as I had eaten dinner here with Joe one evening last year. Undoubtedly the home of a single man, this bachelor dwelling, with its polished wood and traditional designs, is still comfortable and tasteful. My eyes fall on Annette, whose beauty is striking, but, of course, she is the descendant of a princess.

"Annette's ancestor is Mikak," Jonathan had written to me earlier in the year. "The daughter of an Inuit chief who was captured following an attack on a British fishing station in Labrador. Her ability to learn English quickly caught the attention of the governor of Newfoundland, who sent her and her son, Tootac, to London. It was 1765 and the idea of the 'noble savage' was very fashionable."

Annette catches me looking and smiles.

"Jonathan was telling me about your famous ancestor," I say.

Annette laughs and rolls her dark eyes.

"We went to England last year, to the gallery in Guildford, to see her portrait."

"She was painted?" It seems incredible that a woman born to life on the Labrador tundra in the eighteenth century could find herself mixing so easily with the cream of London society.

"Yes, she sat for Sir John Russell and met Augusta, the Princess of Wales, too, during her stay. She became quite a favourite of the court. My uncle still has the velvet outfit given to her by Augusta, all trimmed in gold . . ."

She breaks off as Jonathan stands up to leave.

"Let's allow Alex to have some rest." He smiles at me. "If you need any help before you go, just give us a call."

"I will, thanks."

After they've left, the room is still and Joe and I look at each other.

"So you really are going to do it, then."

"I guess I am."

As I look out the window of Joe's guest room, I can see it is a beautiful day, and it is going to be a big day, too, jet lag or no jet lag. I shall meet Jean Pierre for the first time, my guide and sole companion for the next few weeks. I'm not quite sure what to expect and was enlightened only a little by Joe's response when I told him about my new guide: "You'll be all right with an Innu—they know how to live in the country."

I'm alone in Joe's elegant pine house when Jean Pierre rings the doorbell. "Alex?" My name is clipped, the "x" almost sibilant.

I nod, and a strong, brown hand reaches out to shake mine.

"I'm Jean Pierre Ashini."

Jean Pierre is a big man. Not fat, but tall and strong looking. His face is round under the bright red baseball cap that seems, to my English eyes, slightly incongruous. My first impression is of shyness, but it is a superficial effect. I sense there is more behind those unreadable black eyes. We sit down with tea, strong and well sugared, and make small talk.

We discuss the route, our equipment, the filming.

"Do you have the time to finish the trip?"

"Yes."

I try again.

"Do you know this part of the country well?"

"Yes." Again the quick nod.

"Will you feel comfortable being filmed?"

"Yes." Jean Pierre nods without hesitation.

I'm starting to get a little desperate. Do I want to spend up to eight weeks with someone this chatty? A final attempt is called for. I reach into my now nearly blank mind.

"Why have you agreed to come with me?" Jean Pierre looks at me, at his teacup, then into the distance. I realize I'm barely breathing, willing him on.

Eventually he says, "I want to visit all the old camping grounds, the ones used by the Innu when I was a boy. They are all along the river, many have not been used for a long time." As he speaks, he gains more momentum and the words spill out and he tells me more: about his ecotourism camp at Kamistastin Lake that is to open next year, how it will help the Innu by keeping the traditional practices alive and passing them on to the young. This is evidently very important to him and I sense muted passion behind the words.

"Also," he adds suddenly, "I love to fish."

As Jean Pierre speaks, I realize with some surprise that English is his second language. As he talks, however, a college-level vocabulary and intelligent eyes warn me off snap judgements. The halting words have begun to flow together into a story about his people—a modern tale of politics whose reference points mean nothing to me. What are these band councils, land-claims talks, health clinics?

I ask Jean Pierre if he knows the story of the Hubbard expeditions. He nods quickly and says, perceptively, "So you want me to be your George Elson."

Taken aback for a moment, I laugh. "I suppose I do. Does that appeal to you?"

"Yes." A shy smile. "I can do it."

I realize that while the stories of Mina and Leonidas are common knowledge here in Labrador, the real hero of the Hubbard saga is George Elson. Famed for his skills in the country, Elson was the only man in Leonidas' ill-fated party to reach help and return in time to save Dillon. He was also the man credited with getting Mina to Ungava Bay in one piece. The romance of being a second George Elson has not passed Jean Pierre by, it seems, and the opportunity to emulate his achievements is quite an attraction.

The ice broken, a sudden smile of perfect white teeth transforms Jean Pierre's face and reaches across the gulf. I smile back. How could I not, when a great Innu hunter, as Jean Pierre is revealed to be, confides his fear of . . . the common toad? We strike a deal: toads for spiders and the understanding between us is reached. We will become partners for a time. For our adventure.

Looking at Jean Pierre, I see what Mina saw when she met her guides in North West River:

*My crew numbered four, chief among whom was George Elson ... the other two were Joseph Iserhoff, a Russian half-breed and Job Chapies, a pure blood Cree Indian. These three men were expert hunters and canoemen ... The fourth was Gilbert Blake [Joe Goudie's great-uncle], a half-breed Eskimo boy trapper ... the men were splendid, capable looking fellows, with an air of quiet dignity and self-possession about them, which comes from conscious ability and character. All seemed thoroughly to enjoy the prospect of the trip and their assurance greatly added to my ease of mind.*

My guide seems similarly capable looking and oddly, despite the fact that I barely know Jean Pierre, my reservations about heading off into the wilderness with him have evaporated. I stand on the porch, watching Jean Pierre leave. He reaches his pick-up in three quiet strides and swings fluidly into the cab. I cannot imagine anyone better suited to the task ahead and I realize, with a quick flood of pleasure and anticipation, that the perfect guide has indeed come into my story at last.

I may have found my guide, but the same is not true for my equipment. My canoe is still in a garage in Toronto, awaiting collection by a haulage company, and several crucial items I ordered from a U.S. company while I was still in England have not appeared. Bearing in mind the fate of my luggage (which *has* finally turned up after a sojourn in Halifax), I decide to try to source the items in Happy Valley itself. The nearest store for outdoor equipment is only a five-minute walk away, so I wave aside offers of assistance in a bid to do a little exploring myself.

Perhaps because Happy Valley has existed only sixty years this explains why it still has a frontier feel to it. To a person whose first experiences of Canada were of downtown Vancouver seven years ago, Happy Valley seems to be not only part of a different nation but also on another planet. The first European settlement in the area was North West River. After the region went to the British in 1763, very little changed for almost two centuries in an area whose small white population preferred the hardships and isolation of the Labrador interior to being press-ganged into war for the British or French empires or persecuted for its religious and political beliefs.

Mostly, however, Labrador's early European population seems to have been made up of the landless poor: the people made homeless by the Enclosures in Britain, the starving émigrés from Ireland's convulsions, and the Scottish crofters who owned no land. To them, Labrador's freezing wastes were a dream of freedom and opportunity, a place where the hard work barely tainted the joy of a life lived on one's own terms.

Walking down the road, I think how deceptively tranquil the mountains always seem to look here in Happy Valley. I have a sudden glimpse of them between two buildings, their shoulders framed by peeling paint and fading hoardings. Behind the buildings, across the slow-moving waters of the Churchill River, rises their eerie eternal blue, etched against a lowering Labrador sky. I'm spying on their grandeur through a peephole in the flimsy walls of civilization.

The mountains remind me of that old saying from County Donegal, Ireland: "If you can see the mountains clearly, it is about to rain. If you can't see them, it is raining." A large drop of water puffs in the sand of the sidewalk at my feet and I hurry on my way.

I had met Joe's older brother Horace the previous year. Despite a long life of hard work (he started trapping in 1934), he is as active as a man thirty years his junior and possesses a deep well of experience and knowledge. The door opens and lively eyes peer out from a tanned face, shadowed by the peak of a blue cap. The thin checked shirt he is wearing does little to hide the sinewy evidence of a lifetime of hard labour.

"Alex? So, you decided to come back and see some more of our country."

We sit in his bright kitchen, with blue checkered curtains at the back of a modern house. A clock ticks quietly in the corner. Horace makes us the strong, sweet tea whitened with tinned evaporated milk

that is the favourite brew of trappers and tells of his life in the area
before the airbase. He is one of the very few men who can still remember the days before the modern era arrived on their doorstep. Even
during the twenties and thirties, little had changed since the land was
settled two centuries before.

Almost all the first settlers worked as fur trappers, with the first
Hudson's Bay post arriving in 1843, providing competition to the
French trading company, established in North West River a hundred
years earlier by Louis Fornell. Trapping was a hard, lonely, and often
dangerous life, despite the many survival skills the settlers learned—
some from their Native wives—such as using snowshoes and the
crooked knife.

Even when Horace was born in the 1920s, men would spend up to
half the year fur trapping. "Before the airbase started, our sole
income was from trapping and fishing," says Horace. His voice is low
and almost gravelly, with an unidentifiable lilt, possibly the result of a
French intonation picked up from his uncles. The end of the short
Labrador summer in September would see the men go out on their
traplines, which often held up to three hundred traps. Horace's first
experience of this life was at the age of twelve: "At that age, I didn't
have a gun of my own, but I was travellin' with my dad who had a .22
rifle. He taught me to use that for small game: ptarmigan, spruce
grouse, rabbit, and so on. That year we left . . . around 12 September
to go up the Kenamu [River] and our trappin' ground was located
about seventy miles inland . . . There were an awful lot of rapids.
Really slow progress. It took us about three weeks. We got home a
couple days before New Year's. We came out on snowshoes; you
could [usually] make it out in about six or seven days." During their
time on the traplines, the men would live in small wooden huts called
"tilts" like the one I saw at the museum in North West River last year.
In these tilts, only the warmth of a small tin stove prevented the men
from dying in the sub-zero temperatures of a Labrador winter.

"Anytime after late December, you're looking at probably minus
thirty degrees."

Trappers returned for a few days in January, then went back on the traplines until spring, when they would trade their furs at one of the posts in return for staples such as flour, tea, and guns. There was no cash involved. It was a hard life, Horace admits, yet there is pride in his voice. The people were dependent on themselves and survived by their own strength. Such long periods away were essential. "In order to make enough money," he says, "you would need at least two months just to trap. When I was up at Lobstick Lake, you're lookin' at a five-week trip with a heavy load of groceries and whatever else you would need for four months away altogether."

Horace tells his stories with a practised air, as he's been interviewed about his life many times. He throws in a couple of skittish anecdotes for my benefit, telling how he once met Innu girls out hunting alone on the barrens, and how on another occasion, he was tracked back to his tilt by a pack of wolves attracted to the blood dripping from an axe wound.

Life was no easier for the women, many of whom would be left for long periods alone in isolated cabins with small children. During these periods, a wife would look after home and family by fishing, hunting small game such as geese, making clothes, chopping wood, and protecting herself and the children from the cold and disease as best she could. I had been greatly affected by a book I read on board the *Sir Robert Bond* last year as I sailed back to Newfoundland. Entitled *Woman of Labrador,* it was written by Horace and Joe's mother, Elizabeth.

The life she describes—of physical hardship, isolation, and the need to respond creatively to any situation the environment could throw at you, often as far as seventy miles from the nearest human contact—would be more than most women today could bear. I find myself wishing Mina had had the opportunity to meet some of those strong frontier wives. I've no doubt she would have found a kind of common bond, based on determination, strength, and tenacity.

The arrival of war in 1939 brought massive changes to the communities in the Lake Melville area. The demand for personnel and supplies in Europe meant an agreement between the United States and Great Britain was made, in which the United States gained strategic military stations. One of these was in British-ruled Labrador. Goose Bay soon became the location for a large airport, and the adjoining town of Happy Valley grew to service it. This coincided with a slump in the price of furs, so settlers from all over Labrador arrived at the airbase in search of well-paid jobs. Initially, they pitched their tents along Otter Creek, then moved five miles away to a place called Skunk Hollow and hacked a space out of the bush to build their cabins. And so Happy Valley was born. By 1951, the population was about six hundred. It has now grown to nine thousand.

After a while, the conversation turns to the Hubbard expeditions.

"I guess the main reason why Mina succeeded where Leonidas failed was because she managed to find the right river in the first place."

"Oh, yes." Horace nods slowly. "You got plenty of food? You'll need it out there."

I assure him I have.

"You know, I never could work out how they managed to starve on that first trip," he muses.

"In his book, Dillon blames Leonidas for taking the wrong equipment—wrong kind of guns, no fishing nets . . . and the lack of game, of course," I reply.

"Well, you see that is what I just don't get. I added up all the food they took and the game they shot and there was no way they should have gone hungry."

It is a mystery. If anyone can work these things out, it is Horace, accustomed as he is to packing food for long stays out in the country, regularly living through worse weather than Leonidas encountered.

"Of course, Mina had four experienced men with her. They knew what they were doing, whereas Leonidas and Dillon didn't, not really," I add. Mina wrote a great deal, rather proudly, about her husband's boyhood in Michigan, his love of the countryside and other adventures he'd had, but none of them compared to—or prepared him in any way for—that expedition. "Look at the companion he chose—a New York lawyer, with Elson just the hired hand."

"If they'd listened to him, Hubbard might have survived," says Horace.

"Maybe. Even then Dillon didn't learn his lesson and travelled with friends again in 1905. Some of the men he hired were sent back even before they left the Naskaupi, and only he and Easton made it through to Ungava. It's not really a surprise Mina was two months ahead of Dillon."

Horace nods, thoughtfully. "Who'll be goin' with you, then?"

I tell him.

"They know what they're doin' out there, all right," he says, referring to the Innu. "You'll be all right with them. What was his name again?"

"Jean Pierre Ashini."

"Well, you know I worked with him once at a fishing camp. Years ago. He was so popular with all the guests . . . he always knew just where the fish were. Got big tips."

I smile.

"He's a strong guy. I remember, we were settin' up a camp one time, bringin' sticks out of the forest [I realize he means long, heavy tree trunks, stripped of their branches]. Three of us. Me and another guy, we were carryin' one at a time—they were heavy. But Jean Pierre, well, he was gone for a while and we started to wonder. Then he appeared carryin' three, all tied together. Strong. Smart, too."

After an hour of so of reminiscing and receiving advice, I take my leave of Horace, who promises, like many others, to be on the banks of the river at the old Hudson's Bay Company building on July 17 to see me off.

As I wander back to Joe's via a store or two, I muse on the paradox of the settlement of Labrador. It was the first place to be seen by Europeans at some point in the Dark Ages (either the Vikings in the tenth century, or as explorer Tim Severin suggests, by the Irish monk Saint Brendan in the eighth century), yet it has been the last to conform to the monolith of North American culture. Labrador is the first and last story in the great epic of the North American frontier.

As a result of the rapid growth of this small town, I find to my surprise over the next few days that I can locate just about everything I need from a handful of stores scattered along the apparently interminable road that connects Goose Bay and Happy Valley. Two towns with no centre, linked by an asphalt umbilical cord. Prefabricated stores are clustered at either end, their brash plastic and neon stranded in the midst of parking lots. At the midway point, the road is strangled by spruce and fir trees closing in, reminding the driver of any air-conditioned pick-up, take-away burger in hand, that the great forests are still dominant in this land.

For several days, Jonathan and I ply endlessly up and down this road in his camper van, making occasional detours down a side street, searching out bug jackets, food supplies, waterproof containers, paddles, ropes, and saw blades, for unlike Leonidas, who outfitted his expedition in New York, I buy almost everything except the canoe and my clothing in Labrador itself. In doing so, I have the advantage of both local, expert advice and equipment ideally suited to the environment here. The sheer volume of the stuff seems unbelievable, however, as it grows into an unmanageable pile in a corner of Joe's living room.

Mina's equipment was similarly comprehensive. In her book, she lists "*two canoes, 19ft long . . . each with three paddles and a sponge . . . 2 tents, 1 stove, 7 waterproof canvas bags, one dozen waterproof balloon silk bags, 3 tarpaulins, 3 small axes, one crooked knife and two nets . . .*"

For herself, Mina displayed a level of expeditionary zeal that puts me to shame: "*I had a revolver, a hunting knife, and some fishing tackle; one folding pocket Kodak, one panoram Kodak, a sextant, an artificial horizon, a barometer, a thermometer.*"

I admire her determination not to allow the standards of an Edwardian lady to slip merely because she was travelling across an unmapped wilderness: "*For my tent, I had an air mattress, one pair light gray camp blankets, one light wool comfortable, one little feather pillow and a hot water bottle.*" Far from being unnecessary luxuries for a pampered lady, they made the rugged conditions bearable and allowed her to function properly throughout the trip.

I make do with a three-season sleeping bag, a foam camping mat, and a blow-up pillow. Jean Pierre's sleeping bag comes tied with string. However, it will probably be a vast improvement on the *"pair of light wool camp blankets"* used by Mina's guides. As they might well have expected to encounter snow, this kind of "travelling light" would seem to have bordered on foolhardy had I not already understood just how indestructible Mina's guides must have been.

The technical side of my expedition shows clearly the unbelievable changes and advances that have taken place in the ninety-five years between our two trips. I am taking a single-lens reflex camera, a digital camcorder, and a digital video recorder, complete with blank tapes and forty hours of battery power. The sextant and artificial horizon are replaced by an electronic global positioning system. I let Jean Pierre take care of the gun, knife, and fishing tackle, not so much out of squeamishness, but in acknowledgement of his greater skills and another not-so-minor detail: Canadian gun laws. As a foreigner, I don't have a licence and I don't have the time to acquire one. Besides, Jean Pierre's capable presence means any feeble attempts on my part to hunt or defend myself would be pointless and probably fairly embarrassing.

I also have one item that sets me apart from both Hubbard expeditions. It is the satellite telephone supplied by Labrador Specialty Services in Happy Valley. A little larger than the size of an ordinary cell phone, it provides enough battery power for nine hours and peace of mind. It won't prevent an accident, but it will help get us out if one does occur. It is my insurance policy against Leonidas' fate and will never leave my sight during the expedition.

The next stage in my preparations is a little more taxing. With Leonidas' death ever in mind, Joe and I have decided that it's best that I try to cache some supplies at some point on our route. It means Jean Pierre and I will have the security of knowing there is food stored for us somewhere along our path—a luxury neither Leonidas nor Mina had. My initial plan is to fly the cache out by helicopter until I learn of a rough access road to one of the dams that make up the immense Smallwood Reservoir. Lying to the northwest at the head of the Naskaupi River, it's the only point on our six-hundred-mile route that is accessible from the outside world.

I must remember to mark the exact position of our cache clearly on my maps, for I do not have George Elson's skills. When Leonidas and his companions made their desperate return journey, they were so weak that they left a trail of discarded and unmarked items behind— food, film, and cameras that were too heavy for them to carry. Months later, when Elson returned in the winter to retrieve them, he found each item straightaway, under eight feet of snow. His companion at the time, a trapper, commented with admiration, *"I could never find anything like you, and did not miss one place, but came right on it every time. I would never believe any one could do that if I did not see it for myself."*

The Smallwood Reservoir was created in 1971 to power the Churchill Falls hydroelectric installation, the third-largest hydro project in the world. It was named after Joey Smallwood, the controversial Newfoundland premier of the time, and the reservoir has itself generated a great deal of controversy. It covers an area three times the size of Lake Ontario and produces over five million kilowatts of power. The creation of the power facility itself was a masterpiece of engineering on a scale befitting the landscape in which it is set. The main chamber is over nine hundred feet long and was blasted out of solid rock a thousand feet below the surface.

The creation of a reservoir to feed this monster has important implications for my trip, as it covers the area that previously surrounded Lake Michikamau, which lies at the height of land. From this area, the Naskaupi River drains away to the southeast and the George River drains to the north. It was Mina who established that the unexplored Naskaupi River and the North West River were in fact the same waterway.

Mina had a large and unknown lake to cross, but I have an even more immense stretch of open water. In a Canadian canoe, this can be fatal, as even the smallest wind can whip up waves large enough to tip you over. It is vital that we keep to the shore, the shape of which on the map looks like something akin to the fjord-severed coast of Norway. I decide that in light of this, we should also cache a small outboard motor and gas at the dam. We will need them to cross the reservoir in one piece, although an outboard will be of little use in the rushing fury of the George River.

Reaching the end of the access road at the dam is something of an expedition in itself. First, Joe and I travel about 180 miles along Labrador's only road through the interior: Route 500, which bisects the lower half of the region from Happy Valley to Labrador City, on the western border, next to Quebec. Known as the "Freedom Road," it was completed only in 1992 and consists of a broad sweep of gravel on hardcore, first across the sandy delta of the Lake Melville area, then up into the stunted barren lands near the height of land.

It is at times a picturesque journey, occasionally marred by the clouds of dust and gravel spat up by passing trucks. Twists in the road are tricky and the surface is far from smooth. We take a long time to stop when a mother bear and her three little cubs wander across the road, unaware of the human presence on this alien strip running through their territory. The pick-up's wheels occasionally slip a little too close to the deep ditches separating us from the spruce and muskeg.

Churchill Falls was one and a half times as high as the more famous Niagara Falls, yet it remained unknown to Europeans until the nineteenth century. The first white person to see the falls was Hudson's Bay Company employee John McLean. In 1839 he'd travelled six hundred miles from Fort Chimo (also on Ungava Bay but now in Quebec), down the George, then used rivers and Native portage trails to the west of Mina's route. On his return to Fort Chimo during the winter months, he, like Leonidas, was brought to the point of starvation, as his diary recorded in a desolate way: *"We saw no game."*

Like George Elson, John's Native guide left his stricken companion to travel ahead and bring help. Fortunately, they were just a few miles from their destination and McLean was rescued.

The explorer's route had taken him via a lake called Petchikapau, situated to the northwest of Lake Michikamau. Another Hudson's Bay Company employee, Erland Erlandson, had travelled from Fort Chimo to Lake Petchikapau a few years earlier in 1834. Instead of continuing south at this point like McLean, however, Erlandson missed the falls by turning southeast into Lobstick Lake and Michikamau, descending to the North West River post by parts of the Naskaupi River and Native portages.

Erlandson's exact route remains unclear, due to the lack of accurate maps at that time. His aim, however, was to find a suitable place in the interior for a Hudson's Bay Company post, and this he found at Lake Petchikapau, which was *"most eligible . . . principally because it is surrounded by good fur country."*

A post, Fort Nascopee, was indeed opened at Lake Petchikapau but abandoned only three decades later, in 1864. During the time of its operation, the post was occupied from fall to spring when a group of company men, led by the factor, would reach it after an arduous journey from North West River, travelling west up the Grand (now Churchill) River, past a Hudson's Bay Company post at Lake Winokapau, and portaging up a series of lakes. The falls were never seen, as the portage took the men some thirty miles to the east of them, and the Naskaupi River, though a shorter route to Petchikapau, was far more difficult to ascend.

So despite the establishment of a trading post on Petchikapau, only one European other than McLean saw the falls. He was a Mr. Kennedy of the Hudson's Bay Company, who was for thirty years in charge of Fort Nascopee. An Iroquois named Louis-over-the-Fire was his guide. Of all the Native peoples in the area, only Louis, being Iroquois, would look upon the falls, as the Innu believed that to see them meant certain death. An Innu story associated with the falls tells that the spirits of two girls are trapped beneath the falls and that they appear sometimes to tempt humans over the edge.

In 1887, a Mr. Randle Holme of England attempted to reach the falls using the old Hudson's Bay Company route, but poor weather, difficult river conditions, and lack of food forced him to turn back fifty miles shy of his destination. In Holme's presentation to the Royal

Geographical Society back home in London, he noted that "*to proceed would mean starvation.*"

So by the end of the nineteenth century, only two white people had ever seen the falls by the time A.P. Low, a well-known Canadian geologist, made one of many trips to Labrador in 1894 and 1895, giving us the first description: "*The noise of the falls has a stunning effect and although deadened because of its enclosed situation, can be heard for more than ten miles away as a deep, booming sound. The cloud of mist is also visible from any eminence within a radius of twenty miles.*"

Only twelve years later, the first plan was put forward to use the water's immense power. Even at this early date, the potential power of a river that drops three hundred yards in twenty miles (of which seventy-five yards is accounted for by the falls themselves) was recognized. However, development was hampered by the remote location, rugged terrain, extreme weather conditions, and long distances any transmission lines would need to cross.

When it was discovered that western Labrador had the highest concentration of iron ore in North America, the mines at Labrador City on the Quebec border were opened to exploit the unexpected bounty. This provided the catalyst for a hydro plant, and work started in 1967. By 1971 one of the highest waterfalls in the world was dried up and dammed to serve the hydroelectric plant, making those nineteenth-century explorers part of only a small group of people ever to see the falls in their true glory.

When Joe and I reach the town of Churchill, which is nothing more than a service area for the massive hydro plant, I am stunned. Rows of boxes have been set neatly down in the rugged landscape. These featureless constructions are homes for the workers at the plant, some eight hundred of them. There is also a school, a restaurant, a community area, and a playground. The whole effect is incongruous and disappointing.

The dam seems to be a symbol of human efforts to match, in their own small way, nature's grand achievements. Despite the fact that people are both the designers and beneficiaries of the plant at Churchill Falls, in this town they come a dismal second to the place itself. None of humankind's finer achievements are evident, not even architecture. The legacy of the plant appears to be only destruction. Whichever way I turn, I can hear D.H. Lawrence's words in my mind: *"We can't bring off anything but materialism; mechanism, the very soul of materialism."*

Churchill Falls is a place where humans are venerated over nature and machine over humans. It is the ultimate twentieth-century community.

In order to gain Quebec's cooperation and the use of a toll-free route through Quebec, Labrador ceded the right to tap the headwaters of five rivers in southern Labrador and agreed to provide Quebec with electricity at a loss, and will cost Labrador $300 million by 2041. Although recent talks have "clawed back" some of this money for Newfoundland, Quebec still comes out ahead because it sells much of the power to the United States at a huge profit. Churchill is a sore subject for all Labradoreans for just this reason; there is resentment toward a provincial government that is seen to act only in the interests of the island of Newfoundland, not the province as a whole. Indeed, the predominant feeling among people from Labrador seems to be that they would rather shoot themselves than be called "Newfies."

However, the building of the hydro project at Churchill raised more than Labradorean hackles. It highlighted an issue that was not even much considered twenty years ago—that is, Who owns the land to grant such rights? When the land around Michikamau was flooded, the Innu lost their hunting and trapping grounds, their burial grounds, sacred sites, and gathering locations. It also opened many sensitive issues for them, for the entire Innu sense of spirituality is entwined with the natural world.

None of this was considered when the hydroelectric project was planned and built, and the construction of Churchill Falls went through with little consultation with Labrador's Native people or those of Quebec, as many of the Innu connected to this area are now settled in that province. Both the Innu and the Inuit of Labrador, however, claim this part of the province as their own and have never signed any treaty with any government. When Lake Michikamau and the additional six thousand square kilometres of land were flooded, the Innu lost not only their hunting grounds and historical evidence of their ancestors in the drowned archeological sites, but also a part of their identity.

In 1992, members of the Innu Nation removed the electricity meters from the homes of people in Sheshatshiu (next to North West River) and sent them back to Newfoundland and Labrador Hydro, with this declaration: "*This power . . . is produced at our expense; it is you who owes us restitution. So your meters are being replaced. Our community, backed by the elders, has made this decision.*" (Peter Penashue, President, Innu Nation)

This history weighs on my mind as Joe and I walk across the parking lot. Heat from the sun bounces back on us from concrete walls in a dozen different directions and I feel as though I'm ploughing through treacle. We climb back into the pick-up after a quick lunch at the company restaurant and drive out of the settlement, past acres of transmission lines and towers, a grey metallic army marching across the land. After a few miles, we turn onto the access road to the Orma Dam, one of several on the reservoir and where we are to leave our cache. Joe flicks a switch that takes us into four-wheel drive.

One of the complaints about such access roads is that they open up the country to other forms of exploitation, such as fishing and hunting, but we see no sign of such use today and I find it hard to imagine why anyone would want to spend any time travelling on this track, which lurches us forward and back, sending me grabbing for a hold to prevent my head from hitting the roof.

We seldom go above twelve miles an hour. The country on either side of the track is flat, covered in scrub and stunted spruce trees, and it is overwhelmingly marshy. Bleak ponds of still black water leach the colour and life from the broken trees drowning in them. The occasional burned sections are grey and black, contributing to the sensation that this truly is the land God gave to Cain. Flooded sections are common, and occasionally a dead trunk or a washout blocks our path. I've never seen a road like this.

A shout from Joe snaps me out of a daydream. A young female caribou is ambling slowly toward us along the road. She looks more grey than brown, and she's camouflaged fairly well against the road. To my eyes, she lacks grace and her legs seem slightly too long—she looks like a gangly teenager. I'm puzzled that she seems unaware of our presence as Joe stops the pick-up.

"Look, the poor thing is being driven mad by the flies. They're all around her. They're burrowing into her fur and laying their eggs. Then they'll hatch into maggots that live off her flesh. I've shot many a caribou with large holes in their hides from the open wounds they cause." He sighs and shakes his head with compassion for the creature. I absent-mindedly scratch at a mosquito bite on my hand as another couple of thousand flies zoom into the windscreen and we start off again, the caribou crashing through woods to our left.

The road can occasionally be seen ahead of us, giving rise to hope that the end is in sight, or sending our spirits plummeting down as an endless section of track continues into the distance across the undulating landscape. After about two hours, Joe pulls to a stop and squints into the sun. The road looks no different—all various sized rocks, dirt, and water—so I don't understand his hesitation. Then I realize the trick that perspective has played on me: about twenty yards ahead is a washout about fifteen feet across. We get out and my heart sinks. If we can't get to the dam and leave the cache, I have a major problem. It's now too late to arrange the helicopter drop (not that I can realistically afford it), and we do not have the space to take all the food and the outboard with us.

Joe stands on the edge of the abyss, which cuts across the track. It's at least eight feet deep and too steep to consider tackling in the pick-up. He scratches his head, dislodging several happy mosquitoes, and turns to me. I can see the words of defeat on his lips, but then his eyes slide past my face to a slope behind me. I turn, too, seeing the speculation and sense a spark of hope. A slope to the right of the track might be gentle enough to allow us to drive down it. A sweep of rocks crosses the bottom of the washout to the other side, which is much less steep. As determined as I am, Joe is ready to try anything.

"It'll do. Let's go."

Joe climbs back into the vehicle and I give the detour a last dubious look before following him. I am very conscious that we have no means of communication with us and that a two-hour drive to Churchill would mean several hours on foot if we got stuck. At least we have a gun in the back, I think. And the flies for company.

We turn off the track and slide down to the base before the four-wheel drive kicks in and the wheels spit us back up to the road. I close my eyes and hang on. I'm sure Joe is laughing at me. He's loving the drama.

"There! Easy!" He winks and smiles at me as we continue lurching and bumping our way into what feels like utter desolation.

A whole two hours later, we reach the dam. Its harsh grey bulk is softened by a black bear, who walks nonchalantly along the broad swathe of the dam itself, outlined against the bright sky, before it jumps off and disappears into the woods. We turn off the track and drive down to where the still waters of the reservoir soften the sand of the shore into an orange quagmire. Fifty feet from open ground, we stop and Joe opens the back of the pick-up, pulling out a chainsaw. I then crawl inside and heave out the two metal containers of supplies, the outboard, and three canisters of gas. I write a note stating ownership and asking that the supplies remain untouched, as a matter of life and death. The words give me a jolt as I write them. I can't believe it's my life I'm referring to.

The flies are appalling. I don't have a head net with me, but I do have something to wrap around my head. I also add another layer of clothes when I realize the mosquitoes are biting me right through my sweater. The heat means I'm dripping with sweat, and this brings out the stouts—great yellow and black striped monsters, the like of which I haven't seen since I came across a colony of two-inch-long bees in the cloud forests of Central America. These stouts are more distressing, though, as they are attracted to moisture and their bite is like being burned with a lighted match.

Joe, meanwhile, cuts down four small trees and strips them of their branches. He then cuts several more and uses them to build a platform about six feet high. It won't stop an inquisitive bear, but it might make it pause for thought. The gasoline is left at ground level. Everything else we heave onto the platform, including the outboard, and cover with a tarpaulin, tying it securely to the four corner stakes. I leave the note under the tarpaulin in a plastic folder. Surely no one will ever even find it, much less steal it!

Our work done at last, we realize the afternoon is almost over and decide to eat before the long journey back. In fact, we have overnight gear with us and we may still need to use it. It's a nine-hour drive back to Happy Valley. We move to a rocky outcrop, trying to find a hint of a breeze, although what air there is does little to blow the beasties away. The stouts, I note with thanks, stay behind in the woods. Within an hour, I'm munching on Joe's camp food—caribou steak with a sprinkling of salt. It's hot and tasty and very welcome.

I sit on a rock, steak perched on a fork, wiping a trickle of bloody juice from my wrist and admiring the view. In the late afternoon sunshine, the reservoir is a shimmering mirage of silver and blue, the land a darker edge the eye cannot focus upon. All is still and the plop of fish just offshore makes me jump. It's peaceful, but I sense the moment is transitory and misleading. Like the pools of black water on the tundra, something murky lies beneath the sparkling surface.

With sunset comes nature's most dazzling show. We pack the remains of our evening meal into the pick-up, pursued by the frenzied flies. The cool of the evening has brought them out in even greater numbers and we seem to be the only things around to eat. The light goes quickly as we start to bump our way back to civilization. At nightfall, the ponds turn into unmatched mirrors of the evening sky, the brilliant chaos of colour thrown back up to the gods so perfectly that the only break is a black strip of land, a fold in the kaleidoscope. Occasionally, the horizon is broken by a line of trees or a rock in the water creating a blank spot, like a hole punched in the canvas of a painting.

The desolation of the land creeps through me, edging out into my fingertips. Gone is the sunlit peace of this empty land, replaced by that solid companion, tangible fear. I find a hard, passing beauty in the glory of the sunset. I no longer revel in the emptiness nor exalt in the isolation. Nature here is now neither kindly nor grandiose, simply part of a pernicious hostility designed to destroy from within.

"Alex! There's someone here to see you," Joe shouts from downstairs. I abandon my diary and climb off my bed, wondering if I'd arranged to meet someone and forgotten. No, on entering the lounge, I see a man I've never met before standing in the middle of the room, smiling.

"This is George." Joe introduces us.

My visitor is about forty years old, wearing glasses and dark blue coveralls, the embossed logo of which I see more clearly when he enthusiastically pumps my hand: "Happy Valley Fire Service."

I smile. George lives next door and has a strong personal interest in my planned trip.

"When I heard what you're doing, I just had to come and meet you. I think it's a fantastic trip. Are you prepared for the flies?" I nod and draw breath, but George continues. "I've read *Lure of the Labrador Wild* [written by Wallace about his journey with Leonidas in 1903] and *The Long Labrador Trail* [Wallace's account of his rival expedition to Mina's in 1905] so many times. It's just an amazing tale. It's so exciting that you are making this trip after all these years."

As we speak, I learn that George has something for me to see.

"I have to go out in a few minutes," I say. "Can we make it later?"

"Sure."

We chat for a while, but I have an appointment, and Jonathan will be here at any moment to pick me up. It seems everyone knows about me and most want to come and talk about the Hubbard stories, but I realize, as I show George to the door, that this is not just a story. To the people of Labrador, the Hubbard and Dillon expeditions are part of the local tradition, their history, and now there is a new pressure on me. I find myself wanting to do well for them, too.

I wave goodbye to George and say hello to Jonathan. Time is ticking away. There are only two more days before I am due to leave, yet some of the most important items of equipment have not turned up.

Nothing I ordered from the United States has arrived, but for most of it, I have found a suitable substitute in Happy Valley—though not for the canoe, which has still failed to make an appearance. Jonathan and I are now on our way to collect some additional maps and the satellite phone, first making a small detour to visit someone who knows the country and who may be able to give me a few tips on survival.

Guy Playfair is far from the debonair playboy stockbroker his name had conjured up in my mind. He's a forester in Labrador, a job that keeps him in the country for much of the time. When we arrive, to judge by the state of his military green combat pants, shirt, and boots, he's just come back from a stint in the field. As he shakes my hand, I think how Guy looks like a man who could survive just about anything.

"So what kind of compass do you have and have you programmed the GPS?" Straight away I'm caught off balance.

"Er . . ." I look to Jonathan for help, who roots in one of our many bags and produces the compass bought earlier that week. Guy puts down his mug of extra strong tea with sugar (does nobody drink anything else here? I wonder) and sets to work while chatting about the number of bears he saw out in the country that week.

"We had about six in four or five days. Not too bad—they weren't aggressive and we didn't have to shoot any. There's plenty of food around at the moment, so I guess they were just curious."

Guy exudes energy and capability. The large hunting knife attached to his waistband is used to help Jonathan and me cut and tie the ropes of the tent, so it can be tied to a crosspole in camp. Despite being short on time, Guy doesn't appear to mind this exercise in measuring, cutting, and tying. It lasts just long enough for me to absorb a few tales of derring-do that chill my blood, some useful tips, and a better compass.

As we drive away from Guy's house, I still have a list of "things to do" that seems never to shrink. The pressure of making this whole expedition happen is starting to weigh heavily on me, and I feel as though I'm trapped inside some tacky TV game show, where the contestants have a few minutes to complete impossible tasks and the penalty for failure is total humiliation.

That particular fate draws ever closer as we arrive back at Joe's. The promised canoe has not arrived. Having spent the past few months in a garage in Toronto, my canoe was due to be shipped to Labrador some days ago, but in true farce style, she has not appeared. Jonathan leaves me to my fate with a cheerful wave, while I make another call to the haulage company and have a fruitless conversation half in French and half in English with someone in a depot some-where between here and Toronto, who may or may not have seen her some days ago.

I lean back in my chair, exhausted. Joe hands me a cup of tea, although at this moment I have a hankering for something a little stronger.

"I hate to point this out," he says, "but without a canoe, you are not going anywhere." The phone rings again and I pick it up. It's the haulage company again. My canoe will be with me on Sunday, the day before I am to leave. I hang up, grateful it will arrive at all.

"I think I'm going to postpone our departure," I say to Joe, who nods. "I need more than a day after the canoe arrives. We'll leave on Tuesday."

Joe takes the tea out of my hand and pulls me to my feet.

"I think it's time you had a little break. We're going out."

The sun is starting to set as we drive to North West River. The air has that still, translucent feel it acquires as it hovers between light and twilight. From the end of the settlement, we drive to a point of land and stop on a long, thin beach. The mosquitoes are out, but we are covered up and they don't bother me too much. The water is calm, only the smallest of wavelets lapping on the sand. Before me, the river delta of the inlet opens up, and I feel tiny on the shore. Joe and I walk along slowly, in silence.

There is grandeur to the land here, a sense of space, despite the presence of mountains. They are immense, but always seem to exist far away, just on the horizon. Everywhere there are huge expanses of glossy water, stretching out under endless skies. The Americans call Montana Big Sky Country, but I find it hard to believe that it would beat Labrador. As evening steals closer over the dead-calm delta, the clear blue sky steadily darkens and the sunlight drifts away, somehow getting lost in the trees to the west. We turn around and head back.

"Now," says Joe as we climb back into the pick-up, "I think we need a proper drink."

Half an hour later, we pull up outside a bar in Happy Valley. It crosses my mind that the place seems a little dark . . . where is the music? The man at the door takes Joe's money (ladies get in for free, but gentlemen must pay), and explains that the electricity has gone off, but it's business as usual and they expect it to come back on at any moment.

We go inside to a scene which is a cross between a Gothic novel and a Wild West shoot. It's a typical North American drinking hole with bare floorboards and a central square bar, but the place is lit by candles, the light flickering weirdly on neon signs advertising beer that are now starved of power, as is a band that is set up on a raised platform in the murky distance. Only warmish bottles and spirits are for sale, since the electric pumps are inoperable. I'm the only woman I can see in the series of dark corners and I pay for our drinks with the correct money, getting a written receipt in return. The other dozen or so customers seem unsurprised by the situation and sit in small groups chatting, or alone and morose at the bar, in the compulsory style of barflies the world over.

An acquaintance of Joe's (he appears to know the entire town) joins us and we chat, the topic turning inevitably to my trip.

"Who's your guide, then?"

"Jean Pierre Ashini . . ."

"Yes?"

I spin round. In the half-gloom by the bar, I see Jean Pierre holding what looks like a warm glass of cola. In the course of introductions, a short woman steps out of the shadows and Jean Pierre introduces her as Katie, his wife. I'm curious and pleased to meet her, but she barely touches my outstretched hand and then glances away again, somehow fading out of sight. Joe and his friend say nothing and we move to a table, where Jean Pierre joins us. Katie sits at another table.

As Joe and I drive home later that evening, I ask him about Katie's behaviour. He struggles a little to explain, perhaps trying to find references that I will understand.

"Innu women—their sphere is the home, their community. It was shyness, not rudeness. They wouldn't ordinarily talk to white men they don't know in public places like bars."

"But I'm a woman. I shall be spending a long time alone with her husband . . ."

"You're English. She would have no idea what to say to you."

The following morning, George is again on our doorstep bright and early.

". . . so you need to come over and I'll show it all to you," I hear him saying in my half-awake state.

"Pardon me? Now?"

"I'm on duty in an hour."

As we walk over to George's property, he tells me how he met Dillon's son, also called Dillon, some years ago. They struck up a friendship and George was given some old photographs belonging to Dillon, Leonidas' companion and Mina's archrival. As far as I know, very few people have previously had the opportunity to see them. Suddenly, I'm wide awake.

George has three albums of photos, mostly taken on Dillon's second expedition, the trip he started less than twenty-four hours before Mina, although neither mention the other in their respective books about their adventures. Dillon reached Ungava some sixty days after Mina, but as the supply ship *Pelican* had been delayed for two months, he, too, had the opportunity to sail out back to Newfoundland. Unable, however, to face a lengthy period on board with the woman who had beaten him so thoroughly, Dillon made a choice that demonstrates just how toughened this New York lawyer had become by his time in Labrador.

He decided to travel out to Fort Chimo, a Hudson's Bay Company post to the west of the George River post where Mina was waiting for the ship. He departed in a small boat with Native guides but it became impacted in the winter ice of Ungava Bay. Forced to resort to an overland trail, Dillon became increasingly weak because of the low temperatures and the demands made on him by the trip from North West River. The group abandoned some supplies to make better time, but Dillon had become so depleted that the Native guides left him and his companion, Easton, in a log cabin while they travelled on to the Hudson's Bay Company post at Whale River, midway between Fort Chimo and the George River post. They returned some days later with provisions, which allowed Dillon to continue to Whale River and, eventually, Fort Chimo. Two months later, Dillon was sufficiently recovered to travel by dogsled across country back to North West River.

I turn the pages of the album, looking at image after image of black and white mountains, rivers, canoes, and men, their eyes dark holes gazing at the camera, perhaps wishing it could whisk them out of a living hell of flies, uncertain supplies, and dangerous rivers, or perhaps relishing the challenge of staying alive. There is a curious lack of emotion in the photographs.

Dillon took a different route from Mina's, which accounts for why they failed to meet each other in the country. Mina travelled up the Naskaupi, taking a detour northwest up the Wapustan River and then across a portage route to Seal Lake, but Dillon travelled partway up the Naskaupi, then left it to use a Native portage route that took him out to the northeast, experiencing nothing like the ease with which Mina travelled through the interior.

When George sees I am reaching the last of the photographs, he slips away and comes back with several parcels, which he presents to me with all the glee of a small child unveiling a successfully kept surprise. The first is a hat, worn, I'm told, by Dillon on his trip. The second is a gun, used again by Dillon, and the third is a modern flask, from which George pours me a small glass of slightly yellowish liquid.

"Go on, drink it!" he urges. I sniff. It is slightly musky, definitely not alcoholic, and seems fairly innocuous. I take a small sip.

"Water?" I ask, perplexed.

"From the spring next to the plaque marking Leonidas' death on the Susan River. I fetched it myself." I know I am privileged to see and touch these things. Mina's expedition may have been the one remembered by history, thanks to her research and efficiency, but despite Mina's rivalry with him, Dillon also deserves to be remembered among that noble group of people in the eighteenth to early twentieth centuries who travelled through unknown lands, making rough maps, eating their sled dogs, and burying their friends as they went.

That evening, Joe throws a small farewell party for me and I'm reminded of the kindness of these people of Labrador, who have taken such an interest in my trip. Dave and Ann are there, the first time I've seen them since my visit last year. It's good to talk to them again, for it makes me realize how many friends I seem to have made in this place in such a short time. Indeed, Happy Valley feels like a second home, which is not perhaps such a good thing, as it will make leaving on Tuesday all the more difficult.

Jean Pierre is among the guests and I bite my lip with concern when I see him talking to the former commander of the airbase here in Goose Bay. Relations between the Innu and the base are very bad and have been since it started to carry out thousands of low-flying exercises over the country. The issue is a tangled one, the strands of which include wildlife, land rights, and colonialism. The conversation is animated, but all appears to be well.

I'm slightly embarrassed at being the centre of so much goodwill and attention. What if I fail? What if I break my leg on the first day? Joe notices my mounting trepidation, and after the guests have gone, he sits me down.

"You mustn't worry about what will happen out there. You have your safety nets. The most dangerous thing is your pride. Remember it is far more courageous to admit defeat and return than to go on, risking your life and that of your guide, for whom you are responsible."

I nod, unable to speak. There is a large lump in my throat, and I can feel the tears of relief, tension, and emotion prickling behind my eyes. I swallow and force a small smile.

"I know, Joe."

"You will be respected more for making the right decisions than for getting to the end regardless of the costs, or even not at all." I nod again.

"Remember, I'm at the other end of that fancy phone if you need me. I'll always do what I can."

With that, he gets up, allowing me a moment for a quick wipe at my eyes before we begin to tidy up. It is 2 A.M. and I leave in just over forty-eight hours.

The next morning my canoe arrives. A huge articulated truck trawls down the Hamilton River Road. Fortunately, Joe is at home and between them, he and the driver pull her out and lay her on the sand of the sidewalk outside the gate. I sign the papers, overwhelmed to see her for the first time. Rollin Thurlow, her builder, has done a magnificent job. The canoe has elegance, a pure simplicity that merges the natural beauty of the raw materials—the yellow-gold of cedar wood and her smart, red-painted canvas—with perfect form. She will bear us safely through, I feel. There is integrity about this craft that plastic canoes simply do not have.

Joe turns her over.

"Man, look at the hole in her canvas!" I look, something I should have done before I signed the papers. Three hundred miles of grinding and rattling across the gravel track into Labrador has bashed a hole the size of the base of a soda can in her canvas below the water level. Fortunately, the wood is intact, but a hole like that will mean she will quickly become waterlogged and heavy. A series of scratches also run the length of her underside, a desecration to her paint.

"I can fix it," says Joe, "but I can't guarantee she'll be dry by Tuesday morning."

While Joe spends the morning fixing my new canoe, Jean Pierre and I take one of Joe's canoes out on the Churchill River, formerly the Grand River, launching in via the creek at the bottom of Joe's garden. We spend a few hours paddling about, getting used to each other in a canoe. Jean Pierre paddles stern and I bow. He is tremendously powerful and the canoe shoots along, but I dread to think how heavy our canoe will be when fully laden. The sun is incredibly hot, so we eventually return to cold drinks and the shade of the workshed, where our future companion has been patched, glued, and left to dry.

I have little time to ponder what the future may hold as I rush through my final hours in civilization. This is definitely a good thing, but there is nevertheless a cold knot deep in my stomach every time I think about the expedition, which sends shivers of anticipation racing across my skin even in the eighty-degree weather that has settled on the region. On the night before I leave, Jonathan pokes his head through the doorway to the deck at the back of Joe's house.

"Can I come in? All ready for tomorrow?"

I can only smile, wanly.

"I've brought you something." He gives me a smooth ring of bone, about an inch in diameter and two in depth.

"What is it?" I ask, turning the object over in my hands. A leather cord is tied to the bone and I see the intricate swirl within the core. It is warm and attracts my touch.

"It's caribou bone. The caribou is one of the most important animal masters. Carry this and he will ensure your safe return."

"I love it."

"See you tomorrow at 7 A.M."

And with that, he is gone.

# Part 2

## Into the Wilderness

# CHAPTER 1

I lie awake staring into the pre-dawn darkness, waiting on my 5 A.M. alarm. I'm relishing the last few minutes before I am to depart on the greatest adventure of my life. My eyes rake the sky for light, alert despite the total absence of sleep, and my fists ball up the duvet with nerves. Never previously so uncertain of my fate, I experience almost out-of-body sensations, as though I were looking at someone else lying here in the guest room, about to start out into a hostile land in a wooden canoe. She must be mad, I think.

The alarm rings.

Joe, his friend Merrill, and I drive along the endless road to North West River, windscreen wipers sloshing great swaths of water from our view. It's now 6:45 A.M. and we are due to meet Jean Pierre and a few friends outside the old Hudson's Bay Company building at seven, leaving as soon as the canoe is loaded up. As a distraction, I look at the forest on either side of the road, trying to blank out the well-meant small talk in the pick-up's cab, the talk that pretends we are all just out for a Sunday afternoon picnic, and choose something concrete to worry about. Will Jean Pierre remember the stove (I have yet to see it), the fishing equipment? Will we fit it all in the canoe?

As we pull to a halt at the edge of the river, I'm astonished to find there are about two dozen people there to see us off. When I climb out of the cab, a buzz goes round and a series of camera shutters clicks. Normally, this would be a huge thrill, but this morning I couldn't feel less like being photographed. I try to hide in the cab, pretending to fiddle with some equipment.

Mina chose to leave at the vastly more civilized hour of 3:15 P.M., also from outside the Hudson's Bay Company building, then a working trading post, where there was "*all of North West River to see us off.*"

Not that much has changed, then.

Joe unloads the canoe from the trailer and puts her on the beach, at the edge of the water. It is 7:15 A.M. and there is no sign of Jean Pierre, but I had expected this and feel a little relieved at my few minutes' grace to remain with friends. Joe and I pile all the equipment next to the canoe, reluctant to load without Jean Pierre—such a task is usually the prerogative of the guide, and besides, he has some of the heaviest equipment, which needs to go in first. Already, however, the sight of all my gear leaves me incredulous: how will we fit everything in? It seems that stack of unwieldy items will never fit into our slender canoe, bobbing gently against the sand with each lazy lap of the river.

I move from group to group of well-wishers, talking to those I know, greeting those I don't. Jonathan, Annette, and her son Matthew are there, of course, and Jonathan takes on the duty of recording my final minutes on the camcorder. For some reason, a delegation from the Happy Valley Fire Service is there, too. Then I see George. He looks as excited as though he himself was leaving and I know he wishes he was.

"You know, Alex," he says, "I don't care how far you get. It doesn't matter if you break your leg tomorrow. Don't be ashamed if you don't reach Ungava. You've already done more than anybody else."

Somehow, it's just the right thing to say and I give him a hug in gratitude.

By 8 A.M. there is still no sign of Jean Pierre's shiny red pick-up crossing the bridge above us from Sheshatshiu. There are murmurings, and one or two make their excuses and drift off to work. I am now a little concerned, and the delay has given my nerves time to reassert themselves. Finally, an hour and a half late, my guide appears in wellington boots and jeans. A cigarette clenched nonchalantly in his teeth, he mutters something about a delay and starts to throw equipment apparently haphazardly into the canoe. The final item to go in is the stove and pipe—once no doubt tin, but now a rectangular black husk held together by wire and a wafer-thin latticework of rust. I'm so pleased to see him, I don't care. Not starting at all would be stretching George's already generous definition of success.

We pose for a few final photos and I say my farewells to Jonathan and Joe, the comfort of whose bear hugs I am reluctant to relinquish. Jean Pierre stows the last item close to his seat; it's his gun, wrapped in tarpaulin. The final seconds of our departure are filmed on the camcorder, which is then tossed over the water to me before being stowed at my feet, ready to be grabbed in an instant, should the need arise. As Jean Pierre and I pull away into the dead calm black water, a terrible emptiness fills me, a numbness which allows me to paddle away into the unknown, leaving my dear, newly made friends standing on the shore.

We are not alone, however. Just as Mina was followed by a Monsieur Duclos, crying, "*I have ze las' picture, Madame,*" so we are followed by two local freelance journalists in their kayaks, who take pictures for the Canadian press and the Internet. Gradually, though, they fall away and we have a final glimpse of a dozen or so diehard supporters standing on a point, high above us. I wave, then they are lost from view, and we are alone, at last, on the water.

Mina started her adventure on a resolutely positive note, her diary recording nothing of her fears, just an impatience to begin: "*Did not feel in the least uneasy or unnatural going off. Only glad to be at last off on our trip, really started.*" Perhaps it was the weather that lightened her spirits, as she records a "*perfect day and evening. Grand Lake very very beautiful.*"

When I consider how much more Mina had to fear than I do, I conclude that she was made of far sterner stuff. Where I know my route, she did not, where I have means of rescue, she did not, and where I know this journey is possible, she had only the death of her husband as a guide to what might lie ahead. I decide it is time to follow her example. I straighten my back, pulling a little harder on the paddle. The time for courage has only just begun.

Not surprisingly, the weather is typical of Labrador in summer: grey, damp, and misty. The narrow entrance to Grand Lake ahead is guarded by hills diminished by cloud, which serves to enhance the sinister effect—as though it were the gates to Hades. Indeed, I feel as though I'm paddling through some netherworld, as all is grey, the horizons obscured by wisps of cloud, and every sound—aside from the rhythmic dip of our paddles—is muffled by patches of haze. A light drizzle complements the experience, and for the first couple of miles we move largely in silence, each of us bound in our own thoughts.

It is not long before we reach the point where Grand Lake ahead empties into the "Little Lake" at North West River and eventually Lake Melville. The great volume of this forty-mile-long lake passes through a narrow gap, filled with white water and occasional rocks, standing up like broken teeth in a geriatric mouth. We must paddle through it, upstream.

As we begin our passage into the gap, I find myself kneeling up in the bow, using my body weight to pull on the paddle. It seems to meet with little resistance, and I realize that it is because the water is flowing past us so quickly. I redouble my efforts and we reach the halfway point. We are in the middle of the narrows, forced into a channel deep enough to accommodate us, and the water foams past on both sides.

Above the sound of my own grunts of effort and laboured breathing, I hear Jean Pierre shout something.

"What?"

"We're not moving!"

I look at a rock on our right and try to gauge how far past it each pull is taking us. We seem for a moment to be moving, but I realize that it's a mirage created by the speed of the water dancing past us, like when one sits on a train in the station and it seems to be departing because the train at the next platform slides past.

*"We're not moving!"*

I haul on the paddle until every part of my upper body hurts. I glance over my shoulder and see Jean Pierre's face more animated than ever before.

"I can't paddle any harder!" I shout. I'm aware of my fingers clamped like claws on the slippery wood, and for the first time I feel shaken by the power of this place. This is only the first and probably the smallest of many rapids to come.

Our canoe is so heavily loaded, it would take two men of Jean Pierre's size and skill to push her up this rapid. I feel him guiding us over to the right, into shallow water, where we grate to a halt.

"Get out." I do as Jean Pierre says. Mina had so little trouble with the narrows she barely mentions them, saying merely that they "passed" the rapid and entered the lake. However, I must not forget that she did have two men to paddle each of her canoes.

I see now why Jean Pierre is wearing wellingtons as he splashes into the shallows at the stern and pulls out a rope, which he attaches to the bow. Waving me forward along a narrow spit of sand, he walks the canoe up the edge of the rushing water until we reach the calm of the lake. My feet are wet; it is an ignoble beginning and I am chastened.

We continue to paddle along the length of Grand Lake keeping close to the right bank. It would be suicide to take a fully laden canoe away from the shore on a body of water this size. At this, the eastern end of the lake, we regularly pass over a series of floats and netting, visible on the surface and hanging down into the depths below. Jean Pierre tells me they are for catching salmon.

It was Donald Smith of the Hudson's Bay Company post at North West River who initially started to exploit the salmon fishery in the 1850s and who was the first to can salmon for retail sale. Mr. Randle Holme, on his trip to Labrador in 1887, claimed that the Hudson's Bay Company was netting the lake and rivers and laying claim to the exclusive right to killing salmon, charging each fisherman a percentage of his catch.

Not only was this illegal, as the right to fish salt waters in the public and tidal rivers was vested in the Crown, but Holme notes (somewhat ahead of his time) that the methods used were destroying stocks. In words not out of place today, Holme warned that salmon fishing methods may share the *"consequences of . . . the cod fisheries* [which] *had been very bad for the past two or three years."* His judgement reminds me of the tale told by the captain of the *Sir Robert Bond* last year about the rich waters off Newfoundland enduring a cod-fishing moratorium.

During the six hours of paddling before we stop for lunch, we see only one other boat on the lake, despite the fact that we are barely a few miles from Happy Valley–Goose Bay and North West River. It is a small boat powered by an outboard, which passes us, travelling in the opposite direction. There are three or four people on board, all Native. I gather they must be Innu, as they call out to Jean Pierre, who replies, the sound of Innu-aimun falling for the first time on my ears. I ask Jean Pierre what was said.

"They wanted to know what I was doing in a canoe with you."

By this I realize he means "with a European woman."

"What did you say?" I ask, intrigued.

"I told them we are going to Ungava."

How often would they hear that for an answer? Yet judging by their lack of comment in reply, I assume Innu people must have a powerful ability either to mask curiosity or at least not to express surprise.

It is early afternoon before Jean Pierre steers us up to a large, flat slab of rock against the bank and throws me the rope to tie us up. I've been paddling since 8:30 A.M. and have not slept in thirty-six hours. The adrenaline of our first day is all that is keeping me going. After a lunch of bread, sardines, and tea, boiled over an open fire on the rock, we are ready to start again. Our break lasted a mere thirty minutes.

Before we set off again, I disappear quickly into the trees to answer a call of nature, and as I emerge a few minutes later, I pay little attention to what is underfoot. Suddenly, my feet are in the air, and like a person slipping on a banana skin, I slam onto the rock with such force the jolt gives me an instant headache. Only an elbow thrust out at the last moment prevents my head from making contact with the moss-covered rock, which was quite literally my downfall. I get up slowly, heart racing, elbow skinned, and very bruised. It is a salutary warning about the need to pay attention at all times.

As we set off once more, Jean Pierre and I both try to make a little conversation, but it is difficult, as we have to almost shout at each other from opposite ends of the canoe. I also find it hard to understand my guide's accent sometimes, as I'm sure he does mine. Nonetheless, I learn a little about his wife, Katie, with whom he has lived for twenty-two years, and their five children—three natural and two adopted. The youngest of these is five-year-old Mary, and Jean Pierre tells me proudly of her bilingual ability in both the Innu language and English.

It seems strange to be making this journey with someone I know so little about. I have only the word of trusted friends about my guide, and he himself says little. I have yet to discover his personality, and if the truth were told, I am a little in awe of him.

As the afternoon slips by, the skies lighten, and aside from a constant pain in my back, I start to relax a little and look with interest at my surroundings.

The rain and mist of the morning have been swept away, to be replaced by small white clouds and large patches of blue sky. The entire character of the scenery has changed. Despite the earlier rain, the country had retained a certain grandeur, but it was far from picturesque. Now, all is blue, silver, and green, with the kind of tranquility only wild places ever attain. I can see now how Mina thought it so beautiful. The mountains about us, far from seeming sinister, are enticing, hinting at riches undiscovered and adventures to be had. It brings to mind the feelings expressed by the American explorer Cabot, when he travelled with Leonidas by ferry to Hamilton Inlet in 1903: "*Nowhere are such clear, unfished rivers, such white-moss hills as those of the semi-barren, velvet to the feet and fair to the eye. More than all are the lakes. Its lakes are Labrador's glory . . . their mission only to reflect the sky, with their water horizons . . .*"

I am becoming very tired by late afternoon and I ask Jean Pierre where we shall camp.

"Past the point." He nods at a high spread of forest reaching down into the water on our left. It seems fairly close, but I know it's some miles away. I wonder why Mina declined the use of a yacht, offered by Monsieur Duclos, to reach the mouth of the Naskaupi, though she did point out that it would not cross the rapids at the mouth of the lake. But, then, she did not have to do half the paddling. (Neither, I suspect, do I. Every time Jean Pierre lights another cigarette, he ceases to paddle for a few moments and our speed plummets, despite my best efforts.)

Mina settled instead on another method of crossing this huge body of water. She had the men construct sails on the canoes. *"Soon,"* she writes, *"they were caught by the light breeze, and, together with the quick paddle strokes, carried the canoes at a rapid pace towards Cape Corbeau, which rose high and commanding twelve miles away."*

Cape Corbeau is a point, opposite which Jean Pierre has said we shall camp, but despite our passing it some time ago, we continue to paddle. Each of my increasingly plaintive inquiries as to where we are stopping receives a curt "up ahead" or "just around the next point." I start to feel like a child in a hot car on a long journey and I must be equally irritating. By this time, however, I would give anything for a set of Mina's sails as my back is crossed with lines of fire at every pull on the paddle.

Just as I'm beginning to think this day will never end, Jean Pierre steers us onto the sand of a pretty little beach, almost attractive enough to be worth today's extended agony. I crawl out of the canoe and lie with my back flat on the hard sand. I breathe in slowly, savouring the ecstasy. We've paddled twenty-eight miles from North West River, six more than Mina made on her first day.

We unload all the equipment onto the beach and Jean Pierre separates out what we will need that night, putting the remainder under the upturned canoe, which now rests high on the sand. This includes some of the food, and as I have had drilled into me the necessity of suspending it high in the trees away from the camp to avoid bears, this makes me a little uneasy. But I shrug, figuring that after thirty years of living in this country, Jean Pierre probably knows how to survive. He disappears into the trees, carrying the tent, stove, and axe. I pick up my rucksack and follow. About twenty-five feet from the beach, there is a clearing in the woods. Saplings, shorn of their branches, lie to one side, and small stumps are visible around the edges of the clearing. Jean Pierre moves around the area, picking up the poles, kicking debris out of the way.

"This is an Innu campsite. See?"

Animal bones and empty tin cans also lie around, discarded and rusting, a reminder of the insidious nature of North America's consumer culture. Even hunters drink cola these days, it seems.

Jean Pierre motions to the flat, cleared centre, showing me the clearly defined edges, then hauls the tent out of the sack. I move to help, but he indicates there is no need, so I push my way back onto the beach through the willows and find the rest of our gear.

I walk back and forth, carrying various bags (mostly mine), pots of water, and ropes. Each time I return to our camp, the tent is a little closer to being erected, yet the process seems to take forever. All four corners are each tied to a stake at head height, while a horizontal pole, suspended between two trees, provides the backbone for the tent and is attached by a series of six or so smaller ropes, all of which need to be tied separately. It seems an exhausting process and takes about an hour.

As nomadic people until barely a generation ago, the Innu were familiar with a process very similar to this, and many hunters still live close to the traditional ways. They would move camp regularly, efficiently packing and unpacking, tracking and hunting the caribou, which was their traditional staple food. Caribou herds migrate every spring and autumn across the vast lands of Nitassinan (the Innu word for Labrador), and the territorial lands of the Innu encompass most of southern and central Labrador and a large part of southeastern Quebec. These boundaries are marked by Inuit regions to the north, Iroquois to the south, and Cree lands to the west.

During the long autumn, winter, and spring months in the past, the Innu would move across the frozen rivers and tundra of this territory on snowshoes, pulling toboggans and hunting for the animal that would provide them with their food, clothing, tools, and weapons. If the caribou were scarce, which was often the case, porcupine, ptarmigan, ducks, and other game were taken. Then, in the brief summer season when the ice melted, the people would travel to the coast in canoes to fish and repair equipment, and since the arrival of Europeans, trade furs for ammunition, tea, and other staples. Jean Pierre tells me this is how he has spent a large part of his life.

I ask Jean Pierre what the Innu would have used as shelter before heavy canvas tents of the kind we are using became common. He thinks for a moment, perhaps reluctant to tell me. I am still a stranger, and Native people have seen such destruction of their ways at the hands of whites that they do not always want to speak about their traditions to non-Natives.

"Skins," he says thoughtfully. "Caribou skins. Some used bark."

I wander back to the beach, largely to escape the flies in the woods, thinking how lucky I am to explore this land with someone who is so intricately linked to it.

The Innu who used skins rather than bark as shelter are now known as Mushuau Innu, meaning they belonged to the barren grounds above the treeline, an area north of here that we hope to enter after about three weeks of paddling. Mina met two bands of Mushuau Innu on the George River and describes them as living in a *"camp . . . of two wigwams, one a large oblong and the other round. They were covered with deer skins drawn tight over the poles, blackened round the opening at the top by the smoke of the fires, which are built in the center within."*

It is thought that diseases such as scarlet fever, influenza, measles, and syphilis killed up to two-thirds of the Innu on contact with Europeans and even as late as the 1920s, the population of Voisey's Bay to the northeast fell from 250 to 75. This and the disruptive effects of fur trapping on subsistence hunting first broke down the bands of travelling Innu into family-sized groups and later made them more vulnerable to the pressures of twentieth-century modernism. Today, the Innu of Sheshatshiu and Utshimassit (Davis Inlet) just to the south of

Voisey's Bay are now only about 1,500 in number—representing about a tenth of the overall Innu population that still survives. The remainder live in villages along the St. Lawrence shore in Quebec—a part of Nitassinan arbitrarily divided by a British Privy Council order in 1929.

The sound of Jean Pierre's axe echoes its rhythmic *thunk, thunk* into the stillness of the evening. Sunset is not far away and a golden glow fills our little oasis with serenity. The low green and blue hills on the south side of the lake opposite, the trees, and even the water seem to be poised, ready for the transition into night. I walk along the shore, following a set of prints I cannot identify. When they disappear into the forest, I stop and retrace my steps. A skull lies on the far side of the beach, hidden by the shadow of the canoe. I peer at it and conclude, probably wrongly, that it is caribou.

I take this moment of solitude to record my daily video diary, with mosquitoes zooming into the lens, serving as authentic props. Soon, hunger and fatigue drive me back through the trees into the camp. Pushing the willows aside, I'm astonished at how cozy it looks. The tent is up and the stove is just outside, smoking, the pipe resting in a fork of a tree and the teakettle boiling merrily on top.

Inside the tent there is no groundsheet but a thick, sweet-smelling carpet of spruce boughs. Jean Pierre is sitting in one corner, finishing our home for the night. For each bough, he sticks the sharp, broken end into the ground, with all the fronds facing the same way to make a deep, soft covering which is surprisingly unspiky. I take a deep breath. The scent is intense, but not overpowering, like a forest at dawn.

My feet are still soaking inside my hiking boots, so I remove the boots, placing them under the stove and hanging the socks on a low pole resting diagonally from ground to rock, next to the heat. They steam gently while we sit on a log, eating the dinner of beans and sausages Jean Pierre has prepared. But my appetite seems oddly to have disappeared, despite my knowing that our supply of fresh food will soon run out.

The flies bite my face and hands and dive into my food as I try to eat. Mina described their suicidal antics quite graphically: *"I was willing that day to almost choke with smoke to escape the flies ... there were twenty dead on my plate when I had finished eating lunch, to say nothing of those lying dead on my dress or the large number I had killed. I had to stop caring about seeing them in the food ... When drinking, even while the cup was held to my lips, they flew into it as if determined to die."*

I've replaced my thick socks and boots with thinner socks and runners. After eating, I absently scratch my ankle and look down, discovering with horror that both of my ankles are covered in a swarm of little blackflies, which seem to be biting right through my socks. I bang them all off and spray my ankles with repellent—the camphor-citronella mix they dislike so much. I'm saving my DEET for the George River, where apparently the flies are ten times more numerous than those here on the Naskaupi. Joe warned me this pleasant-smelling mixture would become the "eau de trail" and I can already believe it, as I quickly cover every square inch of exposed skin and clothing with the stuff.

It's too late for my ankles. An hour later, they are swollen and discoloured by about thirty blackfly bites. Each bite has puffed up to about two inches in diameter, making the entire lower half of my legs misshapen, sore, and very itchy. It's another lesson to learn early: vigilance at all times.

By the time twilight descends, we are already inside the tent. The burning mosquito coils make it a passably pleasant fly-free zone, but I'm so tired that little seems to matter any more. Now we are settled and the day's work is over, Jean Pierre opens up a little and talks for a while. I understand that this is how he is: work when there is work to be done, talk when it's time for rest. I must be a sore disappointment as a diversion, as I'm so tired I can barely keep my eyes open. The boughs beneath me are as soft as any bed, and the wildlife outside the tent gives me little cause for concern. Jean Pierre's gun and ammunition are close to hand and I feel safe.

Part of me can barely believe that I am here, sleeping on the shore of Grand Lake after the months of planning and setbacks and disappointments. I think about what happened on that first set of small rapids at the entrance to the lake. There's much more of that ahead. How will we cope? Will I have the fortitude to continue on? Leonidas had not and he was a man of passion, a man who loved the romance of adventure: *"I wanted to get into a really wild country and have some of the experiences of the old fellows who explored and opened up the country."*

To survive, I need to temper this kind of idealism, which bore him to this place as it has me, with practicality and stamina. Will it be enough to have Jean Pierre with me? It occurs to me that although divided by two years, the Hubbard expeditions combined had all the ingredients for success—the benefits of which were reaped by Mina. Leonidas had supplied the idea, the drive, the taste for adventure, his ambition ultimately bringing her—and therefore also me—to this place. Where he failed, she succeeded by making better choices and being better prepared. Mina was the practical half of the ideal relationship.

I am haunted by some of Leonidas' last words before he departed the safety of Grand Lake: *"No matter how a man may add to the fund of human knowledge, it's worth doing, for it's by little bits that we've learned to know so much of our world. There's some hard work before us though, up there in those hills . . ."*

I turn over on the boughs, away from such thoughts, and in the distance, a seagull cries. It is an unexpected sound here among the lakes and mountains, but a reminder that the salt waters of Hamilton Inlet are still close by. The cry makes me think of my home in England's West Country, the land from which many of Labrador's first settlers came before the days of the Hudson's Bay Company and its Scottish employees.

I think of Stuart, of my friends, and of the ocean washing against the cliffs and soft, yellow beaches, where fishermen land mackerel from boats onto small granite quays. I think of haphazard Cornish meadows brilliant with wildflowers, the lanes and paths winding through valleys heavy with the rich green of early summer, when warmth settles on the land and bees pass lazily by, unsteady with their crop of golden nectar.

# CHAPTER 2

The following morning the drone of mosquitoes inside the tent wakes me. Though the coils were supposed to have killed them all last night, they seem either to have found a way in or to have risen from the dead. But there is no time to dwell on this. After a quick breakfast of oatmeal, we are packing up again, taking our supplies from the beach, just where we left them. I have survived my first night in "the country," and as I climb once again into my tiny space in the bow, I feel more optimism than I have for a long time.

Sliding through the water seems unremarkable to me now. It is surprising how quickly paddling becomes "normal." The dip and hush of the blades in the smooth water is calming and comforting. I turn around and smile at Jean Pierre and am rewarded by a smile that transforms his face. It is almost childlike in its sincerity, and the sombre, shuttered, unreadable eyes shine with fun and warmth for a moment. It is infectious, and I realize something I've not acknowledged until now—that my guide and I are going to get along just fine.

We stay close to the edge of the lake as before, as Grand Lake is forty fathoms deep in the centre. Deep and cold. I shudder at the thought and look around at the shores as we pass. What strikes me most about the country is the stillness, the space, and the clean smell of the air. Little stirs as we glide quietly by, and the scale of the entire landscape suggests our passing to be insignificant, our movements barely causing a ripple in the life of this world.

The texture of the water fascinates me, too. Mina describes it as being like "satin," and it does have a strange quality of smoothness, yet it is almost like syrup in the way it slides off our paddles. It is thick and dark, with no splashes or foam to catch light, yet when the sun breaks through the clouds, the entire lake dazzles us with the sparkle of a million scattered diamonds.

The hours pass so smoothly that I cease to notice them. Time expands and flows like water around us. Perhaps, I muse, the rhythm of the paddles is hypnotic. There is a lot of time for musing, which is fortunate, for my mind whorls as I view my journey from different perspectives, alternating from disbelief to a new familiarity that surprises me. A few words from a poem by Philip Larkin flash through my mind:

> . . . this frail
> Travelling coincidence; and what it held
> Stood ready to be loosed with all the power
> That being changed can give . . .

How, I wonder, will this "frail coincidence" change me?

These meanderings are so leisurely that after lunch we chat a little as we paddle. It's awkward to talk with someone sitting directly behind you, a situation exacerbated by how little Jean Pierre and I know each other. I'm slightly nonplussed at some of his opening comments, however, which include the memorable "Do you know Marianne Faithfull? I have stayed in her father's house."

I have to confess I can't match that.

Eventually, the conversation lapses and then I notice the breeze. Turning, I can see something is wrong. The sun has disappeared and Jean Pierre is frowning slightly, his face turned into the current of air coming from the west. I shiver involuntarily, and it is not entirely due to the drop in temperature. Dark clouds are merging with the hilltops at the far end of the lake and the wind has whipped up foamy, frivolous waves that chop at the canoe. Jean Pierre's concern is palpable and we start to move faster, the bow splashing into the swell. The lake, far from calm and pretty, now seems grey and relentless.

"Jean Pierre?"

A small cove comes into view and Jean Pierre unhesitatingly guides us onto the shore. As we get out, the wind really starts to blow, slashing the willows onto the beach, scattering foam and sand. I'm surprised at how quickly the weather has changed, even though I'm accustomed to the four-seasons-in-one-day weather of the British Isles. We haul the canoe up high and quickly start to unload.

"I won't take chances with this kind of weather." Jean Pierre straightens up and looks keenly into the wind.

"A few years ago, I was paddling with my friend and we saw the squall coming, but we tried to get home before it hit us. We almost died for that mistake." I look around me, at the low clouds and the choppy lake. It seems like more than just a squall.

At the edge of the trees, some fifty feet from the water, is a small log cabin. It is the first I've seen on the lake, but no smoke is coming from the little chimney. Jean Pierre strides over to it while I stay, busy with the canoe. A minute later a shout comes from somewhere behind the cabin. I run over, passing a makeshift child's swing creaking forlornly in the wind, noting a padlocked door as I pass. No one at home, then.

At the back of the cabin there is a large window, but all the glass is missing. A loud bang makes me jump as the wind blows the door open. Not locked, after all. We go inside and find the place is wrecked: crockery, books, and cutlery are scattered across the small floor. Every surface is dirty, and the doors of the only cupboard are wrenched from their hinges. I'm shocked at such vandalism, out here of all places. Jean Pierre shakes his head and picks up a bowl.

"Black bear."

There are deep, widely separated tooth marks puncturing the plastic sides of the bowl. He points again, this time at the back of the door, where scratches are scored deep into the wood. I look again and the picture makes more sense. The random destruction, the half-chewed utensils.

"Looking for food and couldn't get out again." Jean Pierre shrugs, walking out the door. I look around me. If a bear can break into a cabin, what would it do to a tent?

I tidy up as best I can, pin a black plastic bag over the smashed window, and close the door behind me.

The weather continues to worsen, heavy banks of rain sweeping across the lake, the mountains opposite to the south now only a memory. After a few hours, we give up all hope of continuing today and set up camp, a frustrating three miles short of the mouth of the Naskaupi River. Already Mina is ahead of me. She may have travelled only twenty-two miles on her first day, but she covered eleven miles the second, taking her far up the Naskaupi. She thought constantly of her rival Dillon's progress; I think constantly of hers.

Around early evening the rain pauses, as though to acknowledge sunset, allowing the sun to break through for one minute and making the black clouds all around seem even more ominous. At that moment, Jean Pierre touches me lightly on the arm.

"Look, in the trees."

My reverie broken, I look and not more than five yards away a fox hesitates. He looks back at us for a second, nose twitching, eyes black and curious, red-gold coat full of light. Then he is gone into the willows that crowd the edges of the forest at the water, their leaves shivering for a second at his passing.

In the not-so-distant past, the red fox was just one of the foxes trapped for fur. The others were white, blue, and silver fox. I think of our little friend lying broken, bloody, and alone in a wintry forest trap and my heart breaks.

"When I was a boy," Jean Pierre's voice cuts across my thoughts, "my grandfather was very angry with me."

"Why?" I sit, curious as to what has prompted this little story.

"He was teaching me to trap. It was wintertime, and we had a fox in the trap. It was still alive, but its leg was broken."

I bite my lip in sympathy and try not to visualize the scene. Jean Pierre continues.

"He told me to kill it so it would not suffer any more and we could take it for fur, but I could not do it."

"But you are a hunter."

"The fox looked straight at me that moment as if it could speak to me, and I told my grandfather I would not kill it. My grandfather"— Jean Pierre laughs a little at the memory—"could not believe what I was saying. He said, 'What sort of hunter are you, that you cannot kill a fox?' But I would not kill it. I have never worked as a trapper. I hunt for food for my family only."

It was with the arrival of European settlers in the eighteenth century that the Native peoples of Labrador started to trap fur-bearing animals. Before that, they used fur only as a by-product of their food hunting. It provided them with material for their shelter and nets. But Europeans were quick to spot the potential profits of trade in furs and used the local Indigenous population to supply insatiable markets with animal pelts.

This arrangement quickly led to problems for Native people, as it bred an unhealthy dependence on the posts, one exploited to the full, as Hudson's Bay Company employee John McLean noted in the 1830s: "*As trading posts . . . are now established on their lands, I doubt not but 'artificial' wants will, in time, be created that may become as indispensable as their present real wants. All the arts of the trader are exercised to produce such a result and those arts never fail of ultimate success. Even during the last two years of my management the demand for certain articles of European manufacture has greatly increased.*"

The dependence caused by trapping suited the white settlers in many ways. It reduced resistance to settlement, and in establishing modified versions of their own behaviour among the Native population, settlers saw themselves as carrying out a moral duty by "civilizing the Indian," a process which, to some, helped justify any other side effects of contact. James McKenzie, a trader, summed up the settlers' attitude to Native people in 1808: "*Very few sights . . . can be more distressing to humanity than a Labrador savage . . . surrounded by his wife and five or six children, half famished by cold and hunger.*"

In the eyes of most European settlers and traders, any process that drew Native people into profitable enterprises such as trapping was a good thing as it helped rescue hunters from a life settlers believed to be precarious and unsophisticated.

Trapping also had another serious impact on traditional Native lifestyles. Not only did access to white products breed dependence, but this dependence was exacerbated by the effect trapping had on hunting for food. The Innu staple was caribou, which was found largely on the barren lands to the north, while the fur-bearing animals in demand by Europeans lived mostly in the wooded areas farther south. Thus time spent trapping was not only time spent away from the hunting grounds; it also meant that hunters had to travel through areas where little food was to be found. After the introduction of trapping, starvation regularly stalked Nitassinan. In a society where hunger was never a stranger, thanks to naturally lean years, it was now a more constant threat.

Awareness of the potential for starvation was constantly in the mind of Mina and her guides. On finding the famous George River caribou herd migrating across the barren grounds, a spectacle few people even today have witnessed, not one animal was shot: *"The trigger of Job's rifle clicked longingly, but they never forgot that starvation broods over Labrador and that the animal they longed to shoot might some time save the life of one in just such extremity as that reached by Mr. Hubbard and his party two years before."*

The storm-shortened day fades into an uneasy twilight, and Jean Pierre and I sit by the stove, listening to the rain hissing on the heat of the pipe. We have already lost both of our teaspoons, and I have managed to chip the handle of Jean Pierre's huge tea mug, so he lies, propped up on one elbow, drinking endless pints of sweet tea with the mug cupped in one hand, cigarette held in the other. The smoke, combined with the haze from the mosquito coils, means that for a few hours of the day at least, we are free of our tiny tormentors. I stretch out in my sleeping bag and relax.

As we travel farther into the country, my guide becomes more at ease and talkative. Likewise, I am beginning to know him better and so the long silences no longer intimidate me. When he is prepared to engage in conversation, I am eager to listen and learn. His world is entirely alien to me, but he is happy to tell me every detail.

Sharp-witted and with an unsuspected dry humour, Jean Pierre is a man who has hunted for food almost his entire life. Usually travelling alone, he would cross large areas of Nitassinan on snowshoes or snowmobile, sometimes staying away from the camp and travelling at night when the starlight glimmered silver across the snow and the trees were no more than dark shadows.

"What do you hunt? Just caribou?"

"No, sometimes goose, duck, ptarmigan. I'd give them to Katie or my mother or to other families if they were not successful." Jean Pierre smiles shyly for a moment. "My mother, she says she does not like to go into the country without me, as I am a good hunter and without me, she would be afraid."

I sense real pride behind the words.

The knowledge Jean Pierre or any hunter acquires in order to survive in this way comes from both personal and shared experiences. Stories, both mythical and "real"—the experiences of a relative or friend—teach a hunter the accumulated knowledge of generations. New experiences are also told within the group, so that these, too, can be absorbed, the better to inform the hunter out alone on the barrens.

As far as I can tell, Jean Pierre was raised in part by his grandparents, in an extended family system, where children watch, listen to, and imitate their elders. It is not uncommon for children to be given wholly to their grandparents, and indeed, Jean Pierre's eldest son has lived most of his life with Jean Pierre's mother. I can't imagine many women in my culture wanting to give their children up in this way, but the practice serves a function which in this case ensures that all members of the family are well cared for.

For Jean Pierre, being taught by his grandfather has also meant that he knows intimately how his people lived in the first part of the twentieth century, even as early as the period of the Hubbard expeditions.

It was his great-grandfather, Tshikapisk, Jean Pierre says, who drew the maps Leonidas used on his trip. I suggest that this is not such a great recommendation, considering what happened to Leonidas, and Jean Pierre laughs but then adds seriously, "They did not ask the right questions and they did not listen to the answers."

Jean Pierre, however, benefited from learning many things other men of his age failed to learn from their fathers, who had perhaps already settled during the 1950s.

"By the time a boy is fourteen years of age, he is thought to be a man and must prove that he is able to look after himself in the country."

"How would he do that? A test?"

"Yes. My grandfather was sent out alone with a gun, a kettle, and some tea. He was expected to stay away a night or two and show he could feed himself."

Jean Pierre smiles at the memory of the story.

"My grandfather had such a great time out by himself that he stayed away for a week, and when he returned, he found his mother in tears. She thought he'd died."

Pien Joseph Selma, Jean Pierre's grandfather, was an important figure in my guide's life, mainly because his father had died when Jean Pierre was just ten years old. At eighteen, Jean Pierre came back home to Labrador after just a year at school in St. John's on the island of Newfoundland, in order to return to the country. If he had not done so, his elderly grandfather and his mother would have been forced to remain in Sheshatshiu, dependent on welfare. An experienced hunter, Pien had a nearly inexhaustible knowledge of his country, which he passed on to his children and to Jean Pierre.

"He knew all the places the animals lived, he knew the animal masters, he respected the land," Jean Pierre tells me proudly.

The key to the Innu sense of spirituality and identity is their relationship with the land and the animals. It is one of dependency and respect, based on knowledge. The process of the hunt itself is part of that relationship, where animals allow themselves to be killed only if humans are on good terms with their world. Similarly, offerings must be made to the animals, such as bones placed in the fire and symbolic gifts of tobacco to bears.

Storytelling isn't reserved only for the hunt, however. Ancient tales are used to educate the young, pass on knowledge and history from the elders, and keep everyone entertained. These stories, often abrupt, indelicate, or merely mystifying to non-Innu, tell of the spirit world. Like all belief systems, the stories together present the universe in a manner that makes it intelligible to people, providing models for behaviour and explaining the world around them. On another level, the stories tell the people everything they need to know in order to survive on the cold wastes of the Sub-Arctic.

The first European arrivals to meet the Innu were fishermen during the sixteenth century. Catholic priests followed soon after—at first to minister to the Europeans and later as missionaries to the Native people. As a result, many Innu are now nominally Roman Catholic, and seem to have successfully developed a kind of religious "dualism," associating traditional beliefs with life in the country and Christianity with life in the settlements. This is a common way of dealing with the arrival of a new religion and can be seen in many Aboriginal groups around the world. Often, some aspects of the traditional beliefs bear some resemblance to aspects of the new religion. In the case of the Innu, the *mukushan*, or bone marrow feasts, resemble the Eucharist, for example. In this way, the two belief systems seem to function simultaneously.

Although many decent and well-meaning men and women have dedicated their lives to the missionary call, Jean Pierre prefers to tell me about past abuses in his community at the hands of church people—physical, sexual, and psychological. For him, the Roman Catholic Church is associated with these horrors and with the suppression of traditions such as the *mukushan*, and must therefore take its share of the blame for the fate of the Innu.

I know Jean Pierre also has an Innu name, Napes, pronounced "Nap-ez."

"Why do you have two names?"

"When I was born, the priest took me away from my parents and baptized me Jean Pierre. When he gave me back to them, he told them my name, but they did not understand it and could not say it, so they called me Napes."

"What does that mean?"

"Boy."

# CHAPTER 3

The bad weather keeps us on the shores of Grand Lake for a frustrating day and a half. Mina is now far ahead of us and I recalculate our route and time in my mind over and over again. Our modern advantages will only take effect once we've travelled all the way up the Naskaupi and reached the reservoir. I'm counting on the outboard at the height of land to shave some time off Mina's eight weeks, but now I'm starting to wonder if it won't just mean we'll make it in roughly the same length of time. But Mina also had rainy days in camp, and she worried about the time they wasted: *"I wished the rainy days might not come often, though I fully expected they would."* Luckily, for her, they did not. I hope that we are as fortunate, so we sit, watching for a break in the weather.

The mist still lies on the hills across the lake. Our canoe rests forlornly on one side, her base to the wind like a wild pony, rump into the winter weather, eyes shut tight and resigned. Little stirs as I write my diary, watch the rain, and think about our future.

We are continuing to eat well, as some of the fresh food from Happy Valley remains, and we have yet to start on the camp rations in all their uninspiring glory. Already I suspect I did not pack nearly enough chocolate, chocolate drink, or chocolate chip energy bars. Mina learned many lessons from her husband's fate and one of them was about food. She departed with both of her canoes packed to the gunwales with supplies, yet even so, they killed a huge amount of game as they travelled, including a caribou (which was dried) and many geese, ptarmigan, fish, and porcupine, all eaten fresh and much of which Mina found "delicious."

Except for the porcupine, that is. On her second night, the men shot one and cooked it for supper. Mina remembers it clearly in her book: *"We had supper of porcupine down on the rocks at the shore. I did not like it."*

I'm not surprised she did not, as perhaps she saw how the men prepared it. Jean Pierre told me today (with some relish, I noticed) how to prepare porcupine for the pot in the country. After killing it, you have to remove the spines before you can eat it, and there's only one way to do this effectively. You have to blow up the animal's . . . erm . . . posterior. Apparently, this inflates the porcupine just under the skin, making the spines easy to scrape off. I look at Jean Pierre closely, but that inscrutable countenance means I can never tell whether he's pulling my leg.

"Really? You're not joking?"

"No." He looked innocent enough and I was partly convinced.

"Okay, but if you shoot one, my lesson in preparing country food will be demonstration only."

Finally, he laughed.

"No problem."

Mina was very lucky to find the game she did. Leonidas had not been so fortunate and neither had John McLean in 1839. Lean years were quite common. In the winter of 1892/3, two hundred people—out of a population of three hundred and fifty—died of starvation at Kuujjuaq on Ungava Bay, and in her diary, Mina records a story about food shortages that she heard at the George River post at Ungava:

*The whole band of George River Eskimos went in west for caribou in Sept 1889. They went on and on and no caribou till they began to drop behind one family after another. When provisions gave out they were so far away from the post they dared not turn back. Finally the last little company had to give up. One young man only had strength to go farther forward and just as he too was giving up, he came on the caribou. He went back to help the others, but in spite of all their best efforts twenty one of the company perished of starvation.*

The twentieth century saw provincial hunting laws enacted and exclusive fishing rights given to private companies, all of which meant it became very difficult for the Innu to hunt and harvest as they always had. The laws were defended in environmental terms, despite evidence that animals such as the porcupine are far from being in decline, yet they added up to a situation in which, for a time, the province of Newfoundland and Labrador was possibly the most restrictive in Canada for Native people.

The notion that conservation is at the centre of government policy making has a ring of hypocrisy. If the country is in so much need of protection, shouldn't it be protected from large-scale industrial projects such as Churchill Falls? In Quebec, where there are several hydro projects, there was little concern for the wildlife when the gates of a dam on the Canaispiscau River were opened during the caribou migrating season in 1984 and ten thousand animals were drowned.

The decline in hunting and the associated dependence on government welfare have affected Innu health, identity, and society, which, in terms of their world view, are all connected. I think of Jean Pierre, of how he describes returning from the hunt to his family before the days of the snowmobile, when he would put several caribou carcasses on a sledge, then, wearing snowshoes, pull it alone across the snow for several miles in sub-zero temperatures. Life in the country strengthens traditions, returns pride to the hunter, supports the family, and confounds the feelings of impotence and futility experienced by most who live in the settlements. Daniel Ashini, Jean Pierre's cousin and chief land rights negotiator for the Innu, expressed the feeling of many in this way: "To reduce the word *nutshimit* to 'the bush' does not describe what it means to us. It is a place where we are at home."

Periodically, Jean Pierre goes outside, walking to the far western end of the cove and facing the point where the mouth of the Naskaupi drains into the northern shore of Grand Lake. He is watching for a change to signal that we can continue with our journey, but even though it is just three short miles before we would reach the protection of the river, he judges it too risky for us to try just yet. I am happy to let such decisions rest with him. It is Jean Pierre's judgement that will keep us safe during this trip and, as a secondary goal, ensure that we get as close as possible to Ungava.

It is widely acknowledged that Mina's holding a similar attitude toward her guides was a major factor in her success. When I read her diaries, it certainly seems clear that she already knew three of her guides very well, especially George, in whom she recognized a man of great worth. Even in the early days of her expedition, the banter between her and her guides and the ease she felt in their company is very evident. Her evenings were spent in much the same manner as mine and Jean Pierre's, with George telling Mina "stories of his childhood."

On the rare rainy days she did endure, Mina kept herself busy taking measurements with her sextant, drawing maps, and talking to the men. Indeed, she evidently enjoyed being an integral part of the team: "*I like them better all the time. They are gentle, considerate and polite, not only of me either but with each other as well and have such grand times together . . . How easy I feel in the midst of them all. Could not feel more so if they were my brothers . . . Would like to know more about Job,*" she continues. "*He is a great character, I am sure. Like him very much.*" Similar things are written about the others. They, in return, show a concern for her that is touching and far beyond the relationship of white employer and Native guide: "*Left my knife back two stages of portage. Wanted to go back myself. Men all so tired. Geo would not let me go so far alone. Bear tracks about. So he went.*"

One day, Mina insists on doing a little scouting of her own and taking some pictures while the men portage their equipment forward. Rejecting their suggestions that it will rain, she sets off to climb a nearby mountain. When she returns to the agreed meeting place, however, the men are not there and it does begin to rain. Determined to make the most of this unexpected opportunity to explore, Mina decides to climb another ridge on the other side of the lake, and when she reaches the summit, she sees the men in the distance sitting and drinking tea. Realizing that she is being punished for not taking their advice about the onset of the thunderstorm, she lets off two shots with her pistol and continues up an even higher ridge. The views are wonderful and she greatly enjoys herself, writing later this memorable line: *"What did flies matter when you were free?"*

Her escapade frightens her guides, who, finding that she did not wait for them, become desperate to find her in case she might fall into the rapids or get lost. On catching up with her, George exclaims, *"Oh, I just thought I was never going to see you again . . . I was thinking about how you would feel when you knew you were lost. It is an awful thing to be lost . . . How could any of us go back without you? And to see you, too, the way you look. Just as if you would never scare anybody."*

Mina laughs at his reproach and says firmly, *"If I can have someone to go with me whenever I want to climb a mountain, or do anything else I think is necessary to do my work without any fuss, I promise not to go away alone again."*

Although all of her guides felt they would not be able to return to North West River without her (particularly George, given his involvement in the first Hubbard expedition), there is a more personal tone in their words. Several incidents show their worry for her comfort, as well as her welfare. On one occasion, George stands over her during dinner, waving a sack to scare away the millions of flies, allowing her to eat. Mina recognizes the role her guides have played in making the country so appealing: *"Realize more and more what strain the trip would be were they not so brave and skilful and good."*

All the same, Mina throws herself into life on the trail, and despite the risk of undermining their valuable role, she makes considerable efforts to become an integral part of the team by making dinner, paddling the canoe, catching and gutting fish, shooting at game, and playing jokes on her fellow adventurers. However, when they arrive at Ungava, British North American social and racial order once again imposes itself—even in that remote outpost of the colonies—and Mina stays in the house of the Hudson's Bay Company factor, while the men remain in their tents. Looking out at them, Mina writes, *"The sight of the two tents made the thought that I was no more to be a member of the little company seem rather a lonely one."*

Such sentiments are to be found in her diaries only, as the strict codes of Edwardian society would not have warmly received a book that suggested a white lady's concern or care for members of a perceived inferior race, or "half-breeds," as her men would have been called. Yet Mina herself never refers to either her guides or any of the Native people she meets with anything but respect. Indeed, she recognizes that she is the first only of her race to see the wonders of the interior, tacitly acknowledging the presence of the Native people all too often invisible behind many a notable European-style expedition, discovery, or venture.

The day drips by, giving me an opportunity to update my diary. Periodically, Jean Pierre goes outside with a cigarette to look at the sky and checks that the kit underneath the canoe is still watertight, but I stay out of the weather and let my mind drift.

I think about everyone in Happy Valley, who will no doubt be wondering how we are getting on. They are really just across the hills on the other side of the lake and, in truth, I don't as yet feel as though I'm on anything more than a pleasant camping holiday in unusual circumstances. The feeling of unreality has worn off and the landscape remains unthreatening.

In the absence of anything useful to do, I start to dwell on the possibility of a visit by a bear. Joe's brother Horace had warned me they were numerous and I'd certainly seen enough of them around Happy Valley to convince me this was true. Being afraid of the local wildlife was not something that had concerned me unduly before I set off on this trip, but now that I'm out here, the prospect of an encounter with a bear in particular seems to be preying on my mind. I tentatively ask Jean Pierre about our chances of running into problems.

"But they'll move away from us, right? if we do come across one?"

Jean Pierre looks thoughtful. "No, not this time of year. They mate in July and become vicious."

"Vicious?" I can't help the slight tremor in my voice. What had happened to the "docile unless provoked" theory?

"Do you mean they'll attack?"

"They might. They are not afraid of humans when they mate and they travel in packs of two, three, or more."

This was just getting better and better.

"When does their mating season end?" Jean Pierre looks at my watch, as though the answer might be 3:30 this afternoon. He breathes in slowly, considering.

"End of the month. As soon as July is over, we are safe. Until then . . ." He bites his lip and shrugs.

I do some hasty mental arithmetic and the answers are not encouraging. Why did I not know this? I ask myself. In all the preparation, years of planning, of *living* in North America in the past, how did I not know that July was open season on humans? Why had no one mentioned, in the bushels of tips and useful information bestowed on me back in Happy Valley, that venturing into the country in July was tantamount to asking to be mauled to death by a sex-crazed black bear with a biological imperative to rip us into small, edible pieces?

"What did you do when you lived in the country with your family?"

Surely Jean Pierre, fount of all wisdom, seer of all things country, will have a fail-safe solution.

"We stayed on the coast, in the settlements—away from the country."

Gulp.

Suddenly, every rustle has sinister intent.

Jean Pierre sees that this information is of some interest to me and decides to share a little story. It is the Innu equivalent of a slasher horror movie, as it turns out. Innu stories tend to take one of two forms: mythical legends about the exploits of the animal masters, shamans of ancient times, long-forgotten battles, and so on, or stories about more tangible events that have taken place in recent living memory. Such as bear attacks.

"Bears are very dangerous in July," Jean Pierre begins without a flicker of emotion. "They are mating and not afraid of anything. They will go toward a sound and attack if they feel threatened, or if the female is threatened. The people travelling in summer would stay on islands to protect themselves. I don't normally keep my gun in the tent—I don't like it—but I do in July. My mother and Katie like me to do it.

"My grandfather told me about a man hunting in July. A small man, out alone, with a Winchester for shooting caribou. He saw seven bears, one female. One sensed he was there; he was sitting on a big boulder. One of the bears heard him and walked toward him on its hind legs. When it was about a hundred feet away, he started shooting. The others heard the shots and all walked toward the sound, standing on their hind legs. The man shot the female first, as she was the most vicious. One by one, they were getting closer and closer. He had to shoot all six. The last one was very big. When it walked toward him, it knocked tree stumps out of its way, tearing them out of the ground with one paw. The man wasn't sure if the gun would go off and was very nervous. He shot it when it was very close, then got off the boulder and went home. He never claimed the bears, as he was too scared to go back.

"This is what we want to avoid on this trip. Since I've been in the country in summer, just me and Katie, I've feared this might happen to us. We avoid bears and avoid the country in July. We can hear them call at night. The males call a long way and you can hear the echoes in the mountains and the river valleys."

It is a long night.

# CHAPTER 4

We rise early this morning to bright sunlight and quickly break camp, loading the canoe and launching out once more onto the brilliant blue of the lake—a tame, shy thing coyly denying its angry excesses of the past two days.

After paddling for less than an hour, we reach the momentous point of turning up the Naskaupi. I can quite understand how Leonidas missed it. A large sandbank covered with vegetation lies directly before the entrance, totally obscuring it from view to anyone on the lake. The sinuous shape of the shore and dense forest also make it very hard to tell that a great river empties itself into the steadfast waters of Grand Lake at this point.

The river is wide and sluggish and the waters are brown—although I drink freely of them. We glide along close to the west bank, feeling closed in after the wide open spaces of the lake. The forest crowds down close to the water, thick and green, and the day is hot, much hotter than any day since I've been here. I feel as though I'm on some great waterway of the tropics. Nothing stirs but us in the still, almost tangible heat. The slightly sour tang of the riverbank catches at the back of my throat. At any moment I imagine, a crocodile could slither out from the undergrowth and merge soundlessly into the water. A trickle of sweat runs from between my shoulder blades to my waist.

The river is flowing, but the movement is as slow and immense as a glacier's. The only indication that we are moving at all is the ever widening V from our bow as we cut through the water. For some reason, the words of Walter de la Mare go through my mind:

> Ay, they heard his foot upon the stirrup,
> And the sound of iron on stone,
> And how the silence surged softly backward,
> When the plunging hoofs were gone.

The deadening silence here surges back after every slosh of the paddle.

Jean Pierre points out an untidy pile of dead wood, half submerged in the water.

"Beaver." He looks at it sadly for a moment, then resumes his strong, fluent paddle stroke.

"Not so many here now. When I was a boy, this whole part of the river had many, many beaver dams."

Mina saw beaver on this same part of the Naskaupi and noted, "There were beaver signs too, willows cut off and floating downstream along the shore . . . Job picked one up and handed it back to me to show me how cleverly they do their work."

I ask Jean Pierre why this has changed and why there are so few beaver on the river. He shrugs slightly.

"Maybe the dam. The river level has dropped by several metres since it was built."

There is certainly some truth in this. Research into the dams of Quebec has shown marked effects on all aquatic, forest, and mammal life. Beaver and other animals such as marten, otter, and muskrat have been the most affected, as their habitats have been flooded or the variations in water level, specifically the drying up of river tributaries, have damaged the ecosystem they depend on for survival.

An osprey rises, screaming, from a treetop nest and circles around, trying to lure us away from its young. We paddle on. I feel as though a dozen pairs of bright eyes are watching me from the greeny gloom of the forest, but I can see nothing. Behind me there is an occasional *flick, flick*, as Jean Pierre lights another cigarette, his only method, as far as I can tell, of combatting the flies that swarm around us, crawling under my head net and biting my neck.

The verdant growth all around us is in direct contrast to the scenes Mina travelled through on this part of the river. *"All this part of the country,"* she writes, *"had been burned over many years ago and was desolate looking."*

How different it appears now, ninety-five years later! Yet I know forest fires are still a huge problem and I pray we do not get caught up in one. I touch the small pocket attached to my waist at all times, which contains survival equipment, fishing hooks, a flashlight, fly repellent, and the satellite phone, sealed in a plastic bag.

It was not far from this place that Mina had her first encounter with an example of Labrador's larger wildlife. High up on a sandbank, silhouetted against the skyline, they saw a large black bear. Despite a rational, initial decision not to shoot at it (for they had no need of the meat and the pelt was worth little), Job was unable to contain himself and fired at it, wounding the creature. That shot unleashed the hunt and Mina herself chased the bear through willows, firing several shots with her revolver.

Reading that account out here in the country, I can barely believe it. I know that if Jean Pierre and I find ourselves at such close quarters to something as large, fast, and unpredictable as a bear, chasing it will be the last thing to occur to me. Although Mina's book records the incident in some detail, rarely does, she present herself as anything other than a lady undertaking an arduous wilderness trip, escorted by four gentlemen. What this incident really does, therefore, is offer the reader a brief glimpse into Mina's true character, which is feisty, adventurous, and almost entirely unfazed by anything the wilderness throws at her.

Crossing paths with a bear so early on in her trip obviously does nothing to dampen her sense of adventure, as Mina spends much of the remainder of her time looking for and wishing to see another:

*"They do not like to leave me very well as bears at this time of year are apt to be dangerous. But think they have come to have a great deal of respect for my shooting and after warning to keep rifle ready, went off. Secretly I rather hoped one would come along, but none did."*

This kind of confession is sadly to be read only in her unpublished diary. George also praises her bravery, and as Mina rather smugly records in her diary, he tells her she can *"walk faster than Wallace."*

However, it is not just the desire to take shots at a bear or the ability to eat caribou gut and enjoy it that makes Mina so much more than the genteel creature she portrays herself to be. She is frustrated at not being able to do everything she wants to do: *"At 3, Job, Joe and Gilbert prepared to climb our hill. I wanted very much to go too. Job said I couldn't. Too Steep. Much disappointed. Such an ignominious sort of feeling to be an explorer and have one of your party tell you [you] can't do something that he has done."*

It is on her arrival at the George River post on Ungava Bay, however, that we see her in contrast to the other white people who have lived there for twenty-two years—who had "never been so far in a canoe before" as she and George take them one afternoon. Mina also relishes the opportunity to learn kayaking, impressing the factor of the post and persuading George to try, remarking to her diary, *"If I were as strong as he, I could beat him."*

Life in the North at no time seems to hold anything but interest for Mina, who embraces the challenges, tries the alien, and copes with the unexpected. The expedition seems only to whet her appetite for more, as she dreams of *"staying away out of the world here for a long time. Wish I were a man would try for a place in HBC service for a while in some of these out of the world places."*

Mina's appetite for the life she experiences in Labrador seems to be even greater than that of her male contemporaries, who on the whole seek to "conquer" the wilderness and to "do battle" with things such as rapids and flies. Rather than representing the country as a hostile opponent that must be subdued, Mina generally seems at home in the wilderness, appreciating its beauty and mystery. Her writing gives the impression that exploring it is a joy and a privilege, not an exercise in pacification.

We paddle on uneventfully for the remainder of the day, making good progress on these quiet waters. By late afternoon, Jean Pierre tells me our camping place for the night is less than a mile farther up the river—just around a large bend to the left. The river has widened, and the trees do not press against the banks, stopping instead about five yards from the water, allowing for an unusual flat expanse of long grass. The earlier sense of oppression has lifted, and I'm relaxed and looking forward to a nice, flat camp, away from the choking, fly-bound forest. Suddenly, Jean Pierre stops paddling and hisses at me.

"Bear! Black bear!"

From the urgency of his voice, I know it is close by.

"On the bank, watching us!"

I scan the riverbank, forested with spruce trees. In a small patch of open grass about fifteen yards away, my eye catches a movement. It's the bear ... sunning himself, looking easily like a shadow in the bright sunlight. It is alone, I notice with relief. Sensing Jean Pierre and me, the animal stares short-sightedly for a moment in surprised arrogance and sniffs the air, pale gold muzzle pointing skyward, its small, rounded ears making it appear misleadingly cute, like an oversized child's toy.

I fumble for the camcorder and waste precious moments trying to zoom in, losing it. The bear sits for several minutes in a test of will as to who should give way and move on. Jean Pierre starts to paddle again, slowly.

"Stop paddling!" I have visions of the bear jumping into the water to show us just whose country this really is.

"Do you have your shot?"

"Yes."

The bear gives one final sniff, but fortunately we are downwind. As we start to paddle closer again, my heart racing, it finally rises to its paws with a disgruntled air and shambles off into the forest.

Moments later, Jean Pierre steers us into a camping place just a few yards past where the bear was sunbathing. We crunch softly onto a wide, curving yellow beach, bordered by long grass, then willows, then forest. All is quiet. Menacingly quiet, to my overactive imagination. Jean Pierre gets out of the canoe and picks up his gun. I follow him, armed only with my camcorder. At any moment, I expect a roar, followed by a charging black bear, but none comes. All the same, I stay very close to Jean Pierre as he walks across the beach, so close, in fact, that I almost bump into him when he stops, like a slapstick comic act.

Jean Pierre points to the sand.

"Prints, fresh."

We stand still and look all around. The beach is covered in prints, the deepest parts of the indent still darkly damp. Very fresh prints. I'm beginning to suspect that this beach is the Labrador equivalent of Miami Beach for bears.

"This is where we were supposed to camp, right?"

"Yes."

"It seems very popular with the wildlife."

"Yes."

"If we did camp here, would they come back during the night?"

"For sure."

My guide evidently doesn't believe in breaking things to me gently.

We walk slowly toward some trees at the far end of the beach, noting the piles of bear dung, some of it very recently deposited. I continually glance over my shoulder, convinced all the things I know are watching me will jump out at any moment. Jean Pierre stops and points to the ground again.

"Wolf, too."

I look. The print is the same size as my guide's hand, and Jean Pierre is not a small man. I've heard timber wolves can grow as high as a man's waist and I would dearly love to see one. Curiosity and interest begin to thaw my worries away, and I film for a few minutes as we walk back to the canoe.

Jean Pierre stands and looks thoughtfully about him, and then, without a word, he strides toward the nearest trees. I hasten after him, but the willows are very thick, growing toward the water, and it's almost impossible to force a path through them. Jean Pierre seems unaffected by their elastic but steely grip and disappears from view. Suddenly, I'm afraid again. In a barely controlled panic, I thrash about in the sea of leaves, trying to force my way ahead by throwing the weight of my body against the springing branches, but I'm too small and light, and they continually thrust me back. Standing still for a moment, I realize I can't even hear Jean Pierre above the silence and my own harsh breathing. I fight the rising alarm, taking deep breaths, forcing myself not to think about what may be only a few feet away from me in the thick undergrowth. Then I take the willows and push them left and right, stepping through the gaps before I let go. They snap right back into place.

I find Jean Pierre on the edge of a clearing in the forest. The lack of sunlight means that everything below shoulder height is brown and dead.

"This is an Innu camp. Here . . . here."

He indicates to two roughly rectangular clearings in the trees, marked by old stumps. It's much larger than the camp on Grand Lake.

"This is where we had our tent." Jean Pierre nods towards one end.

"This was one of yours?" I look around, trying to imagine the place as a home, and failing entirely. "When were you here most recently?"

"Last year. Look." Jean Pierre points to a mark, cut into the bark of a tree, around head height. "My youngest son cut this, the last time we stayed here. It was the last time we came into the country together." He stares at it for a few moments, the expression on his face unreadable. Then, without a word, he walks back to the beach.

It was here, at the confluence of the Naskaupi and Red Wine rivers, that Dillon, unlike Mina, left the Naskaupi and took an old Innu portage route out, travelling north overland via the headwaters of the Crooked River, Lake Nipishish, Otter Lake, Portage Lake, and Namaycush Lake to Seal Lake. While this itinerary presents the advantage of avoiding the dangerous and difficult rapids on the Naskaupi, it creates a much longer journey to Seal Lake (approximately halfway to the reservoir), which is one reason why Dillon arrived at Ungava a full two months later than Mina.

The Hubbard and Wallace expeditions of 1905 were acutely aware of each other and there almost seems to have been an unspoken agreement that different routes would be followed. If this was the case, Mina did well by taking the option of the far quicker route. Her diary burns with undisguised animosity toward Dillon—a feeling shared by her guides: "*Always there is much talk of the other party and their probable doings especially the probability of their getting lost. All are familiar with the story of W's prowess in wilderness travel.*"

Despite the demure countenance Mina showed the world, the competition with Dillon actually consumed her in a most unladylike manner: "*I might possibly get back and some of my pictures in print before W is even heard from and that would be the thing for me. If I am to be successful, that would make it complete . . . How grateful I should be and how complete would be my victory and how completely it would make no account of W's reflections.*"

Jean Pierre tells me that Innu portage routes such as the ones used by Dillon once crisscrossed the entire Labrador interior. They were used by the people when they travelled between the coast and the "country" or when they moved to follow game. In fact, parts of Dillon's route were also used by the American William Brooks Cabot when he travelled with the family of Innuman Tshenish Penashue in 1916. It is only recently, however, that the Innu have begun to formally draw their own maps of Nitassinan, marking each lake, mountain, and river with its original Innu-aimun name in place of those given by the white people who came here.

"I travelled up and down this section of the river every year when I was young, with my family," says Jean Pierre, gazing down at the broad sweep of the river from our sandy viewpoint.

"But not as far as we'll be going?"

"No."

Most of the movement was done in autumn and spring, when hunting was at its best and snow lay on the ground, making it easier to travel along the frozen river valleys. Now Jean Pierre hunts on his snowmobile, covering vast areas of ground and travelling to places once accessible only after long, hard journeys. I ask him how he hunted before he owned a snowmobile.

"I took a sled and travelled with snowshoes. When I killed something, I would load it onto the sled and pull it across the snow back to the camp."

"Even something as heavy as a caribou?"

"No problem."

Of course, Mina was not the first person to travel this route, nor were the explorers of the nineteenth century the first to see the interior. It was already home to hundreds of people who travelled throughout it each year, familiar with every trail, every bend in the river, every campsite. From the day she left North West River, Mina was alert to ways of Native people, noting *"many Indian signs, standing wigwams, fresh cuttings, bones set up on poles, etc."* and wished *"[so] much that we might meet some of them."* She also makes references during her journey to having *"a look at the Indian map."* When they eventually meet a band of Innu on the George River, Mina speaks, through her guides, to the chief, who had spent time in North West River and *"knew the route."* He was also able to calm her fears of not reaching the George River post on Ungava Bay in time to catch the *Pelican* by assuring her that *"you are near now. You will sleep only five times if you travel fast."*

Many white, Métis, and Native trappers living in coastal settlements such as North West River would also use the trails, overwintering in their tilts in the interior before returning in spring with the year's fur. Mina's youngest guide, Gilbert, was one such man, living a life that closely resembled that of his great-nephew Horace Goudie. Among the strands of individual stories woven through the North's great saga, the lives and contributions of men like Gilbert and Horace should never be forgotten.

There is a large and historic Innu campsite on the other side of the river at this point. Probably established at about the time of Louis Fornell's first trading post at North West River in the eighteenth century, the camp most likely formed a sort of staging post for Innu families travelling to and from the post in the summer months until the era of settlement began. Dillon's route leads out from here, although he describes the campsite as having lain unused for ten years prior to his expedition. The truth of this is unascertainable, but the camp may have been a fatality of the changing patterns of Native life, evident as early as 1905, due to the demands of the fur trade. Now, the vast majority of old portage routes and sites such as the one on the other side of the river lie unused, as the Innu who do travel to the country charter light aircraft or come in by snowmobile.

Jean Pierre decides that we will travel on and look for another camping place. I do not know, nor does he tell me, the reason for the decision, so I assume it is because he wants an uninterrupted night's sleep in a location less popular with the local wildlife. We've already paddled about fifteen miles today, and he asks me with some concern, "The next place is more than two miles—can you paddle that far?" It's nearly six in the evening and I am tired, but I don't relish the thought of a night here, so I nod.

"No problem. I can paddle as far as I need to."

After an hour or so, Jean Pierre points to a clearing in the trees, up ahead on the left bank.

"We can camp—"

He stops mid-sentence.

"What?" I half-turn to look at him, sensing something is wrong. He points again.

"Bears . . . in a pack. Three, four. You see them?"

His eyesight must be outstanding, I think, as it takes me a few moments to distinguish the dark shapes from the light and shade on the edge of the forest.

"Ahh, big ones."

I can't tell from his tone if he is impressed or worried, or both.

We paddle on for a while until Jean Pierre spies a suitable camp on the right bank. We are still within sight of the bears, but there is a reassuringly wide, deep, and cold river between us.

After we've set up camp, I climb the small hill behind the tent to watch the sunset. The day has been a long, hot, cloudless one, and the sun barely sinks below the horizon. I think how busy parts of this country must once have been: Innu groups, trappers, the occasional explorer. Yet during all that time, the landscape remained a virtually pristine wilderness. Human activities barely registered against the backdrop of Labrador's forests and barren tundra. Now the country faces greater threats than ever before—from logging, mining, hydro-electric developments, and the military—yet it is eerily silent, like a room where a door has just slammed shut.

All about me, the land turns black as the colour of the day drains away, but the sky and reflecting water remain bright and pale. Far to the west, an orange line of cloud indicates the limits of my perception. The whole landscape is silent and still and I breathe in deeply, strangely content. There is a magic here. I can feel it encircling me, pulling me toward the soft, black earth. It is the same siren song that killed Leonidas and tempted Mina to make a life here.

I realize I can barely see the white of the tent through the twilight, and I rise, stumbling over tree roots and slither down the bank into camp. I find Jean Pierre wreathed in cigarette smoke, in a pensive mood. I pull out my sleeping bag and climb in, arranging my stuff so the water bottle, satellite phone, and my spectacles are close by.

In an effort to break the silence, I ask Jean Pierre about his son, who made the mark on the tree in the camp near Red Wine River. He smiles and says, half to himself, "Mr. T."

"Mr. T?" I'm mystified. Like in *The "A" Team*? I wonder. "Is that his real name?"

"No. He was christened Andrew, but we called him 'Mr. T' because his hair stood up so much when he was born. Just like the guy on TV."

I laugh, thinking, "I bet he didn't pay for *that* in the schoolyard . . ." The question seems to have opened a train of thought, however.

"When he was a little boy," Jean Pierre continues, "he wanted to be a hunter like his father. I came home one day from hunting when Mr. T was about four years old, very young. I was tired; I'd been out following the caribou since before dawn. He wanted a bow and arrow. He begged and pleaded for me to make him one. I stayed up all night carving it, so it would be ready in the morning and he could find it after I'd gone out hunting."

"Did he like it?"

Jean Pierre smiles, his slightly sombre tone suddenly lightened.

"He loved it so much, he made me carve all kinds of things, even a helicopter."

"How old is Mr. T now?"

There is a pause.

"He killed himself last November. He was fifteen years old."

Suicide is not uncommon in many Native communities throughout Canada. The people of Davis Inlet (also known as Utshimassits), the more remote of the two major Innu settlements in Labrador, are thirteen times more likely to kill themselves than the average Canadian and seven times more likely to die before the age of five. The causes of this epidemic of despair are a complex interaction of tangible conditions and an array of psychological causes brought on by the process of settlement.

During the 1950s and 1960s, the tenuous nature of a traditional life already semi-dependent on the vagaries of fur prices and the increasing encroachment by settlers on the land meant that starvation was still a very real threat. The Innu were at this time induced by various means to give up, at least in part, their traditional nomadic lifestyle and settle in government-built villages. Some thought it would be good and were happy to have the things they had seen the settlers gain over the years, such as washing machines, cars, and TVs.

This process took the Innu—in the space of just one generation—from a traditional, nomadic life in the country to a sedentary life in communities ordered by Canadian schools, law courts, police, and health services, all almost entirely alien to their way of life, administered in a language few spoke. The government provided homes and schools, yet conditions quickly became appalling. The homes were little more than wooden shacks, built without flush toilets or even running water. Davis Inlet, the Innu settlement set on an isolated island two days north on the ferry from Lake Melville, still has neither.

The resulting destabilization has created overwhelming feelings of loss of control in a culture that places high value on responsibility and autonomy. Schools taught many young Innu about life in a Canada they did not know, leaving many feeling that their own lives were inferior and not worth living. Although hunting, fishing, canoeing, and wilderness tripping are still very much a part of life in Labrador, the young people in the Innu and Inuit settlements have become ever more separated from their traditional ways. Hunting is a source of great pride for the Innu, the foundation of all social structures and the provider of stability. To take this away from the Innu is to remove their sense of identity. Without that, hopelessness, shame, and impotence are inevitable.

"I tried to give him everything I could," Jean Pierre continues, after a while. "I taught him everything my grandfather taught me, and Mr. T would have become a good hunter, too. He loved the life. My oldest son, he is not interested, but I would take Mr. T out hunting with me whenever I went."

But those hunting trips were fewer than in the past, as Jean Pierre's family has lived in Sheshatshiu for ten years, most of his young son's life.

"I gave him anything he wanted, so he wouldn't start to drink. Snowmobile, pool table, motorbike. It was not enough. Each time he promised me he would not do it again, then he would go back with his friends and get drunk."

In a community where over 80 percent of the adult population—that is, over fifteen years of age—is alcoholic, Mr. T's story is not unusual. Drinking is endemic in the settlements, part of the encompassing sickness that has swept over the people since they have given up their traditional ways. This new reality for the Innu has opened up rifts between the generations, with the younger members caught effectively between two worlds, unable to integrate fully into Canadian society, yet removed from the experiences and knowledge of their elders.

It is difficult to imagine a better role model than Jean Pierre for his young son. An accomplished hunter, with a lifetime of experience in the country, Jean Pierre has also successfully negotiated the shark-filled waters of the non-Innu world since moving to Sheshatshiu, through his work with the United Nations and Survival International. With terrible irony, it was while Jean Pierre was abroad working for this organization that Mr. T took his own life.

"The last thing I said to him as I got on the plane," Jean Pierre remembers, "was don't drink. I mouthed it through the glass, and he understood."

Less than a year ago, while Jean Pierre was in London for the release of the Survival report on the fate of the Innu—*Canada's Tibet: The Killing of the Innu*—he heard the tragic news. Just a day after receiving such an unimaginable blow, Jean Pierre gave a press conference to launch the report, bringing worldwide attention to the fate of his people. Media coverage throughout Canada and in 360 newspapers around the globe made it the most successful campaign in the charity's history. Yet today, little has changed in these communities.

"I can't cry anymore," Jean Pierre told the journalists in the room on that bleak November day in London. "We don't know how to cry anymore because we have too many deaths in our families."

I lie awake, thinking about the sadness in Jean Pierre's heart. It is a story to mark the passing of a life. Helplessly, I realize that this trip is more to Jean Pierre than just another guiding job; it is a way of coming to terms with Mr. T's death, a retracing of his last journey with his youngest son, and an opportunity to experience the healing effect of travelling in the country, away from the world that had taken his son from him.

And so Jean Pierre's voice sank softly into the darkness, recounting stories of a child lost to something as intangible as it was pointless, whispering on until the words grew faint and drifted away into sleep. That voice would speak almost every night we were together, away into the country where once a man taught his son everything he had ever learned.

# CHAPTER 5

As we set off this morning, the river remains glossy and harmless like a picture from a tourist brochure.

Once again, the sky is blue and already the sun is hot on my back. The head net suspended from my Australian bushman's hat keeps the mosquitoes from my face, but the blackflies seem to squirm through it somehow. I'm wearing two long-sleeved breathable fleece tops for protection from the mosquitoes, but even the hi-tech "wicking" feature cannot cope with the thirty-degree-plus temperatures. By 10 A.M. I'm soaked with sweat and do a hasty swap into a suntop and bug jacket, covering any part of me where the jacket rests against my skin with repellent. Jean Pierre, as ever, is wearing jeans, a T-shirt, and wellington boots. The flies appear to ignore him entirely.

As soon as we travel around the first bend in the river, its character changes. Our lazy, deep, and glassy waterway starts to run faster and becomes increasingly shallow. Staying close to the east bank, we start to paddle harder, foam bubbling white at the bow. As far as I can see ahead, the water is fast and rough, with occasional small standing waves. No real rapids, but fast enough to mark the end of the pleasant days of easy paddling.

From below my feet comes a grating sound that sets my teeth on edge. I look down over the side of the canoe. Through the clear, brownish water I can see the riverbed and the small, smooth rocks that have caught us. We heave ourselves from their grip with our paddles, but we run aground again, then again. I look back. We've travelled only about two hundred yards in the shallow water.

The Naskaupi was not always this low. It was deep, fast, and dangerous, with strong rapids and plummeting waterfalls. Now it's been reduced to this pathetic trickle. A shadow of its former self, it is belittled by the monumental landscape that is witness to its demise. This change of character works to our benefit, however, as it may just make it possible for the two of us to travel up the half-tamed parts of this river.

Ahead, a small promontory protects a stretch of calmer water, which looks deep and promising. We haul ourselves across and enjoy five minutes of progress before we reach the tip of the promontory and once again grate to a halt. No amount of paddle leverage will free us this time, so we abandon ship, splashing ignominiously through the water on the sheltered side to dry land, holding the canoe on the end of a line from her bow.

I look around. On each side of the river lies an expanse of exposed rock, a bank several feet deep in some places and only a few inches deep in others. Behind it is a tangled mass of willows, choking the mouth of the forest and clawing its way toward the water. The trees have the hydro project at Churchill to thank for their existence. The dam has vastly reduced the Naskaupi at its headwaters, making the river in places run four metres below its former height. This drop has exposed rocks once deep on the riverbed and allowed that scourge of wilderness travel, the willow, to proliferate.

Jean Pierre informs me he is going up ahead to do some scouting, so I take the opportunity to eat an energy-boosting bar. A minute or so later, I look up from rooting around in the food sacks to find that Jean Pierre has entirely disappeared. I didn't hear him move at all, no sound of boot on rock, no snapping of twigs. Standing up, I shade the sun from my eyes and gaze upstream. There I see a dash of red among the willows, at the next bend in the river, scanning farther upstream. How did he get there so fast? I sit down again and unwrap my snack.

All is very still, apart from the gentle rush of the river, as though the countryside and everything in it were having a siesta during the heat of the day. I recall how Mina marvelled in her book at Job, who *"had a way of quietly disappearing."*

It seems Jean Pierre has that way about him too.

A few minutes later, he returns and wordlessly takes off his boots, replacing them with a pair of waders. He unties the canoe from her temporary mooring and sets off upstream a few feet from the bank, leading the now-floating canoe. Scrambling to my feet, I realize we are moving on. Jean Pierre is moving fast, so I walk quickly as far as the first of the willows, then start my struggle through. At first, it's not as difficult as my experience at Red Wine River, since I am moving sideways through them, not attempting to push through, away from the water. However, they become thicker and thicker, some boughs the diameter of my wrist and impossible to break. Each time I push them away, they push back with equal force. I can't walk in the water like Jean Pierre, as I cannot tell where the current is strong and I know the rocks below the waterline are very slippery.

Hot and frustrated, I can see Jean Pierre travelling farther away from me at every step. I attempt to walk behind the line of the willows, but they reach too far back into the forest and it would take too long to break free of them. Eventually, a petty anger wells up from within and gives me the strength to force a path. I hurl my way through like a person possessed. This seems to go on forever, and the fact that Jean Pierre is too far away to hear me if I shout is at the back of my mind, but I keep it there by focusing on the fight with the willows.

Suddenly, a branch yoyos away, tossing me, sweaty and wild-eyed, onto an expanse of rock. Five yards ahead, Jean Pierre is sitting by the canoe, smoking a cigarette. He views my dramatic entrance impassively and offers me the blackened teakettle, full of cold river water. I sink to the ground and drink deeply, not bothering to remove the head net, feeling my heartbeat return to normal. Then I look upstream and a mouthful of water goes down the wrong way. *This* is where the rapids start.

When Mina confronted the rapids, they fascinated her, but this worried George, who demanded: *"Why Mrs. Hubbard you must not do that . . . You will get dizzy and fall in."* Mina agreed to stay away from the edge of the rapids for the duration of their journey. I, however, do not have that luxury, for if we are to travel up them successfully, I must learn how to do my part and line the canoe.

Mina, like me, was constantly learning about the skills and techniques needed to travel successfully through this country. She records watching her men preparing to line or pole the canoe with some mystification, admitting, *"I was in darkness as to what was to happen."*

Feeling much the same way, I attempt to follow Jean Pierre's one-word directions and idiosyncratic hand signals that indicate what I am to do. Although the water has become deeper, it is no less swift, and the standing waves are frequent and large. Huge boulders just under the surface next to the bank funnel the water past in roaring torrents, the noise and violence making the sleepy wanderings of yesterday a distant memory.

I find myself hanging onto the rope attached to the bow of the canoe. Jean Pierre guides her forward from the stern, while I keep the rope tight, preventing the bow from being caught by the current and capsizing. I'm awed by the importance of this. Until now, I was never in any real danger, but now I understand that my every action needs to be considered and measured. Any lapse in concentration could bring about a disaster similar to the one that so very nearly befell Mina just a little farther upstream from our current location. They, too, were lining the canoe when Mina, walking along the shore, notices *"a big rock round which the water poured in a way that to* [her] *looked impassable."* Further on, she writes how that same rock almost brings her expedition to a very premature end: *"I had just reached the top when looking around I saw the canoe turn bottom up like a flash and both men disappeared . . . the current had swept* [Job] *off and was now carrying him down the river."*

Both of her guides survive, thanks to good fortune and quick action. The reminder that this could happen to men as experienced as

Mina's guides keeps me wide awake, watching every step, gauging every new stretch of water with an anxious eye.

Despite the fact that Jean Pierre is much more forthcoming here in the country, particularly in the evenings when we have long, rambling conversations, he continues to work largely in silence, even, as I have discovered today, when the situation becomes more complicated.

After a couple of hours, I'm starting to develop a knack for lining. As Jean Pierre guides the canoe forward, I pull her toward me, keeping the rope taut, avoiding large boulders just below the surface, and holding her there, the bow nosing among the shallows of an eddy like a dog in trash. Then Jean Pierre catches up and I go forward again, leaping over the assorted boulders and willows bordering the side of the river as fast as I can, always with my eyes on the canoe. I wind the rope in a figure eight, holding it in my palm. I need to continually remind myself not to wind the rope around my hand, as the canoe could be swept away by the current at any moment and the force would be strong enough to tear off a couple of fingers.

The boulders are covered with a fine, grey dust that is extremely slippery when wet. They are often covered by spray and I quickly need to find a crevice to lock my boot into, providing some purchase so I can haul on the rope. This form of extended aerobics goes on all afternoon: scrambling, climbing, pulling, crouching. My boots and gloves are soaking wet from the river and the rest of me is wet with sweat, as we are having another cloudless day. The rapids become stronger and stronger hour after hour, and as our work goes on all afternoon, the concentration level required becomes exhausting.

Lulled by the monotony and the heat, my mind begins to drift, revisiting the conversation Jean Pierre and I had the night before. I look across at him, silently walking through the water, eyes gazing into the distance. What foresight, what chance has allowed him to escape the cycle of dependence the Innu have been forced into—a cycle first created by the European appetite for trapping, now easily transferred to welfare cheques and casual labour.

Here at the turn of the twenty-first century, a generation has grown up entirely in the settlements. A link has already been broken in the chain of their existence. While some, like Jean Pierre, want to return to life in the country, others work in the non-Innu world as teachers and police officers. Each year, the number of those who knew the life away from the settlements diminishes and those born to it increases.

Jean Pierre must surely be one of the last to be born to the hunting life. Indigenous peoples have always been adept at integrating useful tools from the encroaching world at their boundaries, taking some things and leaving others. For the Innu, these tools have been guns, tents, and flour. Yet such things in no way diminished life in the country and many Native communities across Canada are seeking solutions to contemporary dilemmas. The cry "What are the Innu to do?" is one that echoes across the centuries of white settlement in North America with chilling pertinence.

Even as I have been drawn into part of Jean Pierre's life, Mina came to understand the lives of her guides, as they clearly became more than her temporary travelling companions. In an unhappy coincidence, George Elson's child also died—a daughter—several years after his trip with Mina. And on the trip, George, especially, was a close friend. They spent many hours talking to each other, telling each other about their lives. Mina was grateful for George's valiant efforts in returning her husband's body, and Leonidas provided an intimate link between them that seems never to have been broken.

As the friendship grew, so Mina encouraged George to follow his dreams as she had followed hers, and the influence of this encouragement can be read in his diary, where he writes: "I have thought a great deal about what I shall do this winter. I would like to go to school then in the summer I would go down to James Bay and start fur trading and maybe . . . I would write a nice little story . . . I would like now to get married this fall . . . If she was well learnt we could write some nice stories . . ."

Toward the end of their time together while at the George River post, Mina lay awake at night, just as I have on the trail, worrying about the fate of her friend. Elson was a man whose "great heart" she famously admired, and she urged him to explore his ancestry and write the stories inside him that were shut away by breeding, class, and his time in history.

Journeys such as the one Jean Pierre and I are making, and which Mina made, are known for their ability to change perspectives, minds, and beliefs. The country through which we are travelling may be a little different from what it was ninety-five years ago, but, I think to myself as I leap across to a half-submerged boulder, we share an equal voyage of discovery.

A shout snaps me out of my reverie. Automatically, I haul on the rope, but it is too late. The current has caught the canoe with a force that almost pulls me off my feet. The rope plays out to the last inch, flinging water in my eyes, and I slip, half falling, half attempting to keep hold. But there is no purchase on the smooth slope of the boulder and my foot slides down into the cold, leaving me crouched on one leg with the rapid in front of me and several feet of water lying behind, between the rock and the bank.

I am conscious of Jean Pierre running, water at mid-thigh, shouting something as he reaches for the bow. For one long moment, the canoe floats free but unsure, like a wild creature offered an open gate. Then, in a single motion, she swings broadside onto the river, allowing a wave to pour over her side in a mighty swoosh, swamping our equipment. At that same moment, Jean Pierre's hand closes over the bar in the bow, and standing in the shallows, he wrests the fully laden canoe and several gallons of water from the river's grasp, hauling her half onto the rocks in a single Herculean movement.

There is silence for a moment as we both allow what has just happened to sink in. It is an unprecedented rescue. Normally, any canoe lost to the river in this way is gone forever, destined to smash her way downstream, scattering kit as she goes. I get up slowly and step from rock to rock back to the bank. Jean Pierre pulls the canoe onto solid ground and starts to throw everything out of her. Nothing has been lost and all is watertight, except for his clothes and the tent.

We sit, drained, on the rocks, the thin line of salvation between river and forest. Jean Pierre takes off his boots, pouring out the water, then removes his socks and trousers, wringing them out before laying them on the rocks with his other clothes. They lie littered in the strong sun like surviving scraps from a shipwreck—which, in a way, they almost were. We turn the canoe over fully, emptying the water out, and carry her up high onto the rocks, mended patch pointing to the sky. It seems ironic that the only damage she has sustained so far on this trip was done en route from Toronto.

I look at Jean Pierre, who seems surprisingly unperturbed by our little adventure, and find myself agreeing with Mina: "*When you see these men in the bush you needed no further explanation of their air of quiet self confidence.*"

Jean Pierre feels my gaze and says, not unkindly, "Remember to keep the rope tight or we will lose her."

The understatement is masterful. It was indeed my fault, with a little twist of fate to help things along. Next time, we may not be so lucky. I comment on Jean Pierre's astonishing show of strength and he shrugs, looking away. I have no idea if he is flattered or too mad at me to speak.

We camp late that night, thanks to the time spent drying things as best we can and unloading and loading the canoe. Twilight is descending as we finally pull over onto the bank. I cannot see a suitable camping place, but Jean Pierre once more strides confidently through the willows and into the forest, carrying his axe. I follow, with difficulty. We seem to have chosen a spot where the willows are the thickest I've seen all day. As I break out of their suffocating grip, I feel as if I'm entering Narnia, so different is the dark forest from the blindingly bright, noisy world of the riverbank.

Thick moss underfoot muffles the sound of all movement, and every tree seems to look alike. The dead brown branches, starved of the rich sunlight higher up, spike me viciously as I walk by. Flies swarm around, covering every inch of my clothing in their usual desperate attempts to suck my blood.

In the distance, I can hear the steady *thunk, thunk* of Jean Pierre's axe, so I know he's found us a place to camp. When I find him, he is busy clearing saplings away from a small space. Several large rocks lie to one side, recently dug out of the earth. These combined efforts have made a space maybe four feet by four feet. How ironic, that in all this vast land, we have such difficulty finding a flat space large enough to erect a tent. I turn back toward the canoe to collect our kit.

"Not the tent," Jean Pierre calls after me. "It's wet. Bring the tarp."

It's almost fully dark as I crawl into our improvised tent with the final armful of boughs. Jean Pierre has tied several saplings into a dome shape with rope, and over them he has thrown the brown tarp. I wrinkle my nose as I crawl in, my knees sticky with sap from the boughs. It's a good shelter: the edges are held down outside with chunks of moss, making our shelter secure and rainproof. Jean Pierre took less than half an hour to put it up and the boughs on the mossy ground make a soft bed—for me at least. On Jean Pierre's side of the tent (such as it is), a big rock is submerged just below the surface, but he sleeps on it anyway, manfully suffering in silence and allowing me the comfort of the couple of square feet that are rock free.

Inside, it's very dark. There is no tent flap, and the thick forest blocks out the last of the twilight. The flare of a match for Jean Pierre's cigarette lights my way into bed. I'm very tired after a day of wildly vacillating emotions, and I feel much more vulnerable tonight than ever before. Whenever Mina's party felt low or disheartened, they sang: hymns, popular songs, and their favourite "Indian Paddling Song," a recurring melody throughout their trip. Often, Mina complains to her diary, *"Oh how I wish I could speak Indian,"* after listening to their voices drifting out into the night from around the campfire.

It was not just the singing itself that inspired her to this ambition. While working during the day, the men would communicate with each other in "Indian" (she never specifies which language they all share, although it was probably Cree), and she finds her exclusion from this little world frustrating while suspecting, probably quite rightly, that the men prefer it that way. She does manage to persuade George to give her lessons, however—a fact not noted in her book, as the rest of Edwardian society would not have perceived learning the language of one's "inferiors" as a suitable occupation for a lady.

Yet for Mina, it was another important part of her trip through Labrador. It tells us a great deal about her attitude and her level of interest in the people and landscape around her, an attitude that allowed her to consider making such a journey in the first place. Her uniqueness is not easily hidden, even to the most casual reader of her published book.

By the time they reached their final destination, the George River post on Ungava Bay, Mina had memorized and learned to sing all of the many verses of the "Paddling Song." After singing it at a gathering at the post one evening, she notes in her diary that "*the men said anyone would think I spoke good Indian. They wouldn't if they heard me try to read it.*"

She doesn't record what the white employees at the post thought of her new skills.

The idea of doing such a thing did not seem to have occurred to other, earlier travellers in the region. Randle Holme, who'd attempted to reach Churchill Falls in 1887, wrote, "*The country of this unfortunate section of an unfortunate race has so little to offer the progressive European, that the forests and their inhabitants have been left to their primeval owners ... [It] is true, the Hudson's Bay Company has brought them a few things to strengthen them in their warfare with nature animate and inanimate ...*"

To modern eyes, the racism of those words is staggering, but of more interest are the basic assumptions underlying the statement, which still, in part, inform the debate about wild lands and Indigenous inhabitants the world over today.

At the heart of assertions like Holme's (of a kind that continued to be made openly by academics as late as the 1940s) was a basic lack of understanding of the nature of hunter-gatherer lives. Holme speaks of the "warfare" against their environment, a contest they must win to survive. This is a distillation of the white European viewpoint of the relationship between humans and the earth. Humankind has dominion over the land, this culture claims: it exists merely to keep us alive through the intensive production of food and materials. We seek always to control nature, to dominate, subdue, and rule every land-scape and creature. Even "wild" areas remain so on our terms—as national parks, for example. Hunter-gatherer peoples, by compari-son, work in harmony with their land; they survive through knowing its secrets, through understanding its cycles and rhythms. Nothing is destroyed or excluded. There are no weeds, no vermin. Everything has its role, including the hunter. Only that which is needed is taken. There is no hunger for more land and no desire to reshape the terri-tory. It is not a war, it is coexistence.

Europeans judged that one of the most effective forms of helping Native people out of this "savagery" was to force their children to attend schools where the only language used was English. Sadly, this practice seems to have been all too common in Canada. Often, these schools were boarding establishments, set up a long way from the territorial lands of the children and based on regimes of physical abuse and humiliation. Jean Pierre is unusual. As a child born in 1960, he did not learn English until he attended a Canadian high school in Newfoundland for one year at the age of seventeen. His wife, he tells me, was unaware for several years that he could even read English.

"What did she think when she saw you reading a book?" I ask, mystified. He laughs.

"She thought I was joking, I don't know."

Jean Pierre is as curious about my world as I am about his, and our evening chats are not merely one-way affairs. Naturally, he asks the difficult questions: about the British class system, about our schools. He knows about such things, having visited the U.K. while represent-ing Survival International. He also has several British friends, some of them resident in Happy Valley. It was, I noticed, a very cosmopolitan place despite its remote location.

Tonight, however, I am not in the mood for intelligent debate. The incident with the canoe weighs heavily on my mind. What if Jean Pierre had not reached it in time? What if the current had swept it away after all? The enormity of what almost happened is only now beginning to sink in, but I fight it. I occasionally have an inclination toward melancholy, and this trip, I already realize, will be hard enough without brooding on what might have been. I must learn the lesson, put the rest to one side, and focus on the next challenge. Too much is at stake here—everything I have worked for until now and all my future plans—for me to crack so early in the trip. Already I realize that reaching Ungava Bay will depend as much on my mental and psychological strength as anything else.

Even now, however, I am asking myself, Is success defined only by reaching Ungava? In one sense, yes, it is, but already I've felt that there will be so much on this trip for me to face both physically and personally that staying alive and sane is beginning to look like a more realistic ambition.

Jean Pierre senses my thoughtful mood tonight, for he says kindly: "When I was younger, travelling with my grandparents through the country, my grandfather would tell me stories of our ancestors, the legends of our peoples, battles between shamans and tales of the animal masters."

I look over at him, his face half-lit by the glow of his cigarette, the mosquito coil burning between us. Comforted somewhat, I smile and snuggle down a little farther into my sleeping bag.

"Would you tell me those stories?"

"Yes."

And so he tells me a tale about a time long, long ago, when the people all lived on the land and the animal masters watched over them, even through the darkest of winters . . .

"*An Innu hunter and his wife always argued for no reason. She thought him cruel and over time grew less willing to cope with him. One day, they had travelled to a new place where the fishing was plentiful, and the wife told her husband she was going to pick boughs while he put up the tent. When she had gone, the husband finished putting up the tent and looked around for his wife but could not find her.*

"*There were other Innu people living nearby and they helped to look for the woman. They discovered she had picked some boughs, as they found them lying on the ground, but there was no sign of the woman. It had started to snow some time before, and they finally found her tracks in the snow, but the tracks led to a river. It was vast, with strong currents, and they were not able to cross it, although the woman had, because they could see her tracks. So the husband and the other people turned back and returned to the children, whom she had left behind . . ."*

I lie on my back, listening to Jean Pierre's voice, soft in the silence. The coil has burned itself out and he has finished the last cigarette. I can feel the darkness pressing on my eyes, so I close them and let his voice wash over me in a wave of colour, emotion, and magical transformations.

*"Several months passed. As the woman travelled across land, she found another family and killed them, hanging them out like drying meat.*

*"An Innu hunter out alone saw the smoke from her fire and found the tent. He looked inside and saw the woman. She looked as though she was hibernating and he left her there, knowing that something serious was happening to her. There was no shaman there at the time, but it was clear the woman had become cannibalistic.*

*"The woman then woke up and she was stronger than she had ever been. She was possessed with a spirit and was growing in strength. The hunter observed her movements over days. One morning, she left the tent and rolled on a rock three times and started running toward the camp of her husband. A snowstorm started and the woman ran with the storm. The people were frightened and took down all their things, such as the caribou skins from outside, making no noise. They went out onto the frozen lake and the storm passed them. The sun came out and the woman was gone. They found her tracks in the snow. They were large and shaped like the shoulder blade of a caribou. The tracks showed the woman was running toward the north. On the way she killed people in four more tents, then stopped when she reached Lake Michikamau, near the Great Whale River. There was a shaman there, and he told all the people not to look at her, as she had strong powers*

*and could turn them into monsters. It took three shamans to kill the woman on the shores of Lake Michikamau, and when she died, she turned into four big boulders, which lie there still."*

"Do you think the boulders are still there, despite the reservoir?" I ask.

"For sure." Jean Pierre nods. "We may need to search a little, but I know where she rests and I know we can find her."

# CHAPTER 6

My eyes snap open and every sinew strains for sound: the sound I know my subconscious has just heard. I lie perfectly still, listening, pinned to the ground by the blackness of an unlit tent in a dark forest in the middle of the night. The black starts to dance in front of my eyes. I close them again. Nothing. For a reason I can't understand, I'm rigid with fear. I reach for the comfort of the flashlight and remember that it was left behind with the canoe, as was the gun. Both are a ten-minute walk away through the forest. My mind pings into panic. What if claws were suddenly to slice through the tarpaulin?

More silence, pressing in. Jean Pierre sighs, shifting position, and I remember him, lying six inches away. His steady breathing calms me, too, and I drift back into sleep as suddenly as I awoke.

In late June 1905, Mina was forced to climb over the high banks of ice that bordered this section of the river. She was travelling only a little earlier in the year than we are, yet it is far too hot now for any ice to linger, even this far inland. I do not find it so hard to believe the extremes of weather here. Jean Pierre and I have been travelling through temperatures of about eighty degrees Fahrenheit, yet just a few days before we departed from North West River, the temperature barely rose above freezing.

Travelling in summer as we are is the hardest time to travel in Labrador. People who live here hunt or spend time in their country cabins in spring and autumn, often when snow is lying on the ground, but they avoid the harshest part of the winter and the heat of the summer. In mid-winter, temperatures can drop to minus forty degrees, something I am unable to imagine, coming from the temperate climes of England. I recall Joe telling me how he woke up one morning in his cabin during the winter and found his watch had stopped, frozen solid at 4 A.M.

There are advantages to winter travel, however. Randle Holme summed them up well when he wrote, "*It may be readily understood that a man traveling over a frozen river behind a team of perhaps twenty dogs, will cover the ground with greater ease and speed than he who painfully hauls a boat against a rapid current.*" I find myself in some sympathy with this opinion, as nothing could, in my limited experience, be harder than hauling a boat upstream. The deep cold of winter would certainly make it easier to travel over thick snow. Jean Pierre tells me that when he was a child, his family often travelled at night so the snow would be hard enough to cross with heavy sledges. He remembers how, when he was sleeping under a cozy heap of pelts, his father would wake him at 2:30 in the morning, the camp packed away and the entire family ready to move soon afterward. I ask him what would have happened if he'd refused to get out of bed.

He laughs. "I don't know. Get left behind, I guess. I didn't say no to my father."

It is mid-day, and the heat is stifling. We sit, drinking gallons of river water. The rapids roar past us, bigger and wilder at every twist. It seems as though I've been walking, lining, breathing through a net for years, but it's been only a few days. I continue to think about snow and winter, as it takes my mind off the burning heat.

"Have you ever fallen through the ice?" I ask Jean Pierre. I know that to do so would almost always be fatal—only a few seconds and hypothermia would set in.

"I've never fallen in, but I've gone in deliberately."

I raise my eyebrows and turn on my rocky perch in surprise. Jean

Pierre is sitting below me, gazing downriver, but he looks up at me now briefly.

"I saw a man fall in, through the ice, a long time ago. We called the police for help, but he would have been dead by the time they arrived, so I had to get him out. He lived."

"You weren't afraid to die?"

"I knew what I had to do. It was very cold, but I lit a fire straight-away and got warm again."

"That was very brave."

He shrugs.

"I didn't think about it."

Travelling in winter does, therefore, have its hazards, and to those unaccustomed to the cold, it would certainly feel like the tougher option. Mina chose to brave the flies and rapids for most of her journey, rather than taking dogsleds over the snow, as did Dillon and earlier explorers in the region. At one point, however, Mina thought she would be travelling in winter. She had no real knowledge of the area through which she was travelling and did not know how long the George River actually was. Just days from Ungava Bay and the George River post, she was discussing the possibility of turning around and retracing her route back to North West River. The first Innu band that Mina met on the George told her that Ungava was a full two months' journey farther on. Faced with several more weeks of travel before reaching their goal, followed by a long and arduous journey home overland in the depths of winter (since they would have missed the *Pelican*), she reasoned that it would be most sensible to turn around: "*It would mean the entire journey in winter weather and we could not think of that. Half the journey back in winter we might manage, but we could not do it all.*"

Fortunately, they travelled onward, far enough to meet another band which told them, correctly, that the post was less than a week's journey away. But the most interesting point in this event is the discussion that arose between Mina and her guides when the possibility of return was raised. Mina wanted to return via the Naskaupi, so she would be able to take more latitudinal observations. The men refused, however, stating that it would be too dangerous. Mina replied: "*If we go back at all I want to go that way. Now, if you refuse to take me back I cannot compel you to do it and I shall not try but you will record in my diary that I asked you to do so and you refused and state your reasons which you think are good.*"

This could perhaps be seen as the tip of an iceberg called mutiny. Earlier in her diary, while the group was still on the Naskaupi River, Mina records an interesting conversation with George that begins as a discussion about the best spot to place a cache, should they need to return the way they'd travelled. Mina was adamant that they would use the Naskaupi, if necessary, as she had left word to that effect. George, however, suggests rather innocently that they use the Grand (Churchill) River. Mina writes later of her suspicion that the men were travelling slowly in order to return by their chosen route. In light of what happens later on George River, she is quite right in being "uncomfortable" about what her guides decline to tell her.

However, such a spirited response from Mina certainly challenges the image presented in her book: a grieving widow completing the work of her dead husband, a woman grateful to be led by men chosen by Leonidas himself. Although she did value her guides above all else, her diary tells a different story about who was in charge. At all times, Mina was the leader on the expedition and a far cry from the helpless woman she was portrayed to be by some commentators of the time: "*With such skilled helpers, it is plain that Mrs. Hubbard was a mere passenger on the trip.*" (J.G. Millais, *Nature*, Feb., 1909.)

Of course, skilled help was exactly what Mina was paying for. As a woman of means, she could expect—and afford—to pay for four men to do all the heavy work. That they did so is not an expression of her weakness as a woman but of her power as a member of a different class, of white society, with money to pay for the best advice, expertise, and knowledge available. The fact that she seldom carried anything heavier than her rifle and a notebook and appears to have taken instruction from her guides does not mean that she surrendered leadership of the expedition. It merely indicates that she expected the men to carry out tasks for which they were skilled and which she had paid them to do.

In addition to any chivalry the men may have felt toward Mina, they certainly took pride in their roles. Of Job, she wrote, "*He loved to pole up a rapid or hunt out a trail just as an artist loves to paint.*"

I am reminded of Jean Pierre telling me how, while working as one of several guides on a fishing trip for visitors in the country, he and the other men felt confused, impatient, and a little offended when the guests attempted to "help" with the tasks the guides were there to perform. Mina, no doubt, showed more respect. After all, they were not expected to "help" her take sextant readings.

That she relied on the men for their judgement in matters relating to the river and wilderness survival shows her good sense. It was in doing so that she avoided the fate of her husband, and clearly, she had a much more successful expedition than Dillon. Not only did she choose her companions for their skills, experience, and knowledge; she also listened to their advice. Mina's expedition was more efficient, better organized, and better equipped.

It would appear to be true, however, that the men did persist in treating Mina as a "lady," while she saw herself as part of a team. Yet it mustn't be forgotten that if the men were to return without Mina, it was likely they would not be believed when they said they did their best. Indeed, such was George Elson's disadvantage as a lower-class "half-breed" that when he managed to reach help while with Leonidas and Dillon, he was afraid both men would die in his absence, and "*people may not believe me in what I say and will think that I have run away from them . . . and when I got home I would be in trouble.*" This same fear resurfaces when he says in some distress to Mina, "*Don't you know we could never go back without you?*"

Mina's role as a lady is not irreconcilable with that of a leader, however. "*Through George Elson,*" she writes, "*I engaged and paid the other men of my party and on him I relied to communicate to them my plans and my directions and desires.*" And she quickly tires of George attempting to tell her what to do: "*George's tone of authority was sometimes amusing. Sometimes I did as I was told, and then again I did not."* When he steps beyond the boundary of his own expertise, she deals with the situation by laughing at him, adding later that she would do whatever was necessary for her work. The other men tell George, in wonder, that *"they were never on a trip where the women didn't do as they were told."*

Although the men quite clearly tried to wrest some control from Mina, it was likely as much born of an inclination toward chivalry as it was of outright sexism. Mina never acquiesced to play the role of helpless female, and when wider decisions were to be made, it was Mina who bore the responsibility. Realizing, for example, that their progress up the Naskaupi was unnecessarily slow, and calculating the distance remaining against the departure of the supply boat *Pelican* from Ungava, she speaks to George about travelling a little faster, concluding in her diary, *"I think we shall get a little more snap in our game after this."* These are not the words of a "mere passenger," nor was her tactful response when George tried to prevent her climbing a mountain she wanted to scale: *"I gently made it plain that I was going whether I had company or not."*

Such an attitude may strike an outsider as bordering on the irresponsible, but the fact of her gender must not prevent Mina from being given the benefit of the assumption that her judgement was correct. When it came to relying entirely on the word of her guides or making her own opinion known, she seems always to have made the right decision, and the success of her expedition would indicate that her judgement was usually correct. Furthermore, it was due only to Mina's foresight, vision, and courage that the expedition was made at all.

Lower down this first section of white water known as Three Mile Rapids, the standing waves are small, and the water shallow. When we reach the head of this, the first major set of rapids, the roar of water crashing over the boulders is immense. Holding the canoe on a line in these conditions is like trying to hold a skittish stallion on a halter rope. The river is temperamental and unpredictable, at once strangely delicate yet dangerous. I'm astonished at how quickly I've become accustomed to the work and at how strong I am becoming. I've spent a full eight hours holding the canoe against the force of the water today in hot sun and clouds of flies, yet I still have enough energy to be excited by our camping place.

It opens out before us like an oasis in the wilderness. The endless lines of water, rock, and forest are broken by a small cove, sheltered by high, impenetrable cliffs. Soft white sand welcomes our weary feet with a gentle sigh. The late afternoon sun filters through the spruce trees lining the ridge above, and the warmth soaks through me, relaxing my tired muscles. I lie down on the sand, back flat, face to the sky, and breathe in. Slowly.

"Help me empty the canoe. I want to check for scratches."

Jean Pierre's voice cuts through my brief moment of pleasure and I get up. Throwing our kit haphazardly onto the sand, I realize something is wrong—missing, perhaps. Then I realize what it is. There are no flies. Maybe the day has been too hot, maybe fate just decided to give us a welcome break. Either way, I've decided I love this cove and want to stay here for the rest of the trip.

After we've emptied the canoe of all our gear, we drag her high up onto the sand and roll her over fully to examine what the rocks of the past few days have done to her. The patch over the hole from the truck journey is holding up, but only just. We'll need our emergency fixing kit fairly soon. There are numerous other scratches, some deeper than others, all along the length of the canoe. Jean Pierre looks thoughtfully at some of the deeper gouges, then quickly bends over, and creating a seal around a mark with his mouth, sucks hard. Evidently no air comes through and he nods, satisfied, running a gentle hand over the paintwork. I can tell he appreciates the craftsmanship inherent in her.

Tonight we have our "full" tent again. Jean Pierre cuts long poles for stakes, hammering them deep into the sand with the broadside of his axe, then tying them to the corners of the tent to lay the poles, pulling it out into its full glory. It takes forever to pick enough boughs for the floor, but when it's done, the tent looks as cozy as anything I could wish for. I help occasionally, but my main task is cooking dinner over an open wood fire on the beach. Some of our clothes lie draped across the canoe, drying from their dunking farther downstream the day before.

For the first time in a few days, I have an opportunity to do some filming. I set the camera up to capture Jean Pierre as he puts up the tent, cutting sticks and tying them in place. The cameras have proved to be an unwelcome extra burden on this difficult section of river, and I am coming to regret having brought them. Frequently too tired to take them out, plug in the batteries and film, I have not yet shot enough footage to make their extra weight worthwhile. Were it not for the fact that they are extremely valuable pieces of equipment, I would happily throw them in the river.

Later, I lean back, resting on one elbow, waiting for the rice to cook and lazily watching Jean Pierre through the smoke from the fire. He is sitting with his back to the river, sharpening the axe, the rhythmic grinding and the running river the only sounds in the still air. At this moment, I am quite content. I have the prospect of a good meal, a proper night's sleep, and—wonder of wonders—a full wash (the closest I have to a bath) in warm water from the fire ahead of me. I care not for whatever hardships lie in store for us farther upstream. Digging my bare feet into the sand, I wriggle my toes and smile at Jean Pierre.

In a single second, our country idyll is smashed. Two military jet fighters fly over our camp, so close that I can see the pilots' faces and feel, rather than hear, their engines. The effect is as shattering as a baseball bat through a fish tank.

I put my hands over my ears, but the noise is all around me, inside me, and the ground seems to shake beneath my feet. I look wildly around for Jean Pierre, but I can't see him. The noise is so consuming, it is almost blinding. Then, as quickly as they arrived, the jets are gone, and the quiet is once again broken only by the sound of the river. There is no birdsong and the peace seems almost artificial, like the stunned silence following a great explosion before the screaming begins.

There is no screaming here, though. I stagger over to Jean Pierre, who is motionless behind the smoke from our fire.

"Does this happen a lot?" I ask. I know that flight training is conducted out of the airbase at Goose Bay, but I hadn't expected anything as dramatic as this.

"Too often, yes." He looks resigned. "I'm surprised we haven't seen them sooner. They use our highways—the river valleys and lakes—for the low-level flying."

"They must have been very low. For a split second, I saw the pilots. I thought that was illegal."

"Only in Europe." Jean Pierre looks at me. "They fly at a hundred feet above the ground here because they see the county as 'uninhabited.' Europe has too many people. Too many voters."

Of course, I'm familiar with the airbase, as it's an integral part of Goose Bay. However, it's only since 1979 that the Canadian government has permitted NATO forces to use it for air defence training, including low-level flying and bombing exercises. Jean Pierre is not alone in his opposition to the exercises. Many Innu also oppose the presence of the base because of the effects they claim the flying has on wildlife, among other reasons. The prospect of being overflown also creates fear in people spending time in the country, especially the elderly and children, a factor that often drives families back to the settlements.

The non-Innu residents of Happy Valley–Goose Bay, however, appear to be largely in favour of the base, as it supplies many jobs, pouring much needed money into the local economy—still one of Canada's poorest. Indeed, before the airbase was there, Happy Valley did not exist at all. Several of my new friends are involved with it in some way and I feel torn between their interests and those of Jean Pierre.

I watch Jean Pierre as he walks over to the point that shelters our little cove. He is looking downstream, but the jets have long gone. Maybe he's wondering if any more will be slicing through the air this evening.

"What effects do you think the jets have on the environment?" I ask Jean Pierre when he comes back to the campfire.

He points to the river. "I've seen fish floating dead, for no apparent reason, in rivers frequently overflown by the planes. It also frightens the caribou, disrupts their migrating patterns, and separates them from their young."

I can see how smaller creatures could be shocked into heart failure by the jets, just as a mouse is when confronted with a cat or as injured wild birds are when they are picked up by humans. Not surprisingly, anecdotal evidence like Jean Pierre's carries little weight in the eyes of the government, whose environmental assessments have never found hard evidence to support the Innu's claims that the airbase is damaging the environment.

Government statistics show that the George River caribou herd, the largest in the world, has grown from 50,000 in 1960 to 750,000 today, despite the presence of the planes. In 1991, NATO decided that the training base for tactical fighters would not be needed, saving the landscape from several live military target ranges and a vast increase in sorties.

"How many of these flights go out each year?" I ask Jean Pierre, who is now once again sharpening his axe by the fire, as though nothing has happened.

"Thousands," he says, then thinks for a minute. "I think there are about seven thousand each year. They claim this is not very many, but we are certain to see more planes when we are out here."

The discussions over low flying also ignore the larger question of ownership. Just as with the Churchill Falls project, this military activity is based on the assumption that the Canadian government has a right to use the land as it pleases, despite the fact that no treaty giving Canada rights to the land was ever signed between the government and the Innu. The current land claims talks are based on the Comprehensive Land Claims Policy document, which states that "*the aboriginal rights to be released in the claims process are . . . those related to the use of and title to land and resources.*" This implies that the question is how, not if, title to the land will be ceded.

So the Canadian document goes against the spirit of the UN Convention on the Elimination of all Forms of Racial Discrimination, ratified by Canada. In 1997, the monitoring committee called upon

States to act as follows: "*Where they* [native groups] *have been deprived of their lands and territories traditionally owned or otherwise inhabited or used without their free and informed consent, to take steps to return these lands and territories.*"

The Innu Nation, the group that negotiates on behalf of the Innu communities of Labrador, is claiming just 22 percent of Labrador, which is equivalent, on a per capita basis, to the remarkable land-claim agreement that created from the Northwest Territories the autonomous area of Nunavut in 1999. This is in addition to 23 percent to be governed under co-management proposals. It excludes areas already developed for industrial use, such as Churchill Falls.

These figures do not suit everyone, including Jean Pierre, who growls unrepeatable things when I mention the land-claims process.

Most members of Labrador's Native communities—Inuit and Innu alike—do agree, however, that all "development" projects must cease on the land until Native rights has been recognized and title to the land and its resources have been decided. Until that point, they claim, the land belongs to them and Canada has no jurisdiction over it.

To Jean Pierre, as to many Innu, land equals culture. Daniel Ashini, chief land rights negotiator and Jean Pierre's cousin, speaks for many Innu when he says, "Our land is being turned into a military wasteland and there's nothing we can do to stop it. This land is Innu and Inuit. It does not belong to the Newfoundland government or to Canada. We never gave it to them and we continue to use it. But it makes our lives very difficult when there is more low-level flying, more fishing camps, and more mining without our consent. The companies who come here are parties with the government in stealing land from the Innu people."

The flight has changed the mood of our peaceful camp. Jean Pierre is preoccupied and quiet. I cannot tell if he is thinking about Mr. T again or if he is disturbed by the jets. The sun slowly moves farther from our sanctuary and takes the light with it.

Washed and refreshed, I lie in my sleeping bag, but there is no bedtime myth to soothe me to sleep tonight. I lie awake for a while, listening to the river. It is the first time our camp has been so close to the water, and I can hear the rush and crash of each rapid, not just a distant roar. Despite the noise and violence, I find it oddly comforting. As I drift into sleep, I fancy I can hear the swirling notes of a piano playing jazz, the tinkle of champagne glasses and laughter, lots of people laughing as they dance and talk, while all the time the piano plays . . .

# CHAPTER 7

The river directly north of the sandy cove is mostly fast water, but we have come to the end of our first set of big rapids on the Naskaupi River. I surprise myself by desperately wanting to return to paddling the canoe. After lining it so far and in such heavy waters, the aches and pains of a long day wielding the paddle seem like a pleasant, if distant, dream.

My prayer is answered and we have not travelled far upstream from the cove when we do manage to paddle, but these passages are tempered with stretches of lining. I'm sure at these times that Jean Pierre would be able to paddle if his companion was any other than a 110-pound weakling. But, then, I console myself, I'm the only reason we're here at all. We are, however, already two days behind Mina. Our initial advantage of covering so much distance on the first day was quickly lost through our enforced stay on the shores of Grand Lake and our slow progress up the rapids. We now need to travel at speed, and the only way we can do that is by paddling.

The river at this point has opened out into a wide, lazy sweep reminiscent of our early days below the Red Wine River tributary. A large, wooded island in the centre makes the waterway appear to fork into separate tributaries. This confuses me, but Jean Pierre unerringly takes the route to the left, so we glide on into the stillness, our paddles seemingly muffled by the immensity of the landscape. There is a sense of anticipation in the quiet, as though birds and animals alike are holding their breath. Each human-made noise seems so insignificant that once it is made, it is swallowed up by the universe and lost, the weight of the atmosphere denying its existence and wiping it from memory.

We continue through this cloud-darkened world for several hours, stepping ashore on another, smaller island for a short lunch of yesterday's bread, half-melted cheese, and energy bars.

Sometime in the early afternoon, the sky grows darker still and the temperature drops. Jean Pierre seems uncomfortable, as he was the day we were almost caught in the squall on Grand Lake, but I sense no breeze. Instead, the grey sky underscores the forest's silence—an empty, menacing absence of sound that is soon filled with the soft but persistent drumming of rain, falling straight and steady.

I'm wearing a light top that is showerproof only. The weather has been so hot over the past few days that I've stashed my all-singing, all-dancing waterproof deep in the kit.

"It'll pass," says Jean Pierre, nodding at the sky. But I'm not so sure. I've seen skies like that many times at home, and they always herald the start of several days of nonstop rain.

We pull over to the left bank of the river and stretch the tarpaulin over the kit to protect it and to make sure the rain doesn't collect in the canoe. Huddling under a tree, I stare disconsolately at the sky. At home, I'm often accused of being a weather junkie, and it's true that I'm addicted to forecasts. On fine days, I find it impossible to stay indoors, but I constantly and obsessively scan the horizon for the first suggestion of cloud, which in England arrive frequently. At the merest hint of a shower, I rail insanely at the weather gods, and should it be raining when I first get out of bed in the morning, my overwhelming desire is to return and pull the covers over my head until the sun appears.

Jean Pierre, on the other hand, seems unconcerned about the rain. He is happy there is no wind and is standing out on the bank, apparently oblivious to his darkening jeans and a T-shirt that is beginning to stick to him. He strolls over to me smiling, but notices my glum face.

"My grandmother always called rain medicine."

"Really."

I'm not convinced and sourly refrain from commenting on the possibility of pneumonia that such an attitude must surely induce.

The phrase reminds me of the stoicism that so astonished Europeans when they first met Native peoples in the seventeenth century. Hardships and suffering—much worse than a simple wetting—were borne with cheerfulness. The attitude came, I suppose, from acceptance of and resignation to the vagaries of the natural world. Whereas Europeans sought to challenge, change, and dominate, the inclination of the Native people of North America seems to have been to adapt, survive, and learn. These differences set us apart. Those who live so close to the land can never conquer, and find instead a kind of harmony that has been all but extinguished under the boot of modernity.

The rain slows down a little, then stops altogether, and we paddle on into a silent, grey, reflecting world. Our respite is short lived, however, as the rain begins again—this time with a heavy, determined ferocity that has me abandoning my paddle and reaching for my waterproof. It's too late. Drenched and cold, we head toward the first section of riverbank that offers any kind of harbour.

"Are you cold?" Jean Pierre asks me, a worried look in his eyes.

"Yes."

We pull up against an apparently hospitable bank, but when I get out, its innocent-looking red sand sinks beneath my feet, sucking me down past my ankles. I gasp in surprise and lunge for the grassy bank. The evil gunge clings and slobbers, but I wrench myself free, scrambling into the undergrowth. I'm cut, wet, muddy, and a little shocked. Jean Pierre jumps out, balancing from rock to rock, avoiding the large holes in the sand left by my feet, now filling with water. He ties up the canoe and pulls out the axe.

"Into the trees."

I really am cold now. All my clothes are wet and I'm starting to shiver, probably more from fear of hypothermia than from actual cold, but Jean Pierre is concerned. The wood looks too wet to start a fire, but he finds some large logs and pulls them over to a small mossy hollow in the forest floor. Taking the axe, he chops them lengthwise, somehow extracting the dry wood from inside the log. Using this, he starts a fire that quickly grows into a fine blaze, which soon has my discarded clothing steaming on a nearby branch.

We boil a kettle of water and drink hot tea in the forest, listening to the sound of a billion raindrops falling on water, their healing caresses washing the land clean. Jean Pierre's grandmother's view of the rain as medicine is typical of the Innu. In the settlements, many attend mass, but in the country, only the traditional beliefs seem appropriate. It's a kind of double faith, matching the double lives the Innu lead. I touch the caribou bone in my pocket. I can't believe we've done anything to offend.

During our often-rambling conversations at the close of days or during lazy, heat-heavy afternoons, we've often found ourselves back at the subject of hunting. Before the beginning of this trip, several people told me that Jean Pierre is well respected as a hunter in his community. And I've come to realize that the greatest praise I could give him would be to tell him he is a good hunter.

The Innu believe that humans, game, and land are all bound together. As in all animist belief systems, there are no distinguishing lines between "religion," society, and work, as the hunter operates within a framework where all animals and forces of nature are associated with spiritual beings. The walls between the earthbound world and the spirit world are flimsy, though only shamans have the power to cross through those boundaries. It is they who have the power to find animals and to describe the routes hunters must take to find them—a discernment often made through dreams. By moving between the human and animal worlds, between times and place, shamans are able to make decisions that could mean the difference between life and death. Naturally, this is considered to have a mystical element, but the process itself is quite believable.

The information shamans use to dream answers is stored through

(*top*) Leonidas Hubbard
(*bottom*) Mina Hubbard (From the drawing by J. Syddall)

(*top left*) On the trail
(*top right*) George Elson, Mina's head guide
(*bottom*) On the riverbank, 1905

(*top*) Camp life, 1905
(*bottom*) Breakfast at camp, 1905

(*top*) The Montagnais-Naskaupi (Innu) men Mina met on the George River
(*bottom*) The women of the Montagnais-Naskaupi (Innu) band

(*top*) The last pictures at North West River
(*bottom*) Paddling into the unknown

Surveying the landscape. Alexandra on the banks of the Naskaupi River

(*top*) Jean Pierre in fast water, Naskaupi River
(*bottom*) Jean Pierre paddling on the lower reaches of the Naskaupi River

(*top*) After the thunderstorm. Jean Pierre in a forest camp
(*bottom*) The mouth of the Naskaupi River from Grand Lake

generations of experience and passed on through stories of the kind Jean Pierre tells me almost every night. The stories are blends of current fact and experience, of patterns, relationships, and other forms of knowledge, which, when combined with intuition, can be powerful tools. Essentially, shamans use their subconscious to filter all the available information and make the right decisions.

Drumming, charms (such as the caribou bone, bulky and reassuring in my pocket), and scapulimancy are all considered essential for a successful hunt. The latter involves placing the shoulder bone of a caribou, putting it into the heat of an open fire, and "reading" the patterns in the crack. The information is seen as no less reliable than that drawn from more mundane patterns of weather and animal movements.

However, possibly the most famous—but most secret—of the Innu traditions associated with shamans and the finding of game is the "shaking tent" ritual, or *kushapatshikan*. Possibly the Innu's most important ritual, the shaking tent was used not just to find game, but also to communicate with the animal masters and make contact with groups of Innu in distant areas. Some have described it as a form of telepathy, or like electricity in the air. The tent itself, erected inside another tent, was made of caribou hide stretched over four, six, or eight poles, depending on the power of the shaman. Boughs also covered the floor, as in all Innu tents.

The power of the shaman also decided which spirits came to the tent. Young hunters would assist the shaman to set up the tent, and one of them would likely be expected to take on the role of shaman in the future. However, the elders did not go inside the shaking tent itself, as it was thought to contain the power to kill people who did not have enough power of their own. Those with a great deal of power could talk directly to the caribou master himself, but this was very rare, and often a shaman would work up through the sprits until he found the one to whom he needed to speak. The arrival of these spirits in the tent is described as sounding like the rushing of a wind, each spirit having a distinctive voice, some easier to under-stand than others.

Power of the kind needed to conduct a shaking tent was accumulated through a lifetime of successful hunting. It increased in direct proportion to the number of animals the shaman killed and power was therefore given by the animal masters. The Roman Catholic Church has made great efforts to eradicate *kutshapatshikan* and other traditional customs since it first arrived on Labrador's shores, but this ritual in particular survived until around 1973 among the Sheshatshiu Innu. The reason for its disappearance since then is thought to be a decline in hunting, which, in turn, causes a decline in the spiritual power needed to conduct the ritual.

I realize that Jean Pierre, born in 1960, would be old enough to have seen a shaking tent—or possibly several—but when I ask him, he dismisses it, saying, "Everyone keeps talking about the 'shaking tent.' That is not what it is about. Our future is our land. That is what we need to be fighting for."

Next to shamans, hunters come closest to crossing the boundaries between realms. Jean Pierre could therefore be assumed to have some such power. He tells me again and again about the importance of hunting to his and his people's identity, but he never mentions an ability to dream or drum, and just as he dismisses my inquiries about shaking tents, he dismisses other similar inquiries about the spirit world. He knows only too well how the life-and-death issues facing the Innu today—land claims, industrial processes in Nitassinan, life in the settlements—can be overshadowed by the romance of practices like the shaking tent. He wants me to understand the realities of a life that no longer requires the services of shaking tents—because there is no longer a hunt.

Somehow, a belief system that speaks of and to the living things around us seems more credible here—more so than the beliefs I learned in church as a child. While the rationalist in me balks at the notion of animal spirits guiding our steps, even deciding our fate, I have a great deal of sympathy with a world view that sees humankind as integral to a larger system of interdependence. In a world where survival depends on an understanding of the weather and animal migration patterns, it is not surprising that the Innu make a spiritual link between their collective well-being and the wider well-being of the environment.

Jean Pierre confirms my thoughts when he tells me that all drinking and abuse stop when the Innu return to *nutshimit*—the country.

"Here, a man has purpose, an identity. In the settlements, there is nothing to do but drink."

I can believe it. Even though Jean Pierre is teetotal, I've noticed a distinct change in him since we left "civilization." On our first meeting in Happy Valley, he was not talkative, almost subdued. He moved and spoke like a man bearing an immense weight. I'd been concerned that I might be about to embark on a very solitary few weeks, yet as we've left the roads and houses of Happy Valley and North West River farther behind, Jean Pierre has become more open and chatty, his impenetrable silences replaced by a calm confidence and quiet ability.

"All of the things the settlers have brought to our land," says Jean Pierre, "add to the destruction of our land and the life we lead on it, drawing us into this cycle of drinking and ill health. My people believe they have little choice about how and where to live their lives. I never wanted to leave the country."

After a while, the rain diminishes and we dampen out the fire. I pull on my stiff, wood-smoky clothes, rinse our mugs, and climb back into the canoe, carefully avoiding the lethal red sand. A hot breeze has sprung up that is slightly unsettling, but we continue to paddle on for another few miles. It is hard going. The water is increasingly shallow and very fast. Several times we are caught on the riverbed.

I'm kneeling in the canoe, using my body weight to haul on the paddle. My arms are so exhausted they feel like string and my heart is beating fast, not from the exertion, but from the knowledge that if we do not paddle hard enough, the current will sweep us downstream, helpless and vulnerable in the grip of our watery master. I think of the rapids that lie behind us and shiver.

Not for the first time on this trip, my own insignificance, my power-lessness are brought home to me. Previously, I'd enjoyed the impervi-ousness of youth. Although in theory I knew that something could happen to me out here, I hadn't believed it actually would. Before I encountered the Naskaupi, I had never understood the true nature of fear—a fear bred of the certain knowledge that the environment is greater than I am. I have come to understand my own mortality. Not in a single, shattering, terrifying moment, but in a low-grade, constant, and pernicious way, the country of Labrador has made me aware that I am at its mercy.

Maybe Jean Pierre senses some of this, for as we reach calmer waters, he calls out gently, "Not so hard . . . you don't need to paddle so hard. It's okay."

The day is growing darker and we must soon make camp. We've travelled a long way, and it's been hard and fraught. We soon reach a high, sandy bank on the right where the river is calm, and we glide in, the break plate bumping on a small rock. Wary of my recent experience with an unknown bank, I test the ground with my paddle before jumping out and pulling us farther up.

As we survey the available ground, it becomes evident that the only suitable place for a camp is above us, on a nice flat plateau. It's a steep climb, but a scramble up loose earth and shingle brings us out onto the plateau, about twenty feet above the river. Caribou moss covers the ground among the sparse and stunted spruce. Jean Pierre disappears into the trees along the edge of the bank and I follow, emerging into a perfect little clearing. Old stumps and sticks are lying around. Someone has used this place as a campsite, but not recently. The site could be several years old, and the absence of any kind of trash makes me think this is so.

I return to the canoe and begin to unload, ignoring the rather fresh-looking bear prints in the soft soil by the river. After a short while, Jean Pierre follows me and calls for his axe from the top of the bank. I look around, but it's not in its usual place near his seat in the stern. Jean Pierre slides down the bank in a shower of grit, concern making him heedless of the mini-landslide he is creating. We take everything out of the canoe, but there is no axe.

I know very well what a serious matter this is. We have only one axe, and without it, we will not be able to cut sticks to erect the tent, cut trails through the forest, or even chop firewood. No hunter goes into the county without his gun, his axe, or a teakettle.

Mina confronted this situation as well. After one of the canoes was almost lost, they found that all the axes, pans, pole shods, and other essentials had disappeared with it. *"The loss of the axes,"* she wrote, *"was the most serious result of the accident . . . I feared the men would not go on without the axes."*

They do go on and find the going hard, until they come across a tilt belonging to Duncan McLean, a trapper, where they find an axe and take it, leaving some supplies in a bucket as payment.

We will not likely be so fortunate. There are no trapper's tilts on the land anymore. If we cannot find our axe, we'll have no replacement unless we come across a summer fishing camp on the George River, several hundred miles from here and a long, long way to travel without an essential piece of equipment. Jean Pierre is about as close to frantic as I am ever likely to see him: he's silent and tense, searching our kit with a single-minded thoroughness that we both know is pointless.

"Where did you last use it?" I ask—the obvious maddening question.

He thinks.

"When we made a fire—back there—" Jean Pierre jerks his head. "We must go and get it."

He throws the last of the kit out of the canoe.

"Get in. We need to hurry before it gets dark."

I climb in and Jean Pierre pushes us away from the bank with a single, powerful thrust. We shoot into the current, and it snatches at us, gleefully bearing us downstream at tremendous speed. After the weight of the fully laden canoe and the desperate struggle to haul it upstream, I find that manœuvring this light, flighty craft is like riding an unbroken horse. I can feel the power below my feet and know I have little control over it, but the roller-coaster ride of running the fast water and small rapids that we spent several hours negotiating earlier is exhilarating.

"Watch below!" Jean Pierre calls out to me. "You must watch for rocks just below the surface and steer us away from them. Ahead!"

I look and see some large boulders lying menacingly just below the smooth surface of the river.

"Steer!"

I try to pull us in the opposite direction, but little happens. The rocks come closer.

"*Steer!*"

I whip the paddle over to my left side and draw it away from the side of the canoe, as I have been taught. The canoe obediently moves to the right and we avoid the boulders by a matter of inches. The exhilaration is gone now. I'm on my knees, eyes darting across the varied shadows on the water, looking for the rock that could smash us to pieces and abandon us a long way from our camp. The sun is setting quickly and the light is poor. All around, land, water, rocks, and canoe are just different shades of grey and brown.

I don't remember the section of bank where we stopped for our fire earlier in the afternoon, but Jean Pierre could probably find it in the dark—which is just as well, given the circumstances.

"Here! Pull over."

We pull in and I recognize the red sand. Jumping out of the stern, Jean Pierre splashes through water and strides across the shore, into the trees. I tie the canoe to a rock and wonder if I should follow him, but it would probably be fruitless. If the axe is there, Jean Pierre will find it in a heartbeat.

Silently, Jean Pierre emerges from the forest. He has the axe. I feel the knots in my stomach disentangle. I hadn't realized they were there at all. For a man so relieved, Jean Pierre is not smiling as he gets back in the canoe. But my relief is amplified by the knowledge that this was my fault. I was responsible for picking everything up from our brief stop in the forest that afternoon. It was my job to check that nothing was left behind, and my carelessness almost cost us the trip.

It's a difficult journey back upstream again, even though we can paddle the empty canoe. By the time we reach the bank and our camp, it's twilight and we have yet to sort the equipment and haul it up the bank, put up the tent, and eat something. I'm a little shaky and Jean Pierre is, too. He turns to me, looking at the ground.

"I need a bar of something. I feel weak."

I give him one of the "power bars" and he takes it, eating it as he goes to put up the tent.

There are more bear prints in the soft ground by the canoe, but I don't care tonight. They soon become obliterated in the deep gouges made by my boots as I drag the heavy bags up the slope. It's another quick, dome-shaped tent tonight. My search for decent boughs among the sparse trees takes me deeper into the forest, which is still and silver, eerie in the half-light. I can't even hear the sound of Jean Pierre's axe. The moss has sprung back and my footsteps are gone. Swallowed up. I feel as though I'm in a magical place. A thousand eyes are upon me, yet nothing moves. Red Riding Hood never felt so alone. Do I know my way back? I do, but I let the thought of being lost tingle down my spine momentarily.

A twig snaps and ends my moment of insanity. Turning, I hurry back to the camp.

The following day, I record in my diary that it was "a night without sleep, despite being dog-tired and taking three herbal sleeping pills."

I lie awake, listening to the sound of the breeze in the trees, the distant roar of the river, our constant companion. The sweet smell of the boughs is masked by the choking swirl of mosquito coil, a chemical tang that always catches in my throat. I turn the events of today over in my mind, worrying at them, pondering. Until now on this trip, I've relied on Jean Pierre so naturally for my survival—my life—that I haven't considered my responsibility for his. Of course, as the driving force behind the entire expedition, I've always known that both final decisions and accountability lie with me, but in an everyday sense, I've all but abdicated these responsibilities to my guide. In some ways, this has been a sensible decision. It's not my place to question judgement calls relating to the river when I have so little experience— another lesson from Mina that I've taken to heart. However, my actions out here have as clear an impact on Jean Pierre as they do on me. In forgetting the axe, I not only placed both of us in danger, but also neglected my responsibility for him.

I sigh in frustration and try to roll over as best I can, wriggling to find a comfortable position on my uneven bed. Maybe I woke Jean Pierre or maybe he was also lying awake thinking, because out of the darkness, his voice breaks softly across my thoughts.

"Do you believe in ghosts?"

The man has a talent for grabbing one's attention.

"I suppose I do, somehow. You're not telling me this camp is haunted, are you?"

He laughed a little. I'm coming to realize that Jean Pierre has quite a mischievous sense of humour. He's the perfect straight man, with his usually impassive countenance.

"No, it's not. I'm not trying to frighten you. It is just that, being in the country here, it reminds me of my family."

"Katie and the kids? Mr. T?"

"Them, too, but I meant others—my grandparents, cousins. Every-one who lived out here." I realize that, when talking about ghosts, Jean Pierre also means that the land remains home to those long-dead, the spirits of all the Innu who ever lived here. Maybe Mr. T is one of those spirits.

This is the first time Jean Pierre has been in the country since his last trip with Mr. T nine months ago. I'm constantly aware that our every day here must bring memories to the surface that cause him pain, but I don't have the words to comfort, so in my English way, I say nothing.

"Why do you mention ghosts?"

"You were asking me about Innu spirituality today. Ghosts are a part of it. They can send messages to anyone, not just the shamans."

"Have you seen any?"

"I have."

I remember that hunters are believed to have more spiritual power because of their central role in Innu society, but Jean Pierre doesn't mention this. He never mentions anything that could make him seem self-important.

"What happened?"

"I was on a lake in a canoe—there were two of us. Very suddenly, a fog came down and covered the lake. It was so thick we couldn't see the shore, but the water was very calm and we were not frightened. Then I heard the sound of another canoe being paddled through the water. I was surprised, because we knew no one else was out there with us. I turned and saw a canoe with two people in it go by. They were grey and their outline was indistinct in the mist."

"How did you know they were ghosts?"

"Seeing people on the water like that, people you know are not there, is a premonition of death. Two passengers meant two people were going to die. Within a year, two of my close relatives were dead. It was their spirits I saw on the water that day."

With that thought, we subside back into silence. Sometime toward dawn, I snooze a bit, but my mind will not let go and allow me the blissful relief of full unconsciousness. This morning, I awake with puffy eyes and heavy limbs. Sometimes I can't feel Mina here at all and the George River post at Ungava seems a very long way away.

# CHAPTER 8

Jean Pierre's increasingly apparent concern for my welfare bears echoes of George Elson's concern for Mina. In a thousand little ways, George did his best to ensure that the expedition was as easy for her as possible. Simple acts, like standing to flap a bag and keep flies away from her while she ate, spoke of thoughtfulness beyond his duty to return her in one piece, alive and well. It is this similarity between the actions of our guides that makes me think there is little in the suggestion that Mina and George were having a love affair.

There has been a great deal of speculation in recent years as to the true nature of Mina and George's relationship. The origins of this lie mainly in cryptic comments in their respective diaries and not least the famous "missing diary"—a second, possibly more personal, record of the trip kept by George and now seemingly lost forever.

There are hints aplenty in Mina's diary, such as passing references to watching the sunset together and long talks into the night in her tent, which have raised many an eyebrow. Perhaps more telling is the absence of descriptions of such events in her book. Was there in fact something to hide or was Mina simply trying to avoid the inevitable criticism of her conduct that such references would engender? Any suggestion of scandal would, of course, have detracted from her main mission, which was to complete her husband's work and clear his name. One incident that goes unrecorded in the book occurs when the group comes across a caribou herd on the upper reaches of the George River—past the height of land, as they begin their descent to Ungava. Mina is very excited, as they have tracked the herd for some distance, trying to get the best photos. In her eagerness to reach the deer, Mina writes that she *"gave Geo my Kodak and taking his hand we started down the hill at top speed . . . Geo had the open Kodak in one hand and had hold of my hand with the other."* Holding hands might suggest a degree of intimacy, but did the two really go beyond friendship?

At the conclusion of the expedition, during their enforced wait at the Hudson's Bay Company post, Mina writes several times of her concern for George's future, and she does hint rather intriguingly that there is something to hide: *"Better ask him to sign an agreement not to write about the trip without my written consent and approval. There would be no questioning the thing then."*

Very often, however, there follow immediately after such "hints" a few lines about her dear "Laddie." Her memories of Leonidas seem to walk with her at every step of her expedition. Several occasions see her turn from a moment of jubilation to sadness, his absence a reminder of the cause of her success. Two years after her husband's death, Mina is still in mourning, although this itself may have triggered some sort of emotional connection to George.

However, it is the ghost of her husband that seems to form the deepest bond between Mina and George. He was Leonidas' most trusted guide and the person responsible for returning her husband's body. After coming back to North West River with Hubbard's body, a task he undertook with three local men, Duncan McLean, Douglas Blake and Tom Blake, George then took Hubbard's remains by sled to the ferry at Fox Harbour, on the east coast. Monsieur Duclos, of fur traders Revillion Frères, provided his teamster, but the teamster had only four dogs to work with: *"A mixed team, some water dogs, some Esquimaux dogs. The water dogs do not stand the hard work near so well as the huskies and get played sooner."* George carried Leonidas' body and baggage. Dillon, however, had *"six good dogs and no load."*

It is clear from George Elson's diary that he, too, felt some of Mina's resentment against Dillon. Also clear is his respect for Leonidas. These two things combined could have produced a strong bond between Mina and her guide, almost on meeting. She was already deeply connected with him in ways she was linked with no other: he represented a vicarious part of Leonidas' last days and she owed him a debt of gratitude as the man who returned her husband's body to her at great personal risk.

Mina often records in her diary the depth of her respect for all her guides, praise that does not appear to single George out particularly. Indeed, she has a great deal to say about her admiration for Job as well: "[He] *knows just what the water is doing and knows just what he can make it do for him. He is wonderful.*"

In this context, it seems to be little more than a romantic idea to suggest that Mina and George were having an affair. It merely serves to heighten further the interest of an already fascinating tale to add the dimension of an illicit love affair in the wilderness, hidden from the disapproving eyes of society. While Mina almost certainly had a profound feeling of friendship, respect, and admiration for George, it seems difficult to believe that a recently widowed woman on a difficult and dangerous expedition accompanied by three other men would take the further risks associated with a love affair.

It is, of course, human nature to speculate on such things, and I have been asked on more than one occasion about the nature of my relationship with Jean Pierre. It causes us much amusement one day on the trail, when there is little else to laugh about. Jean Pierre explains the reaction to his decision to join the expedition: "When I told men I know about this trip, they winked at me and suggested I would have a very good time with you."

I am partly surprised, partly amused, maybe even a little shocked. I'd received similar suggestions, albeit phrased more delicately.

"I had a similar reaction. Did Katie not mind your travelling alone with a young woman for several weeks?"

Jean Pierre laughed.

"No. But your boyfriend must be very trusting."

I am taken aback, thinking about the frantic days of preparation prior to this trip. Jean Pierre is right, of course.

"I can honestly say I never gave it a moment's thought. Maybe it was naïve of me, but it never crossed my mind. Besides, I could tell what kind of man you were the moment we met."

It seems bizarre to me, thinking that I may have taken risks with a man upon whom my survival depends. The two facts do not seem to correspond in any way. But I am no longer amused. I can see that people were right to question—not because Jean Pierre and I would become lovers, but because I had taken a risk. There was no guarantee that my guide in the country would be the honourable man that Jean Pierre has turned out to be.

My relationship with Jean Pierre, like Mina's with her guide, is based on respect. In that way, for her time, Mina was a very unusual woman. That was and has always been her charm. The attitude of other white explorers and of white society in general during this period was disdainful, in many ways, of the Native people who lived in Labrador. New European arrivals would claim they were "the first person to see the Labrador interior" and the like.

Erland Erlandson, the Hudson's Bay Company employee who missed seeing Churchill Falls in 1834, spoke about his Native guides as though they were little better than animals: "*One was really snow-blind, a difficulty which I overcame by directing another to lead him by a string. Another and another then pretended to be ill, but I soon saw through their artifice.*" Such descriptions fall into the category of representing Native people as sly, untrustworthy, and unreliable. It is the antithesis of the romantic ideal of the "noble savage"—an innocent, free from original sin—which sprang from the writings of eighteenth-century philosophers, such as Rousseau.

Mina's treatment of her guides as equals, as people with names and personalities, not merely as functions of the expedition, is rare among the adventuring classes. Her husband, too, shared her attitude, as is apparent from an entry in George's diary, saying that Leonidas had "*gone by my* [George's] *plans a good deal, though he was head of the party.*" However, on the first Hubbard expedition, in many ways, George *was* still regarded as little more than a hired hand. Indeed, after George had retrieved Leonidas' body from the bush, Dillon asked him repeatedly to return for the canoe. George defied Dillon, calling this "*a piece of nonsense*" that he resisted, as "*I thought it was hardly fair to try and force me to go any way, because I knew I wasn't under either of them* [Wallace and McKenzie]. *I was hired by Mr. Hubbard on the trip and we had to do all the planning. It was Mr. Hubbard's trip and we had to obey him and try to help him all we could whilst we were together.*"

Although all were men, there were clear dividing lines based on race and class. George obeyed Leonidas because of his position as employer. In commanding George to undertake certain (dangerous) tasks, Dillon evidently saw himself as the natural inheritor of leadership from Leonidas, and he thought he had every right to direct his employee. George, however, never did return for the canoe and no doubt surprised Dillon when he chose later to support the ambitions of a "mere woman."

The perception of many white people at this time that Native people were in some way inferior contrasts with Mina's apparent sense of ease and the equilibrium evident on her expedition. Mina was the leader and employer, but her lack of formality and the pleasure she derived from the company of her guides distinguished her from many white explorers at the time. This may go some way to explaining why her actions could be interpreted as standing for affection, when in reality they were unusual only because of a lack of an imposed hierarchical order and the presence of genuine friendship.

Since we passed the Innu people in the boat on Grand Lake, Jean Pierre and I haven't seen another soul except each other. Leaving the bear-mauled cabin behind marked our passing into real wilderness, and now we are truly alone. Each day, I stumble along the unending line of riverside boulders, conducting rambling conversations in my head or inventing a hundred different fantasies or plans for the future to distract myself from the bear and wolf prints, visibly damp and fresh in the sandy bank despite the heat. These boulders are the skeleton of the Naskaupi. Its watery flesh has withered and died, leaving these bony fingers to wrap a grey skein across the landscape. No one has mourned its passing, as those who used it to roam are now all but ghosts themselves. There is just us, alone out here and wandering through a brilliantly unreal photograph from a different age.

As we struggle on, pinned between churning waters and thick forest, my mind drifts back to an evening a few days before the trip started. Joe and I were sharing a bottle of partridgeberry liqueur, for which I am developing quite a taste. Maybe it was the effect of three glasses of the warm red syrup or maybe he wanted to take my mind off what lay ahead by giving me something even worse to worry about. In any case, he decided to tell me all about the Labrador Big Foot, a "yeti"—part human, part animal.

"Well, now, there are lots of local stories—of course, I've never seen it myself, but my Uncle Tom did, a few years back."

"Really?" My attention was caught; the glass of liqueur stopped halfway to my mouth. "Big Foot? Come on."

"You don't believe me? That's what *I* said. At first. But like Uncle Tom said, you just don't know what's out there." He jerked his head toward the back of the house, where the long garden was bordered by a creek, which was all that separated us from the hills running away north for hundreds of miles.

"He was out hunting one year, away for a few days with his pal Bill. They'd travelled farther than Uncle Tom had been before, and it started to snow a little. But they were two old timers who knew their way around the country well enough, so they set up camp anyway and Uncle Tom went to fetch some wood for the fire."

Here Joe leaned forward and took a long drink from his glass before setting it down carefully and giving me a long, serious stare.

"When he got back, Bill had gone, but there were some pretty scary prints all round their camp. Huge things, the size of a shovel. Human shaped, but . . . 'Round about then, anyway, Bill turns up and wants to know what the hell Tom thinks he's doing."

"What did he mean?"

"It seems that as soon as Tom got out of sight, Bill heard a cry and thinking Tom was in some kind of trouble, he went after him."

"What about the prints?"

"Well, they couldn't work those out, but thought nothing of it. Until they went into the tent, that is."

"What was in the tent?"

"Long hair. Long, dark, coarse hair."

There was a pause while I digested this.

"And you are telling me Yeti have long, dark hair, right?"

"You don't believe me?"

"Er, *no*. Has anyone actually seen this thing?" I mocked, reaching again for the half-empty bottle.

Joe took off his glasses and rubbed his eyes.

"Well, I don't want to scare you."

"I'd like to see you try."

"Okay. Back . . . way, way back, before Happy Valley existed, over toward Mud Lake, the settlement on the banks of the Churchill River, there was a family living out in a cabin away from the town. Not too far, but the forest made it seem remote, I guess. Anyway, the father was away trapping with their son, leaving his wife and their young daughter at home, as most families did back then. Well, the girl was alone, hanging out the washing on a line in the field maybe thirty yards from the house, when she heard her mother calling her frantically. She dropped the washing, and thinking it was maybe a bear or something, ran for the house, but something came out of the trees behind her, fast."

"What was it?"

The washing machine in the cellar switched itself off noisily and I jumped, but Joe continued.

"She didn't know, she just screamed and ran, but the mother saw it and she pulled the shotgun off its hook above the porch door and shot the thing chasing her daughter."

"Did she kill it?"

"There was a terrible scream and the girl reached the porch just in time to see something that looked like a bear walking upright, disappearing into the trees. They found blood on the ground, but nothing else."

Maybe that fourth glass was one too many. For both of us.

At night, Yeti notwithstanding, Jean Pierre and I camp as best we can between the trees on rocky ground. I often have the sensation that I am being watched, but cannot separate out the onset of something like paranoia due to the moving parameters of my consciousness from my newly heightened senses. Am I going mad or are my instincts simply more attuned to my environment?

One night, we set up the tent at an intersection of small paths that run between the trees. It takes a moment for the significance of this to sink into my mind.

"Are these bear paths?" I ask Jean Pierre.

He nods.

"Aren't you worried?" I eye the trees around me, expecting to see an aggrieved bear on its way home for the night.

"I would be if I didn't have a gun," he replies and strides off calmly.

This is the night the tent goes on fire for the first time. We have the stove burning inside the tent, despite the heat. It means we can boil water for tea and cook away from the continuous onslaught of flies. The sweat pours off us, but at least we aren't being bitten, and it's so hot inside the tent that we don't need the mosquito coils. That kind of assurance lifts a huge weight from one's shoulders. It's a relief, no matter how temporary, of the kind that keeps one buoyed up until the next small victory in the country. It's astonishing how life here makes preoccupations shrink while perceptions simultaneously open out like a wide-screen cinema.

I unzip the front flap of the tent in order to fetch more water, throwing the empty pot out ahead of me and following it on my knees into the mess of wood chippings and churned-up moss. Zipping up my bug jacket, I detect an unusual note to the pleasant tang of wood smoke in the air. Then, turning, I see that a canvas flap has been caught by its tape and is resting against the hot flue of the stove. The temperature of this is extremely high, and a small flare of red heat and sparks hovers constantly at its mouth, like the burn of exhaust from a jet engine. The canvas has caught fire, and dry now in the constantly good weather, it's burning at a speed that seems unstoppable. I freeze, managing only to call out Jean Pierre's name. The note of panic must be apparent, as he appears, takes one look in the direction of my rigid stare, and reaching inside the tent, douses the flames with the contents of the teakettle.

The main wall of the tent is fortunately intact, but an additional flap is burned to nothing. We look at each other, but there's nothing to say.

By now, the landscape has begun to change a little. Gone is the claustrophobic, steamy forest of the lower Naskaupi, with its impenetrable tangles, lazy brown water, and afternoons hanging motionless in the heat. Gone, too, are the twisting, roaring fury of rapids and the steep sides of the river valley. Now, although we are gaining height, the river is wide again, but shallow. Impromptu islands of scrub grass and purple flowers dot the river. Flat islets of shingle occasionally break the surface of the water, forcing us to zigzag a path through, wading gullies and jumping streams. The banks are high, but behind them lies flat land that would be almost pasturelike, were it not so rough and covered with the inevitable stunted spruce. Often, the water flows only at the very centre of the riverbed, but it is always fast, shallow, and unpredictable.

Through this water Jean Pierre walks, the canoe close at heel like an obedient terrier, his red baseball cap a vivid and constant point of reference for me in my own personal journey up the river. Sometimes it seems we are each locked in our own capsule of strain and triumph, heading in sympathetic parallel along our separate journeys' routes. Maybe if I reach out, I can touch him. Yet try as I might, our lives seem only to lightly brush, and he slips away from me, borne on a tide of white water into an entirely different world.

Mina thought this area beautiful and so it is. On the not-so-distant horizon, mountains reach their bare heads to the sky, burning brown and black on their crowns. Below, in perfect geological waves of colour, are marked the limits of the riverbanks, dense forest, sandy ridges, and sparse wood. Despite their constant companionship, these mountains never reach down to us, allowing the river space to wave its erratic course down the valley.

This miniature archipelago of sandy islands and shallow water has meant that we are now on the opposite bank of the river. Not since the day we passed Red Wine River have we travelled on the western side of the Naskaupi. The bank, however, has suddenly reared up to forty feet or more, steep and forested, falling straight into the river. It evidently shelves deeply below the waterline also, as the river here is deep and fast.

There are few boulders for me to negotiate. A thin, sloping horizontal line of small rocks marks the boundary between trees and water, but this line is often smudged by deadfall. At each of these broken bodies, Jean Pierre must cut us a path through with his axe, the flesh of the wounded spruce left bright against its dead, grey skin.

Many times, the fallen trees lie half in the water and I hold the canoe against the current, feeling the pull of the river strengthen with every passing moment until the trunk is hacked away, tumbling past in a tangle of spines, half-softened by submergence. Sometimes I cannot climb past the tree without following Jean Pierre into the water, but he won't allow me to take such risks and I must instead face alone the battle much farther up the slope, through the lower branches or a jungle of churned-up roots rising several feet above my head. I feel like Alice in Wonderland, so tiny am I, fighting through the whiplash boughs and sharp twigs that grab and tear at every inch of me. Climbing through this and over the trunk itself demands a high level of gymnastic ability from my stiff and tired limbs. Half falling, I push through, caring nothing about my ripped trousers and bleeding hands, before sliding down to the water once again in a shower of tiny stones and dislodged earth.

Today, we continue on like this for three hours or more, the river offering us no quarter, no place to cross, the banks no less steep. Again, we find a fallen tree in our path. This one, however, is different. It must have been one of the tallest trees on the slope. As it fell, it ripped up most of the bank, leaving huge, gaping scars in the earth. In its fall, the tree brought down several other trees of similar height around it, resulting in an impenetrable mesh of dead branches and dry brown needles. Jean Pierre and I look at it together. Without speaking, we both know there is no way—no way at all—I could possibly find a path through it.

As one, we turn to where the top of the tree lies half drowned in the water. The river is fast here, smooth and black. I know this innocence is deceptive and that the water is also deep and strong. Jean Pierre hands me the canoe rope and I tie it to an upright tree, mindful of the accumulating power of the river. Using my hands, I kick and snap away the smaller dead boughs while Jean Pierre gets to work with his axe, hacking into the core of several of the smaller trees brought down by our fifty-foot monster.

We cut a path several feet long this way, arriving eventually at the last trunk. We cannot even get close, however, as there is no bank to stand on. Jean Pierre wades into the river, the splashes glinting a pale yellow in the sunlight. The angle is wrong, the tree huge. All he can do is shear away the mess of smaller branches and twigs, leaving the main trunk inches above the water. I do not see how we can get past this. The tree extends almost fifteen feet out into the river, which is too fast to try to cross, and the bank is too steep and cut up to climb. And then there's the canoe.

Wordlessly, Jean Pierre walks back with difficulty and unties her, pulling her along the bank. Wading deeper into the river, he pushes the canoe toward the tree trunk. The bow bumps, then dips a little and passes under. Jean Pierre nods with satisfaction and pulls her back. Turning to me, he jerks his head minutely at the canoe.

"Get in."

"What?"

"Get in. Down, below the gunwales, and I'll push you through. There's no other way."

He sees my hesitation and adds a little more reassuringly, "I'll be holding the canoe. You'll be okay."

Knowing I can't wade into water to above my waist without being swept away, I climb awkwardly into the canoe and crouch in the bow, where my feet normally rest. I can see nothing but cedar wood, smell its essence that is still fresh, and sense the motion of the river below me, amplified now as it rushes past, inches from my face.

Half in the river, Jean Pierre leans out and pushes the canoe under the trunk. I curl into an even tighter ball, hearing the creak of wood on wood directly above my head. Then I hear him call and I sit up a little. The trunk is resting across the centre of the canoe, so I grab hold of it to steady the craft while Jean Pierre starts to scramble over the trunk from the river. I see him stagger a little as his footing slips on the underwater bank, then I breathe again as he catches hold and hauls himself over the trunk, immediately reaching for the canoe as he splashes back into the river. A few moments later and we are free of the deadfall, the riverbank once again becoming less steep and passable.

There is no doubt that the country is ever more rugged at every mile. And at every break for lunch or tea, we now pore over our maps, as though by committing every twist and turn, every marked rapid and boulder to memory, we can somehow beat the country. We think we must be very near Seal Islands—maybe even past them. The proliferation of shingled islets that have appeared since the Churchill Falls dam was built has reduced the volume of the river, and we are finding it very difficult to identify our location from the map alone. I take a reading on the GPS, but the numbers don't seem to fit. Only the longitude reading makes any sense, and that would put us a good six miles behind where we thought we were.

Disheartened, we turn back to the previous page of the map to stare at ground we think we've already covered. And as ever, the pull of the trail lures us on to turn through the pages ahead: rapids, falls, and lakes sliding by easily in the mid-day sun. The well-thumbed corners tell of an optimism yet to be dimmed by the conditions.

"There . . . it will be bad. And there, there." Jean Pierre points to a narrow, twisting section of river, where the contour lines cluster close to the banks, pushing shoulder to shoulder like a crowd on the move.

"That will be hard. I don't know where we shall camp. No flat ground." Jean Pierre looks concerned, as he always does when he sees the maps. It is the George River, past the height of land, that really worries him, however.

"The flies will be bad and the rapids big."

"I know. Let's just get up the Naskaupi before we start to worry about the George. We need to reach Seal Islands soon if we are not to fall behind Mina."

The trials of the past weeks have focused my mind on more immediate things than reaching Ungava. As each day passes, that goal seems ever more remote and the struggle of the next few miles takes on overwhelming precedence. I've always believed that one can achieve seemingly impossible tasks by breaking them down into smaller, more manageable aims. So for now, my thoughts are concerned with reaching Seal Lake, and beyond that, our cache on the shores of Smallwood Reservoir. To reach that point alone is a major expedition in itself, and unlike running the George River, getting there would be an important "first" since 1905.

Secretly, I treasure the idea that we could "come out" at Smallwood, thereby retaining some sense of achievement. At times of stress, that escape is a comforting thought, yet I know myself too well to pretend that it is anything other than a device to keep me going. Once—*if*—we reach Smallwood in one piece, nothing will prevent me from continuing.

As ever when the route ahead is discussed, the map of Mina's journey is pulled out for comparisons. As far as we can tell, our progress is no more than a day or so behind hers through this section. Although our route is slow and very difficult, Mina travelled along Innu portages that often took her some way inland, away from the river. Even with four men, she had a hard struggle to portage all her supplies across the rough country. It feels as though Jean Pierre and I are travelling very slowly—which we are—so I'm surprised to find that we are not as far behind Mina as I had anticipated. It is, in fact, a matter of some pride for both Jean Pierre and me. Our attempt is much more difficult, and we have a lower margin of error than Mina had. With only one guide and one canoe, the burden of physical endurance lies more heavily upon us as individuals. There is no one else to take up any slack.

For me, this endurance test continues later in the day when we come to a broad section of river interspersed with the usual flat islands of small rocks and shingle. We weave a path through, returning once more to the bank on the right. This time, the river is not shallow, but runs deeply between the islands. Here, a curving indent in the bank has created a ⊃-shaped channel, the river running between the bank and an island. On the other side of this island, the river is very fast and rapid, but the channel seems as though it may be suitable for some paddling. Looking up at the bank along the length of this indent, we see that we have little choice, as it rises to a steep, sandy point about halfway along, above water that is far too deep to consider lining through. I can see Jean Pierre weighing our options. He turns to me and says, "We may be able to paddle through this, but the current is stronger than it looks."

I eye the surface, which is deceptively smooth.

"Try to stay close to the bank and don't allow the bow to be caught by the current."

"Okay."

The detailed instructions are uncharacteristic of Jean Pierre, and I realize that something more than a short break in our tedious routine of portaging and lining may be in store. I sense some mild concern, which, in turn, generates some real concern in me. Not because of the (admittedly) slightly higher risk involved, but because I know only too well the limits of my physical strength.

Launching the canoe back into the river feels effortless and natural, yet soon I feel the power of the current pushing against us. Jean Pierre steers us close into the bank on the right and we make some hard-won headway upstream. After several hundred yards, however, the top of the ⊃ shape means there is a small promontory ahead. The current swirling around from this point of land catches us full force, sucking us back as though on elastic. Fighting hard, we manage not to swing sideways, but in doing so, we move far over to the left, out of the centre of the current and into calmer waters—but onto the wrong side of the channel. We grate to a welcome halt on the island.

Getting out, we take a walk around to see which is the best possible way of getting off our temporary refuge. Is the left bank of the river closer? Is it easier to reach? Trudging through a confusion of pink flowers and pebbles, we see that the river on that side of the island is rapid and impossible to navigate. I trail slowly back toward the canoe behind Jean Pierre.

"We must cross the channel again."

I nod. Jean Pierre continues.

"We will put the canoe in here." He indicates the tip of the island closest to the promontory with a flick of his hand. "And the current will take us downstream, but we should have enough time to cross back to the right bank. You understand?"

I nod again, silently, wondering what we will do when we're back where we started.

"Are you frightened?" He seems more curious than sympathetic.

"I'm a little concerned."

"It's nothing. Just be alert."

Alert. Concentrate. These are two of his favourite words. Since our first day on the rapids above Red Wine River, Jean Pierre has constantly reminded me to pay attention. This is not because my mind is elsewhere—although it may seem so to him—but because a great deal of what we do and have done so far on this trip is part of a steep learning curve for me.

Again, we push out into the water, Jean Pierre guiding us on a diagonal course across the channel toward the right bank. The current takes us, and we are quickly across and reach the bank where the sandy point flattens out a little, giving us a place to put ashore. We are travelling fast, however—too fast for the "brakes" we put on as the bow reaches the bank. We are swept past our landing point, again bumping against the land as Jean Pierre resolutely keeps us out of the current.

I jump out, taking the rope to tie us up to a rock, but the loss of my weight means the canoe is tugged farther downstream, along the bank. Digging in my heels, I'm caught off balance, with nothing to hold onto. Jean Pierre, at the stern, is seventeen feet away in the middle of the river with only a paddle to keep the fully laden canoe from being dragged back downstream into the river. I haul on the rope with my full body weight, leaning almost horizontally above the shingle. The canoe, side onto the river, drags downstream several more feet, the bow carving a deep groove in the shingle.

Somehow, I realize, my left leg is straightened out and lying to the side of the canoe. Another strong pull from the current and the top of the canoe will go right over it. I cannot pull it back without loosening my grip on the rope, forcing me either to let go and see Jean Pierre washed away or to be dragged in after her. At that moment, Jean Pierre, sizing up the situation, manages somehow to bring the stern of the canoe alongside the bank and quickly jumps out, pulling her after him. I collapse onto the ground, half-crouched, my leg still outstretched as he ties her up to a tree six feet back from the water.

"You okay?"

"Yep."

Jean Pierre takes the teakettle out of the canoe and scoops it through the water. Then, putting it to his lips, he takes a sustained draft. He then looks at me and nods thoughtfully.

"We line from here."

I look back. For all that effort and drama, we've covered only a few hundred yards, at best. Yet we had no choice but to paddle, and I think about the countless times ahead when we may also have only one choice but may not be so lucky.

# CHAPTER 9

The hot sun and the physical demands of the trip are taking their toll on me. My weight has dropped and I am constantly hungry, yet also entirely lacking in energy. At the end of today's efforts, I sit right down on the ground where I step out of the canoe. The sun is blinding and I am desperate to escape it, but the only alternative is the dark, fly-infested forest behind me. Besides, I cannot move. I need to go and find us a good camping place, but as I rise, the blue and green of the landscape swirl and merge into one and I am forced to sink back down to the cool, damp earth while the dizziness passes.

Peering from underneath the blessèd protection of my broad-brimmed hat, I see Jean Pierre pause for a moment as he unloads the canoe. He's picking something off the ground. He then pulls a small, glittering thing hanging on a cord from around his neck and holds it next to the object he's picked up.

"What are you doing?" I struggle to my feet, holding onto a rock until I'm confident I won't fall over.

"Looking for evidence."

"Of what?"

Jean Pierre throws away the object and slips his tiny magnifying glass back under his T-shirt.

"Archæological evidence of the occupation of Labrador by the Innu."

It's impossible that humankind could have existed in Labrador before the end of the Ice Age, so the first people must have entered the peninsula sometime between thirteen thousand and three thousand years ago. There seems to be a general consensus among academics that these people came across the Bering Strait from what is now Russia and Asia, though many Natives all over the continent disagree. Whatever their origin, the first inhabitants of Labrador are known as "Maritime Archaic" Indians, though there is some doubt as to whether these people were the direct ancestors of the present-day Innu.

Very little archæological research has been carried out in the interior of Labrador, as its rugged landscapes have sealed it off from the rest of the world and preserved its secrets for millennia. Indeed, only within the last thirty years or so has there been any real research into the origins of the Innu and Inuit in the region. Much of this has been geological in orientation, with different kinds of stone and other matter being used to identify which ethnic groups used particular sites. The distance that stone was removed from its origins can also indicate population movement, trading routes, and group interaction.

On the basis of such evidence, it has been suggested that the Innu once lived on the coast of Labrador, fishing and hunting seals. The move to life in the interior would have meant a much more precarious dependence on fluctuating numbers of caribou and other game. In order for this to happen, something fairly cataclysmic must have occurred. The Innu themselves have an explanation for this, told in several tales about battles with another tribe, some of which Jean Pierre has already recounted on this trip.

Randle Holme, the late-nineteenth-century explorer who tried to reach Churchill Falls, also concluded that a great battle had taken place: *"Twelve miles west of Rigolet lies Eskimo Island, the scene of a traditionary battle between Indians and Eskimos* [i.e., Innu and Inuit], *the two races having always been and still being, hereditary foes."* He goes on to explain that this animosity resulted from an Innu belief that a sign had been given by the Great Spirit distinguishing the territories of the two races. All that was forest belonged to the Innu, and all that was barren, to the Inuit. Holme also records finding evidence of the battle in the form of seventy Eskimo graves on the island, although modern archaeologists doubt the graves are a result of such warfare.

Jean Pierre prefers to explain the matter in more conventional scientific terms of population pressures on the land in prehistoric times. His theory is supported by some archæological evidence, and it is certainly easier to swallow, if a little less romantic. However, my appetite for the more colourful versions of stories about the interaction between Inuit and Innu is more than satisfied by other tales Jean Pierre tells me each night in our tiny, glowing tent, lost in the dark vastness of a Labrador night. Warring shamans, brave warriors, and a story strikingly similar to *Romeo and Juliet* enacted on the barren wastes of a prehistoric land not only reflect eternal human themes, but also concur with the idea that the event that pushed the Innu into the interior was violent confrontation with the Inuit.

The antipathy between these ethnic groups is evident even today, the two communities living separately in Labrador, with little apparent connection between them. Indeed, as I discover, Jean Pierre is rather nervous about reaching our final destination, the largely Inuit town of Kangiqsualujjuaq on Ungava Bay.

"Don't tell anyone I'm Innu when we get there," he urges me.

"Will it not be obvious to them?" I ask, genuinely curious, but he says nothing more.

Mina's guides seemed similarly nervous of meeting the Mushuau Innu bands on the George River. Despite having some kind of common language (they all belonged to the wider Algonquian group), her men had a marked fear of the unknown Innu tribes they were sure to meet. As Mina noted, "*Geo said 'Oh they won't shoot you. It will be us they will kill if they take the notion.' Gil said 'No they won't hurt a woman I don't think. They want a woman for themselves.' That is a phase of the question I had not taken into consideration.*"

Knowing the Innu to be a particularly gentle people by nature, reading this makes me feel uncomfortable. I cannot tell from Mina's writing whether the nervousness expressed by her men was a result of traditional rivalries between the different Native groups or an indication of the extent to which all of her guides had become assimilated into the white European culture and had come therefore to see Indians living in a traditional manner as little more than "savages."

Innu myths and legends tell of the Innu always having been here in Labrador, and in 1998, some evidence was unearthed which seems to support the belief that they have indeed lived on the land for much longer than the mere 2,500 years some experts suggest. A study of terrain included under the proposed Churchill River Power Project, a second phase of the dam already built, revealed evidence of Innu habitation dating back four thousand years and at Nain, further north up the Labrador coast, there is evidence dating back seven thousand years. Among the findings of the Power Project were twenty pre-European-contact sites, some near Mud Lake on the Churchill River.

The Innu carried out much of the fieldwork on this project themselves, as part of a program that sought to blend Western scientific discipline with the traditional observations, myths, memory, and knowledge of the Innu. The combining of these two seemingly disparate approaches has already been productive in studies of Aboriginal culture in Australia. "Dreamtime" tales, which often run into hundreds of verses, tell of creatures that, according to archæological studies, actually did roam the continent tens of thousands of years ago, when a land bridge to other land masses still existed.

One man who has done much to explore the history of Labrador and who believes the Innu did, at some point in history, move from the coast to the interior is Stephen Loring of the Smithsonian Institution in Washington, D.C. It was through a connection with Loring that Jean Pierre became involved in archæological work in Labrador, and he is very keen that we "keep our eyes open" on this trip, particularly as we will be travelling through areas that are not frequently seen by humans.

This task, however, like much of the work done by researchers in the area, is hampered by both the conditions and the fact that many old Innu camps left only perishable evidence, such as wood and animal remains. Camps were also often on low beaches, which were easily overrun by water or bush. I look around me. The forest of alders that has grown up since the dam lowered the water levels has obscured everything in its path. If there was anything to find here, it is almost certainly now lost for eternity.

Roughly two weeks' travel to the northwest of us lies Lake Michikamau, a place of extreme significance in the oral history of the Innu. Now, of course, it is part of the great water mass that makes up the Smallwood Reservoir, but Jean Pierre is eager to see the area, hoping that the boulders he told me of previously—the remains of the woman possessed by animal spirits—still lie above the waters.

Flooding has, in fact, great significance for the Innu. They believe that they once inhabited *Mishtapeuat*, a world similar to that of Labrador, with mountains and lakes. It was part of the spirit realm, and the Innu lived there with the spirits until it was flooded. Then the people were forced to flee to this world, which is connected to the spirit world by a bridge. The tale bears a striking similarity to stories prevalent in European religions and historical legends: consider Noah's Ark, the Irish Tir-na-n'Og, or the ancient British tale of Lyonesse, the mystical city once connected to the Cornish mainland. It is said to have sunk beneath the waves of a great flood, leaving only the hilltops visible—and these now form the Isles of Scilly, twenty-five miles west of Land's End.

Work started on the Churchill Falls dam in the late 1960s, only a short time after the majority of Innu had settled in Sheshatshiu, Davis Inlet, and Quebec. Many, however, like Jean Pierre's family, still lived on the land, and other families spent several months of the year hunting in the country. Despite this, when the additional land for the reservoir was flooded around Lake Michikamau, there was little, if any, consultation between the government, Labrador and Newfoundland Hydro, and the Innu. Many Innu did not speak English and claim they did not know the flooding was to going to happen, "luckily" losing only belongings to the waters and not their lives.

Not only were hunting territories and equipment lost when Michikamau was flooded, but many graves and other archæologically rich sites also disappeared—a blasphemy in the eyes of the Innu. A single survey of the area before the dam was built revealed several important sites, including some camps with bones over a thousand years old. With the rising of the waters, evidence of the Innu occupation of Nitassinan was lost forever—a record that would have been vital in their battle today as they lay claim to parts of Labrador as their ancestral homeland.

"Alex! *Alex!*"

There is an entirely new note of panic in Jean Pierre's voice as it floats through the thick undergrowth between me and the beach. Mystified, I drop my armful of boughs for the tent floor and scramble through the willows, across some rocks, and finally onto the bank again. Twilight is upon us, the heat of the day draining away moment by moment. Mosquitoes are swarming in their trillions as the sun becomes nothing but a hazy red line beyond the head of the valley, away to my right. Jean Pierre, however, is fairly easy to spot. Standing in shallows about two feet from dry ground, he seems unable to move.

"What's up?" I look around, but cannot begin to imagine what is making Jean Pierre need my help so desperately.

"Toad."

"What?" I hadn't caught the word, half-whispered, half-swallowed, through fear or pride, I can't tell.

"TOAD!"

"Ah." I look down, but I can't see anything in the dying light. All the stones at my feet are shades of brown and grey, the pools of water tiny mirrors for the darkening sky. I don't see the toad until it moves, a half-hearted hop away from my threatening boots.

"Aw, it's just a baby . . ." I try not to smile for Jean Pierre's sake, but I fail. "Don't worry, I'll just move him."

I've never actually picked up a frog or toad before, and if the truth were told, it's not something I would ordinarily volunteer to do. This small favour, however, is probably the only time on this trip that Jean Pierre will rely on me entirely. So, buoyed up by the courage it often seems so easy to find in the company of someone more afraid than you are, I reach down and pick up the toad.

It is very small and, surprisingly, not slimy. I had expected it to feel like a fish, but it was just cold, light, and a little leathery. I walk a good dozen yards downstream and put the little creature under some bushes next to the water. When I get back, Jean Pierre is already more relaxed. His teeth flash out of the gloom in a half-embarrassed smile.

"Thanks."

"Hey, no problem. I said I'd move them for you, didn't I?" I smile back and for a moment enjoy closeness between us born of the scales, albeit temporarily, being levelled. I try to build on our new comrade-ship by turning the subject around to something that is long overdue.

"You said you would teach me how to make bread. Tonight?"

Jean Pierre nods.

"Yes. Okay."

Trappers in Labrador traditionally make unleavened bread on wood-burning stoves and call it "flummery." I ask Jean Pierre the Innu name for it.

"*Pakueshikan*. The 'P' is pronounced like a 'B.' But," he adds, "my grandparents, they would eat hardly anything but meat—not even salt."

"But they had flour—for bread?"

"Sometimes."

I make a couple of ham-fisted attempts at pronouncing the Innu word, then give up and settle down to watch the unusual scene of a great hunter doing some baking.

Jean Pierre opens up one of our bags of flour and scoops some out into our blue plastic bowl with his hand.

"You don't measure it?"

"No." Jean Pierre manages not to look at me as if I've lost my mind. He then throws in a good handful of baking powder and mixes it in. Taking a kettle of cold water, he pours it in slowly, mixing it to the right consistency. He looks at the dough with approval and starts to knead it—first with one hand, then with both.

Our stove is made of tin, blackened now from much use. It's about a foot and a half long, a rectangle with a flue, held together with wire that has seen much better days. Jean Pierre takes a piece of wood that has been chopped so it has a hard, fresh edge and scrapes it across the uneven surface of the rusty stove.

Now, anyone who knows me will tell you that I can be a pain in the kitchen. I compensate for my lack of natural culinary ability with an obsessive degree of cleanliness. Despite my weariness with camp life in general and my role of camp cook in particular, it therefore takes all my will power to refrain from shouting, "You can't put the dough on there! It's filthy!"

A shower of nameless black bits are flung onto the ground, and the virgin dough is slapped down, hissing as it touches the hot surface. A second rounded loaf follows and Jean Pierre sits back, satisfied.

"So who taught you to make bread?" I ask. "Isn't that a woman's job?"

"Normally, yes, but all hunters need to know how to feed themselves in the country. My grandmother taught me."

The undeniable aroma of baking bread begins to fill the tent, mingling with the smell of freshly picked boughs. Jean Pierre sits up, and wiping a fork quickly on his shirt, lifts up the edge of the first loaf. It's a little black, but I can't tell if it's burned or if it has picked up residue from the stove. Jean Pierre quickly flips the loaves over.

"It cooks very quickly."

He opens the front of the stove and pokes in another three or four pieces of wood, shutting it again with a heavy *clank*. Through rusty cracks in the side of the stove, I watch the flames leap and surge in their greed. A rushing noise like an infernal wind comes from the flue, and the temperature rises by another few degrees in the already sweltering tent.

When Jean Pierre deems that his creations are ready, he flicks one loaf onto each of our plates. I wait a few moments for mine to cool. Then, taking my penknife (the only knife we appear to have left, for some mysterious reason), I rip open the now familiar red and yellow packets of margarine. It's half melted and exists only as a congealed mess, but such considerations were forgotten long ago. Scooping up a good amount, I spread it thickly on the bread, ignore the fine black dust, and take a big bite.

It's delicious.

As I rummage through my bag tonight, shaking out my sleeping bag and tracking down some clean clothes, I notice how everything we have reeks of camphor and citronella oil, our homemade fly repellent. It has become, for me, the one smell that will be forever linked in my memory to this trip through Labrador. In the months and years to come, whenever I use a piece of equipment that was on this trip, I catch a faint whiff of citronella and instantly I'm back in the forest, boughs beneath my feet, the sound of the river filling my ears, and a teakettle boiling on the stove.

"Tell me a tale," I plead as we get into our sleeping bags. This almost nightly ritual is oddly—and childishly—comforting. I often find myself forced to fight sleep as I drift into my own dream world, where magic and monsters reign in unpredictable fashion. Each story also banishes the strange voices I still hear at night, whispering in the river's endless song. Jean Pierre's soft voice begins the tale, spread out in long, slow sentences, and soon my eyelids are drooping. I open them wide and prop myself up on one elbow, the better to concentrate, and our little tent becomes a sanctuary from the mythical world that ebbs and flows into eternity beyond the canvas and out into the infinite black night.

# CHAPTER 10

*"Beyond this point our progress was slow and difficult . . . However, by poling and tracking, by lifting and dragging the canoe through the shallow waters near the shore, or again by carrying the entire outfit over the sand hills or across boulder-strewn valleys, we won gradually forward."*

Mina's words haunt me as we make our way through the same landscape, using exactly the same methods. The river has entered a steep valley now, bordered on both sides by high sandbanks that make our normal mode of progress impossible. We are entering the Seal Islands expansion, where *"there are five of these islands, low flat and evergreen covered, some poplar. Water just piles up in ridges round some of them."*

It feels quite strange to be walking so closely in Mina's footsteps. At no previous point could our paths be pinpointed so precisely, each of our experiences so clearly a mirror of the other. She found herself disheartened by the slow progress on this part of the river—we both make little more than two miles a day, two miles of back-breaking work. I share her concerns about this, and at no other place so far on our trip have I felt her presence so distinctly.

We camped just short of a point last night below the expansion, knowing that this morning we would face some difficult decisions. I knew what we'd have to do even before Jean Pierre returned from his reconnoitring of the route ahead. Like Mina, I will have to walk alone through forest, making my own trail along the top of the ridge while Jean Pierre drags the canoe along the edge of the river at the base of the sandbank. This bank is so steep that I cannot walk across the face of it.

Jean Pierre dons his waders in preparation for the task ahead.

"Wouldn't it be safer to take my chances with you?" I ask, one last time.

"No. You'll be safer up there." He nods up toward the forest.

"What about bears?"

"You won't see any."

Right.

I walk away, fighting through the willows, then into the forest proper, following a spur from the point up onto the ridge, far above Jean Pierre. It's not long before he's completely gone from my sight, the bright scar of sand swallowed by the forest that reaches and clings to me at every turn.

There is no remnant of the bear paths that Mina followed, and at every step I must stamp, snap, and push a trail through. Farther away to my right, I can see the forest thinning out, with the bases of spruce and fir rising unchoked from the moss. I veer in that direction a little, with caution. It would be very easy to lose my way, despite my usually excellent sense of direction. I find myself sealed into another, almost silent world.

The light is faintly green but steadily shaded by the tall, luxurious trees that grow here. This place is not like the poor, stunted patches of forest we've seen in places. It's so closed in that I cannot see the edge of the ridge above the river that I know lies not far to my left. Instead, I am surrounded on all sides by the trees, thick and close, the gloom crowding out any sense of space high above the river. Nothing moves, and every dry snapping of twigs that accompanies my passage sounds like gunshot.

I've pushed my mosquito head net up onto my hat, as the flies are not so bad here and with it across my face, I cannot see so well in the poor light. Beneath my feet, the moss presents a deceitful surface that pulls me down several inches at every step. *"Through the wooded land,"* wrote Mina, *"the soil appeared to be simply a tangle of fallen and decayed tree trunks grown over with thick moss of another variety, in which you sank ankle deep, while dark perilous holes yawned on every side, making you feel that if once you went in you might never appear again."*

Mina had obviously walked through this forest.

After what seems like a lifetime, I can hear Jean Pierre calling my name. Despite the distance, I detect a note of concern, particularly when he calls a second and a third time.

"I'm okay!" I call back. I can't tell if we've come to the end of the sandbank or not and I try to make my way toward the light so I can see our relative positions. I had not, however, reckoned on the willows. I had thought that they would not be so thick so high above the water, but I'm soon reduced to a standstill. In front of me is a tangle of trees seven feet high and impossible for me to climb through. They are so dense, it's only their presence that offers a clue that I am near the edge of the ridge, as I cannot see anything through the wall they create. Behind me lies the dark forest, tempting me away from the river, Jean Pierre, and safety.

Taking a deep breath, I call out again, to reassure Jean Pierre (and myself). Then I retreat a little, moving slowly along the line of willows until I find a patch slightly less dense than elsewhere. All thoughts of bears completely banished, I select a point of entry and slip into this world of triffids, kicking a path through, bending and pushing until, finally, I can see light ahead. One last heave and I'm out, dazzled by the sun and immediately aware that I'm still high up on the sandbank, at least fifty feet from the nearest point where I can rejoin Jean Pierre.

He is far below, eyes anxiously searching the forest that lines the top of the bank. I wave and he acknowledges me, then watches as I descend diagonally. The sand is soft and deep, like dunes behind the beaches at home. Yet I cannot surrender to gravity as I would there, allowing myself to be pulled down in a shower of sand and giggles before landing in a heap at the bottom. No, here I must carefully judge every step, as a loss of balance could land me in the cold embrace of the rushing waters below.

When I finally reach Jean Pierre, he is sitting on a rock, waders at his side, wringing out his socks. This has been an almost hourly ritual for the past few days, but this time the amount of water he pours out astonishes me. Normally containing no more than a cupful, the waders seem to be holding a whole new water system all of their own.

"I thought they came up to your thighs."

"They do."

Jean Pierre is over six feet tall.

I feel a trickle of blood on my neck. Blackfly. I put my hand up to pull down my head net and find nothing there. It must have become snagged in the forest. Somewhere behind me it hangs, hooked on a branch for the birds to nest in. This is quite an important loss, as protection from the flies is vital out here. Fortunately, I have a bug "jacket" made of the same mesh, but it doesn't fit my hat so well and is less convenient. Damn. Then a shudder goes through me. This is precisely the same place where Mina tore her veil so badly that she was later forced to put a canvas bag on her head and use what remained of the veil as netting for her eyes and mouth.

The next section is no less challenging, if a little less lonely. Above us, the incline of the sandbank has decreased slightly, but the sand has been replaced with rocks ranging in size from tiny pebbles of scree to huge boulders. For a while, I stagger happily along next to Jean Pierre, idly noting how most of the largest boulders are at the bottom of the slope. Then, looking up, I can see that not all the boulders are at the bottom. A good many are still at the top of the slope, with fifty feet or so of a clear run right down to . . . us. At each step, I create mini-landslides of the smaller rocks. If any of their larger cousins were to be destabilized by this . . .

I point out our situation to Jean Pierre.

"Yes," he says and carries on walking. I grit my teeth and turn my head, so as not to see death poised in the corner of my eye. I recall the horrific injuries one of my friends sustained when he walked along similar scree in Banff National Park some years ago. "If I make it out of here in one piece," I promise myself, "I'm getting a nice safe office job." Of course, I would never do that, but it is a comforting thought at this moment.

The valley itself is heavily wooded on the slopes, but farther up, the mountaintops are barren. Mina calls them "true virgin forests" and I realize with a shock that they still truly are—here at least. Living as I do in a country where the landscape has been constantly shaped and reshaped by the hand of humankind over millennia, to be somewhere that is truly "virgin" gives a sense of perspective I never gain in less grandiose, human-made surroundings.

I am even luckier than I realize, however. Newfoundland's boreal forests of birch, poplar, and conifers—black and white spruce and balsam fir—are possibly the last remaining parts of an immense, circumpolar forest not decimated or immediately threatened by logging. Stretching from this, the far eastern edge of Canada, to Russia, this forest constitutes one-third of the planet's entire forested area, and it is as precious—and as fragile—as the more famous southern rainforests. Quite apart from sustaining the culture and lifestyle of people like Jean Pierre, it also harbours over two hundred species of birds, as well as the elusive lynx, wolf, and moose. The twentieth century has already seen huge tracts of Labrador's landscape lost to hydro projects and mining. The next big threat is unsustainable clear-cut logging, unbelievably already the scourge of the old-growth temperate rainforests of British Columbia. How long, I wonder, before Labrador's forests are virgin no more?

As in much of Labrador, areas are named for practical, solidly descriptive purposes. Seal Islands, like Seal Lake, now not very far to the north of us, are so named because they are associated with a supposedly mythical population of seal-like otters, called *wentsuck-ahmeseteyoh* and *misintsuk*. An Innu story tells of a man who killed a young otter and was chased by the mother, who could move on land and under water equally well. She killed the man, but his friend escaped, living to tell the tale. The animals are described as being very large (up to ten feet long) and shaped like seals, with black or brown bodies and white legs and feet.

This story, like many Innu legends, has some roots in the truth. It was apparently well known that seals could be found in this part of inland Labrador. The Hudson's Bay Company employee Erland Erlandson reported in 1834 that *"in descending a river, which falls into [Seal] Lake, we met many seals ascending it."* It seems this was a variety of fresh-water seal also familiar to Dillon Wallace, the geologist A.P. Low, and the medical missionary William Grenfell, though none of them record first-hand sightings. Low wrote in 1898 that *"here, in former years, the Indians killed annually more than 30."*

It is Mina's record of meeting seals at the lake which remains the most detailed eyewitness account: *"Geo shot two muskrats . . . and almost shot a seal. Gilbert pleased that we saw one. Said lots of people do not believe the trappers when they say there are seals here. The one we saw tonight was a good big one, too."* And the next day, she wrote: *"Saw another seal tonight. George took a shot at him with his rifle but shot high. Seal swam off to southwest and men met him and near point Joe shot at him with pistol. Also missed. Legend has it they are invulnerable."*

This legend of invulnerability held no water for scientist Arthur Twomey, who wrote of his trials attempting to locate seals at a lake of the same name farther north, near Ungava in 1938. Travelling in winter by dogsled, he eventually reached the lake and described it as *"less humanly bearable than some windless regions of the far Arctic north."* Native people in nearby Richmond Gulf on Ungava Bay itself had told him that as many as eleven seals had once been killed on the beaches of the lake and that they were regularly hunted in the summer when they came ashore.

Twomey followed a route to the lake that had defeated A.P. Low with ice storms and potential starvation in 1884. Spending many days lying on the ice, drilling holes to look for seals, Twomey and his guides soon reached the point of no return. Crippled by snow blindness, their rations all but finished and with little game to be found, they were considering eating their dog. It was at this, the eleventh hour (for the dog at least) that they found a pregnant female seal—not beneath a blowhole as they had supposed, but at the rapids where the seals would congregate in the open water. Some also clustered near air pockets along the shore.

The dog was spared and the legend lives on. We don't see any seals at the islands here on the Naskaupi, but if we were to see some at Seal Lake just to our northwest, that would be quite remarkable, as at last record, their numbers were dropping fast and none have been observed now for several years.

The habit of naming places for wildlife and unusual sightings has already given me a few jolts.

A few days before I left Happy Valley, Joe showed me a map of the Churchill River. On one page, the name "White Bear Island" appeared.

"Is that named for the reason I think it is?" I asked in surprise, knowing that polar bears, though usual in northern Labrador, don't venture this far south.

"Sure," he said, enjoying the effect. "Sometimes they just get stuck on an ice floe that brings them right down the coast, and when they get off onto land, they run straight back up north."

I didn't know whether to believe him (Joe is an inveterate leg-puller), so I just raised an eyebrow: "Are we likely to see one then?"

Joe sucked in his breath and shook his head in doubt (managing simultaneously to suggest it was highly likely). "Oh, I wouldn't worry."

Hmmm.

Perhaps more worryingly, Erlandson refers to a "barren ground grizzly"—despite the fact that only black and polar bears exist in the east. Other explorers, including Randle Holme, also mention this creature, but there seem to be no recorded sightings. Needless to say, after hearing Jean Pierre's bear story during the first days of the trip, I have never quite forgotten the whole bear issue, including mythical grizzlies. Often, a shadow on a nearby hill takes on an ominous shape, only to dissolve into a clump of bushes as we near it. Occasionally, Jean Pierre calls out, "Bear!" But the dark shadow on the opposite bank or far mountain is hardly visible to my untrained eye and even less threatening.

Mina seems to have shared my obsession with our local inhabitants: *"My imagination turned every black spot I saw on the hills into a bear, to the great amusement of the men. But no bear appeared."* I rather suspect that her fascination was born of a desire to give successful chase to it, rather than of a fear of an encounter with one of these crazy hormone-driven owners of sharp teeth and big claws.

It is around mid-day. The sun is high above us, the Naskaupi throws back a relentless blinding mirror to the empty sky, and a small plane passes overhead. For a moment, I pay little attention. Despite my readjusted consciousness, the sound of aircraft is so indelibly imprinted in my mind as an everyday sound that I give it little thought. It is only as Jean Pierre pauses, shades his eyes, and looks up that I realize I have not heard that sound since the day on Three Mile Rapids when the military jet overflew us. I also look up, squinting, my mind caught between the inescapable roar of the river and the blue void of sky. For a moment, I feel weightless, disoriented, until I see the plane.

The black outline seems so tiny against the dome of our perceived universe. This floatplane going to a fishing camp, maybe somewhere on Seal Lake, is our only evidence that the world I once knew—my world—is still out there somewhere, turning and intact. It's a reassurance that there is more in the universe than these mountains and this river, the forest and the tundra. I imagine we are the survivors of some huge catastrophe and the plane means we are no longer alone.

Mostly, though, it reminds me of home and of what the poet Philip Larkin called the "hollows" of afternoons. Rising from my keyboard in my study back in Cornwall, I would look out a window onto the harbour at the brightly painted fishing boats with their coiled ropes and stacked lobster pots bobbing gently against the side of the harbour wall, lined into neat rows of three or four according to size, the smell of fish and engine oil hanging faint and motionless in the heat.

At these moments, time seems not to exist, and I have the overwhelming feeling that the world and all the lives in it are happening somewhere else, in someone else's time. Suspended on the canvas of an abstract landscape, I am isolated, out of time, irrelevant. The only things that seem real are the words I write on the screen in front of me. And now, only the plane disappearing over the horizon seems real. When it disappears after a fleeting moment, we are back on our own and start our slow progress up the river.

Much later that afternoon, a strong, hot wind starts to blow down the river, flattening my clothes against me in mock relief from the sun's heat and sending the plastic coverings on the kit into a frenzy of flapping.

"It's going to rain. Soon." Jean Pierre's eyes flicker over the land above the bank to our right. It is thickly forested but has become much flatter, the mountains rising steeply from water level some distance away. He shakes his head.

"Not here. We must hurry."

The light has changed to a hard, artificial yellow, as though all the sunlight from earlier in the day has become caught beneath the black clouds now sweeping down the valley, and with no blue sky to disappear into, it is bouncing angrily between heaven and earth.

"Here. Quickly." Jean Pierre points to a section of bank thick with large rocks, rising steeply to sparse forest.

We pull and throw the kit onto these rocks, slipping in our haste and tripping over fallen boughs. When the canoe is empty, Jean Pierre hauls her up high onto the rocks, several feet above the waterline, and turns her over. Realizing that this is to be our shelter during the coming storm, I rummage hastily for delicate items, including all the cameras, and push them under the canoe to join us. Just as I snatch my waterproof from under the food sack, the rain begins, beating black down the river toward us, attended by an entourage of grey and silver shadows. The noise is tremendous, much louder than the sound of the river alone, and it has its counterpoint in the thunder.

I smile wryly on the advice we all took so literally as children: never shelter under a tree in a thunderstorm, for fear of being struck by lightning. The sky is torn apart in a flash of silver. Not much chance of avoiding the lightning here. Jean Pierre and I are both crouched awkwardly on a jumble of rocks under the upturned canoe. Forced into silence by the storm, we smile at each other helplessly. I feel like a commuter trapped on a delayed train in rush hour. There is nothing to say, so I take out the little camcorder and film the storm, our kit under the tarpaulin, and Jean Pierre's brilliant smile in the cedar-smelling shade.

Eventually, the storm abates and the sky brightens to reveal a rainbow reaching across the mountains and into the river. I smile to myself as I remember Mina's attempts to convince George of the existence of the pot of gold at every rainbow's end: "*I have never seen such rainbows . . . Geo never before knew that there is a pot of gold at the end of the rainbow. I suspect that he does not believe it yet, for I could not persuade him to try to move the rock to look under.*"

As the rain finally abates, a bright band of bronze points across the river toward us, filling our little corner with a soft, warming light. I crawl stiffly out from under the canoe and survey the scene. The canoe pulled so high on the bank and turned on her side, the haphazard lie of kit and tarpaulin on the rocks, all together look like the flotsam left by a tidal wave. Jean Pierre decides that this shall be our campsite for the night and we set about making order from the chaos.

The more time I spend with Jean Pierre, the more I realize how little I understand him or his life. The more I think about our developing relationship, the more I realize there is a great cultural difference in the way we communicate. While I can never pretend that a few weeks in *nutshimit* will make me an expert in the Innu manner, I have at least begun to *try* to understand the different ways of communicating, of being.

The lack of emotional expression is a significant difference. Even coming from my reticent nation, I find the absence of negative emotions and the restraint new. Although Jean Pierre is always ready to laugh, or at appropriate moments tell me stories, even about personal trials, I need to rely on my instinct to feel the sadness behind his manner at times. When he's spoken of Mr. T or his anger about land rights and other political issues, the passion is evident yet always controlled. Any hint of these feelings is rare and mild. At first, I thought my guide a particularly gentle person, but I quickly realized that it was simply one more indication of the cultural gulf that lies between us.

In a society that historically and culturally cannot be expressed in words alone, I am beginning to comprehend that to really understand anything, I need to experience something of what it is, what it means, to be Innu. This trip is far from a stay at an Innu hunting camp in the country, but it is in many ways an immersion in a different way of being that infuses every aspect of our communication. When we part, even if it is two or more months from now, the sum of what I have learned will be little more than the realization of how much I still have to learn about the Innu and the life of a hunter.

On this trip, it has been Jean Pierre's stories that have opened my eyes to some of the many differences between us. The stories are not always mythical. There is a type of story known as *tipatshimuna* that is more journalistic in nature. It does not necessarily come from the personal experience of the storyteller, but it does derive from the personal experience of an Innu—a first-hand description of events, of meetings with people or spirits, or of dealings with outside forces, such as the church or the government. The bear story Jean Pierre told me that first rainy day in camp would fall into this category. This evening, I inadvertently prompt another such story as we lie down to sleep.

"Were you not very cold after getting so wet while I was walking in the forest today? You are wet so often. Yet you seem never to be cold."

Jean Pierre shakes his head.

"I don't get cold easily."

I can see him smile a little in the faint light of the mosquito coil and the citronella candle burning between us.

"A few years ago, I was out in the country with some white people. It was November and I was living in Sheshatshiu, but we had gone into the country for a few days. The weather turned bad and the other guys didn't know which way to go home. I always had a good sense of direction. I always know which way to go and I said, 'It's this way.' They asked me how I could be so sure, but I couldn't tell them—just that I knew. We walked and walked. There was a strong wind and soft, wet snow. I was wearing only a T-shirt and jeans, maybe a light jacket."

I believe him totally, as he has worn nothing else since we left North West River, but I cannot imagine how inadequate that would be at the beginning of a sub-arctic winter.

"How long did you walk?"

"Eighteen hours. Then we walked straight into Sheshatshiu. They couldn't believe I had taken them straight to the town."

"Didn't you get sick from the cold?"

Jean Pierre laughs.

"No. Katie thought I would, but I was fine. I felt nothing."

The flies are bad tonight. Even with the mosquito coil burning and Jean Pierre's cigarettes, my ear picks out their persistent, dreaded whine. Like a wartime Londoner listening for doodlebugs, I have learned to fear the ceasing of a mosquito's drone more than the noise itself. The ominous sound of silence means it has landed, probably on me, and that I will soon find another painful and itchy swelling on my person. Despite being almost continuously clothed from head to foot, with my head in a net, my hands in gloves, and repellent seeping from every pore, I am still covered in red weals and antiseptic cream. Every night, I wash dried blood from my face and neck, where bites have gone unnoticed and the beasts have drunk their fill, falling off in a sated daze.

My ritual before bed, despite the warmth of the sub-arctic evening, involves pulling my neckband up over my head and—before I lost it—putting the head net, or now the hood of the fly jacket, on top of that. I puff it out, so that few parts of the net rest against my skin, thwarting the flies' attempts to feed through the mesh. I then try to sleep with only my nose outside of the sleeping bag. Yet each morning, as if from nowhere, the tent is filled with light spindly bodies drifting on the early coolness like the cast of *A Midsummer Night's Dream* against the backdrop of the bright tent walls.

# CHAPTER 11

I awake the next morning with a jolt. Jean Pierre jumps out of his sleeping bag and rips open the tent flap in one unbroken movement. All I can see is the orange of flame where the sky should be.

Our cooking fire, thoroughly dampened down the previous evening, was kept that way only by the heavy rain that fell during the night. As this ceased at dawn, the fire resurfaced, a horrible reminder of how a fire can stay alive underground for hours, even days.

I don't have time to think, to scream, to move, but Jean Pierre is out of the tent and dousing the flames with a bucket of water, kicking the earth over to smother the blaze. Having saved me temporarily from being burned alive in a torch of heavy cotton, he then douses the hearth again and again with river water, pouring it on in great swishing puddles, digging down, pouring again. Finally, he is satisfied and we have our morning tea and oatmeal, cooked on the stove, sitting in a weary, post-calamity silence that is becoming rather familiar.

In the rush of setting up camp between rain and thunder last night, I did not notice a patch of dead boughs on the ground several yards away from our tent, in the forest. I find Jean Pierre looking at it today, however. He paces the four corners of what was evidently someone else's camp. The dead boughs were that person's groundsheet.

"Innu?" I ask. Jean Pierre shakes his head.

"Not here." He picks up a bough, brittle and brown, despite the damp. "Some time ago, though."

It must have been a small tent, I notice, stepping across the space. Not more than four feet by four feet, but the ground is rocky all around here and anyone camping would have the same problem that we've had. Something occurs to me.

"How would someone get out here? Not by canoe—that I know!"

Jean Pierre puts down the bough and nods, slowly, his eyes darting along the line of trees opposite, looking for something.

"Prospectors. They come by helicopter to stake claims in areas they think might contain minerals."

I look around, half expecting to see a man carrying a shovel pop out from behind a rock.

"All the way out here?"

"Oh, yes." Jean Pierre sits down, his hand moving briefly across his face to dislodge a mosquito or two. "Anyone can stake a claim here on the land—for about $240, I think. Thousands are staked every year, and the government helps them do it. It pays people grants to match the money they spend on the prospecting."

"They just come out here and claim it?"

"All you have to do is pick it out on a map. Five hundred square feet. If you work it, then you get your money back."

In fact, over a quarter of a million dollars was awarded to individual prospectors by the provincial government during 2000, in a bid to open up new mines generating employment and, of course, taxes. There are now almost three hundred thousand claims staked all over Labrador and the number is rising each year—by just under thirteen thousand last year alone. There is gold—quite literally—in Labrador's hills and a lot of people want a piece of it.

However, these claims have provoked occasionally violent, often emotional, and extremely political tussles over land rights, drilling practices, investment levels, and just about everything else to do with mining. Specifically, there has been a great deal of Innu and Inuit opposition, on environmental and archæological grounds.

A recurring criticism of large industrial projects in areas that have

Native populations is that the only jobs made available to these sections of the community are the low-pay, temporary positions. Often acting as guides or working in similar roles, Native people help create projects that then lock them out of the economic benefits.

Some potential mine developers have attempted to mitigate these problems, but even these solutions will not prevent the acculturation and assimilation that result from the introduction of major industrial operations. Jean Pierre resists such acculturation with every breath.

Employment in a mine would lead to economic self-reliance, yet it would also remove what remains of the Innu's true self-reliance as hunters. Innu in Sheshatshiu and other Native communities point out that jobs will not solve all social ills. Industrial employment would merely add to the original problems that have stemmed from enforced settlement. It was not until the Innu were taken from the land forty years ago that jobs were needed, that violence erupted, and that drinking and abuse began to be a serious social problem. How is it possible to fix a problem by applying more of the pressures that created it in the first place?

In asking these questions, the Innu are engaged in a process that few people today have the opportunity even to think about. Does being involved in the wage economy equate with freedom? How can control over lives be maintained when control over the thing that defines those lives—the land—is lost? While extra money may pay for a better snowmobile or a new rifle, the largest profits from the exploitation of Innu land—and Innu labour—go to the mining companies and the government. As Jean Pierre asks, "I hear people mentioning money. Who is going to have it? Where is it going to go?"

Several times on this trip, Jean Pierre has found evidence of various "interesting" minerals. He has made me promise, however, not to reveal their locations either directly, or indirectly, in anything I write or say. He fears that this would attract more prospectors. I look around me—at the pristine waters; the bright, strong colours of the trees; the uninterrupted sky; and the land. I cannot imagine it torn up, minerals gouged from the earth, the animals gone, the fish poisoned. Even if a mine were operated in a way that minimized environmental damage, great harm would still be done to this precious and unique landscape.

The day is hot, but at about mid-day, a shout from Jean Pierre catches my attention. I follow his eyes and look upstream, where I see a crazy, wobbling stack of air. A tornado. Maybe it's the high level of danger I'm becoming accustomed to on a daily basis now, but I feel little fear. The twister is only about ten feet high and nothing like the relentless, destructive monsters I have seen on American news programs. It's my first real tornado, and I watch it hover, moving this way and that, an opaque whirl of energy in the leaden light of midsummer. Eventually, it moves away from us, upstream, dissipating as it goes, until there is only a ripple on the water, then nothing.

We move on.

The hawks diving at us from tall trees, trying to divert us from their nests, are the only wildlife we see all day. I call out to them, "It's okay. We don't want your young. We won't harm you." Behind me, the *flick, flick* of Jean Pierre's lighter is magnificent in its lack of comment. Perhaps I'm going insane. It wouldn't be surprising, out here in this heat, only one other person for company, on a trip that seems to have no end, with trials that seem to increase after every successful solution. Like a computer game, each time we manage to move on, fate puts us up a level, with one life less to play.

We have a good camp tonight, in a small clearing among the trees. It's a short, easy walk down to the river, where the water glides by slowly enough for me to wash the pots and dishes with ease. But every night, I miss the glorious sunsets, as we camp in the forest and wash-ing-up time comes too late. Sometimes I am asleep or cooking or pick-ing boughs when spectacular colours are spread across the sky. All the chores must be done first, and by the time I have finished, I am often too tired even to write in my diary, much less climb a hill and watch the sky. Instead, I talk to Jean Pierre in our temporarily mosquito-free tent, half choked on mosquito coil fumes and cigarette smoke, but released from the perpetual torment of being bitten.

Tonight, however, I make a great effort and go to the river with the dishes just as the sun is sliding out of sight behind a mountain, to the northwest. I have also neglected the filming. So, I give Jean Pierre the little camcorder and tell him to follow me. Startled at being given an instruction for a change, he agrees, a little bemused. Some domestic detail would be appropriate, I decide, so I make him stand filming as I scour the inside of the pans with sand from the river's edge, rinsing them out in the clear brown eddies below the rock on which I am perched. Mosquitoes whine around my unprotected face and neck, landing lightly on my hands in a parody of harmlessness.

"Elson never had to do this," says Jean Pierre.

I laugh.

"You fancy yourself as George Elson a bit too much."

A smile flashes out of the half-light from behind the camera.

"Okay."

Once the sun has finally left us to the night, we sit and discuss our progress again. Although we are still making good time, Jean Pierre is worried about the George River. We will most likely need to walk around sections that Mina—and others who have travelled the river since—were able to run. Jean Pierre talks about it whenever we discuss the future route, but all I can think about is getting up the Naskaupi. We still have the most difficult section below Seal Lake to navigate. After that, the long paddles west across both Seal and Wachusk lakes will be very welcome indeed, yet both seem a long way from here. Obsessively, I count the weeks. We will be lucky if we make it in anything close to Mina's eight weeks.

During our all-too-short evenings, spent chatting in the tent, I'm reminded of the evenings when Mina's guides sat around the campfire, singing the "Indian Paddling Song." I can imagine her perfectly, sitting in the soft warmth, maybe on a rock, with a lamp beside her, scribbling in a diary, or listening hard, trying to memorize the strange-sounding words.

I also listen closely as we lie in the dark, side by side. The last of the coil smoke rises and disperses through the tent, but I'm so close to the ground that all I can smell is the tang of spruce needles. Settling back with his last cigarette of the night, Jean Pierre tells me a story from a time long ago, when the Innu and the Inuit were at war and the powers of the shaman were absolute . . .

"*Shamans used shaking tents in the battles between peoples. On one occasion the Inuit shamans transformed themselves into giant caterpillars, which lived under thick ice. The Innu hunter had only one harpoon—a spear—and only three attempts before the Inuit shamans would kill him.*

"*The first time, the ice was so thick he could not penetrate it. The second time, the ice was again too thick and he could not penetrate it. The shamans were getting closer. The third time, he broke the ice and killed one of the giant caterpillars.*

"*The Inuit shamans all died.*"

Sometime in the middle of the night, I awake suddenly from a deep and restful sleep. There is definitely something outside around our camp. My mind spirals away into what we may have left outside, but there is nothing—until I remember the tea, dried milk, coffee, and chocolate inside the tent with us. Enough to attract a hungry, curious bear perhaps? Nothing else would . . .

A mighty snapping of branches and a rustling as loud as an elephant in a cornfield comes from a few feet away. Whatever it is, it is certainly in the camp and there's no way I'm imagining it this time. I look over at Jean Pierre. Normally awake within seconds on hearing some telepathic warning of danger, he sleeps peacefully on. I can feel the cold of the rifle barrel if I lean out of the sleeping bag just a little . . .

There's a shuffling sound I'm convinced is a bear sniffing its way through our kit. It ricochets around the tent, deafening my tightly strung nerves. Jean Pierre sleeps on. The idea of waking him dances through the back of my mind, but somehow I'm too preoccupied with not breathing too loudly so I can hear whatever is outside. Also, I have a sneaking, no doubt-deluded, belief that as long as Jean Pierre stays asleep, it can't be anything too serious. By not waking him, I can make the creature outside disappear.

After what feels like æons—probably only ten or fifteen minutes—

the sounds stop and all I can hear is the dulled growl of the river through the trees.

The next morning, I tell Jean Pierre excitedly about our nocturnal visitor.

"It was definitely a bear," I conclude with triumphant conviction.

"Hmmm." Jean Pierre looks around outside the tent, pushing at odd pieces of bark or twigs with his foot.

"There, look." He points to a paw print.

"Big, big"—he looks at me mischievously—"rabbit."

"*Rabbit?* There's no way. It broke branches . . ." I trail off as Jean Pierre shows me a dried-up twig and cracks it in half. He smiles.

"Rabbit."

Now, this is pretty embarrassing, but again I have Mina for comfort. As I read her book, I hear her reassuring, practical tones telling me about her experience with bear-sized rabbits:

> *How long I had been asleep, I could not tell, but some time in the night I was awoken by sounds outside my tent . . . Presently something shook the branches of the tree near my tent close to my head. I reached for my revolver and remembered that there were only two cartridges in it. Quickly filling the empty chambers I waited, ready to give battle, but the sounds in my tent obviously alarmed the intruder, for there was silence after that. In the morning the men said it was a rabbit jumping through the low branches of the spruce tree.*

By now, I understand Mina as being very sensible, down to earth, a true explorer in the Edwardian mould. If a rabbit could fool her, well, then so could I be fooled. Jean Pierre just gives me that wry smile that says, "You're a crazy woman, but I guess that's pretty harmless . . ."

The day seems determined to be another scorcher. After a couple of hours, we come to part of the bank that is little more than sheets of smooth rock with sharp ridges, sloping into the water. The river laps against them, making their surface as slippery as an ice rink. Willows reach out from the forest across these razor tops, making the terrain virtually impassable.

We have to portage, an unwelcome development in the heat. First, we sit and have a long cold draught of juice made from a powder concentrate and unadulterated river water in our blackened teakettle. In the past few weeks, we've been losing "kitchen" equipment at an alarming rate. We now have only one cup (with a chipped handle—my fault), no teaspoons, one knife that is on my Swiss Army set, a cooking pot, and the teakettle. If we lose any more, we'll be eating with our fingers and drinking straight from the river. But at least there's less for me to wash up.

We unload the canoe in what is becoming an all-too-familiar ritual. Jean Pierre carries the heavier bags and I the lighter to a point about a hundred yards along the bank. Not a great distance, but the going is terrible. Loaded with a heavy pack, I find it almost impossible to keep my balance on the rocky ridges. The willows constantly push me out onto the slopes, my feet slipping into the cold river while their cruel whips scratch my face. A rip opens up in my waterproof trousers and leaves work their way under the elastic of my gloves.

Mina was fortunate in that she was often able to follow portage routes away from the river itself. In pre-reservoir days, trappers or Innu people cut trails when the river was high, and the banks that have become our main highway did not exist. Now, even if we knew exactly where these trails led out, they would be vastly overgrown. Perhaps more important, despite the almost continuous rapids and fast water, we have been able to cover the ground as quickly or even more quickly than Mina. By keeping the kit in the canoe as much as possible, we can move faster than when we must portage. That is hard work for just the two of us.

Most of the time as we stagger along the slippery edges of the river, I cannot see Jean Pierre, since he moves at twice my speed. We pass occasionally, he on his way to collect another load, a silent nod acknowledging me, or a curt "Don't hold onto the willows. They will snap."

Dumping the kit, I turn to go back to where I started for another load and am suddenly overwhelmed with an intense feeling of aloneness. Not loneliness, but a peaceful, silent sense of separateness. An osprey swoops downstream across the blinding sweep of river, shimmering in the bare sun, and the forest sleeps under the haze of heat. Then I hear the scrape of Jean Pierre's boot and I scramble over the rocks to pick up my next load.

At the end of a long, tiring, and very hot morning, we have covered three hundred yards.

Given that I barely have the energy to write in my diary at night, I find it incredible that Mina was able to take meteorological and geographical readings on her trip. Such activities seem astonishing on a journey like this.

In the Victorian and Edwardian periods, explorers, particularly women, bore a responsibility to return with useful scientific knowledge as "justification" for their adventures. When Mina traversed Labrador, she effectively filled in a blank space on the map. Indeed, her work based on this expedition detailed entirely new maps of the region, recorded encounters with Montagnais-Naskaupi (Innu) groups, and proved that the George and Naskaupi rivers flowed from the same source. Mina also witnessed the migration of the great caribou herds of Labrador's barren lands.

Using only a surveyor's compass, a sextant, and an artificial horizon dependent on water as a gauge, Mina took great care to record correct readings for their latitudinal position, recalling in her diary every mishap with frustration: *"My watch has gone wrong and I did not get my observation right today. But I think my map is pretty correct."*

Indeed, when Mina and her guides were considering turning around just prior to learning from the Innu band that the Post was only a few days away, Mina's dedication to her observations caused the one significant argument she had with the men. They wanted to return via the Grand River, whereas Mina insisted that they use the Naskaupi for the purposes of her work. As she put it: *"Well I want to go down the Nascaupee. I have failed to get any correct observations on it and if we go back at all, I want to go that way."*

As these extracts indicate, Mina also drew the first good maps of the area, relying a great deal on the local knowledge of her guides.

Although she was one of the first white people to see many of the wonders of the Labrador interior, Mina was probably also one of the last to see it in a pristine state.

Mina's findings led to recognition by the American Geographical Society, which described her work as "An excellent piece of pioneer research which has been recognized by the geographical authorities of America and Europe."

The attitude of the period was less magnanimous, as expressed in this letter to the *Times* of London: "The genus of professional women globetrotters with which America has lately familiarized us is one of the horrors of the latter end of the 19th century." Despite her accomplishments, Mina returned to a world of disbelief, and though she did speak before the Royal Geographical Society in London in 1908, she was prohibited from becoming a member of the Society by the fact of her gender.

It was undoubtedly an effort to forestall such criticism that led Mina to write a book that differed substantially from her diary entries. Not only was she the first white woman to travel through this part of the interior, but she also lived with the men without a chaperone, something few white women of her class had done before. Her lessons in Cree, her adventurous spirit, her clear responsibilities as leader, and the scientific work she carried out all go unremarked in her published book, but they are important features in her diary. In particular, her published account of the trip mentions only once, in the preface, the work she undertook in the wilderness: *"I should put on record here the fact that my journey with its results—geographical and otherwise is the only one over this region recognized by the geographical authorities of America and Europe."*

Similarly, her book does not mention the more active side of her participation in the trip. Work such as catching and gutting fish, shooting at bears, paddling, and carrying packs is either left undescribed or glossed over. The overall impression given in her book is that of a lady accompanied by four unusual servants, which was far from the truth in terms of the work done and her relationship with the men.

According to Edwardian attitudes, the country was no place for a lady, and the society to which she returned would have considered her to be either mad or wild to undertake such a thing. Mina, mindful of the importance of appearances, explains that her journey was *"a result of a determination on my part to complete my husband's work . . ."* By placing her endeavours in the context of Leonidas' ambitions, she is able to circumvent Edwardian notions of what was appropriate for a woman of her class.

Any reader of her book would find only one other hint that she knew how people would view her as a "woman-explorer." At one point, she talks, via George, with the chief of a band of Montagnais-Naskaupi (Innu) people on the George River. On hearing that the explorer Cabot had travelled with that same band until just a few days before, Mina records her disappointment at their failing to meet:

> *When during the winter I had talked with Mr. Cabot of my trip he had said 'Perhaps we shall meet on the George next summer.' How I wished he had sent me a line by the Indians . . . I wondered at first that he had not done so; but after a while, laughed to myself as I thought I could guess why. How envious he would be of me, for I had really found the home camp of his beloved Nascaupees.*

As a widow, Mina had gained some tenuous entry into a man's world through her husband, but in order to maintain her credibility and the support of "civilized society," she was forced to represent herself as decidedly feminine, inexperienced, and lacking in skills. Her remarkable stamina is similarly played down, as it is something for which only men could be admired. The generally good-natured authority she clearly exercised over her guides is masked in the book by her tacit acknowledgement of their superior abilities and knowledge.

Without the protecting shroud of widowhood, Mina's choices would have ceased to be virtuous. They would instead have been seen as reckless and a challenge to the ideal of Edwardian womanhood. For a woman, lacking strength and expertise were not just acceptable traits; they were expected. If she had shown herself to be the practical, strong-minded woman she was, she would have risked condemnation, and her goal to vindicate Leonidas' name would have been lost, regardless of her actual success in reaching Ungava. In this sense, Mina not only had to succeed at the hard work of exploration, she also had to fight and win a public relations war in the context of Edwardian sensibilities, in order for her achievements to be acknowledged.

Yet did Mina really do all this for her husband's memory or did she use her situation, as some have claimed, to "validate her own choice" to venture into the man's world of wilderness exploration? Was this albeit tragic circumstance an opportunity for Mina to satisfy her own adventurous spirit?

Mina's writings about her expedition leave little doubt that she missed Leonidas, or her "Laddie" as she fondly called him, at every step of the way. Often, in her diary, a moment of joy or exhilaration is immediately tempered by a lament that her husband's experience of the country that was so kind to her had been so cruel to him.

Furthermore, had Leonidas' death merely been an excuse for Mina to travel as she wished, she almost certainly could have used her success in Labrador to demonstrate her abilities and demand the right to undertake other expeditions. Yet she did not do this. Although her diary records a longing to spend more time in the North and a strong appreciation of the tough life of the trail, she instead followed a very different path in the years to come—one that took her to England. And from there, she returned to North America only infrequently.

I believe, therefore, that Mina's original intention really was to finish what Leonidas had started, as she states so often and so forcefully. There is no doubt that the stubbornness and single-mindedness required for such a decision were elements in Mina's character. However, after the decision was made and Mina found herself in the country, having made the right choices with regard to guides, supplies, timings, and above all, route, I would suggest that she discovered her own spirit of adventure. Each test or decision displayed that Mina had the temperament, leadership skills, endurance, and natural curiosity eminently suited to wilderness travel. As George Elson said, *"Well, we got through and I want to say that our little lady . . . has done very well. She has done what no other lady could do, for sure."*

The kind of "untamed country" through which Mina travelled was perceived by the society from which she came as a symbol of freedom. The wide open spaces were not just blank spaces on the map, they were also a clean, fresh page on which a man, regardless of class or race, could write his own fate. Hence, the allure of positions with enterprises like the Hudson's Bay Company. That is one reason why Mina is so fascinating. At that time, "man" really did mean "man," yet this woman grasped the opportunity to enter the "free country" and she made it her own, defiantly and practically—using her own finances.

In many ways, therefore, Mina's journey was also a triumph of money and class over the restraints of gender. Not only were women barred from the freedom of the wilderness, but no poor woman could ever have hoped for even the limited choices available to her male counterparts, a situation which still exists more than we would wish today. In time, of course, it would be the poor who would people the frontier, but it was almost always the rich who could afford the glory of "discovering" it.

Money helped Mina remove some of the obstacles facing a woman travelling in rough country. She was fortunate enough to be able to buy labour where she herself could not perform the tasks. Yet despite this advantage, Mina was still a woman, and as such, bore the criticisms and slights of her peers. Commentators at the time of Mina's trip, and even now, point out that she had four strong men to do the heavy work, as though by not carrying the heaviest of bags, she was in some way not a full participant. On more than one occasion, I have wished for the funds that would have allowed me to engage enough guides to make Jean Pierre's work easier or take a second canoe. Only a very male-oriented observer would suggest that the heaviest lifting was the only kind of work that mattered.

Not only did Mina produce some important observations and measurements, but if it had not been for her determination, planning, vision, and courage, the journey would not have gone so well. Leonidas had two male companions and he died. Mina not only survived; she triumphed. As women, we may only be able to carry one piece of kit instead of two, but as anyone who has experienced Labrador will tell you, it's rough country out there and living to tell the tale is what counts.

It is a great loss that a woman who found the courage to complete the expedition felt she was unable to write a book that portrayed her experiences truthfully. If she had been able to do this, in opposition to a world where the actions of women outside the home were regarded with horror, perhaps her book would have sold as well as the more dramatic accounts by Dillon Wallace.

We try some fishing later in the day but fail to catch anything. Jean Pierre gives up surprisingly quickly. Sometimes I wonder if there is anything else alive here but us. All we ever see are prints and more prints—but few animals.

"I thought you loved fishing," I say.

He nods. "But if there are no bites in the first few casts, there are no fish."

What would he make of the overfished seas around England? I wonder.

The heat is a big problem today. It is definitely getting hotter, and all my energy is leached out in sweat and blood. I bend to untie the canoe after a short break and I feel like an old woman—back aching, hands stiff. I fumble, and Jean Pierre looks on, waiting patiently.

We are examining the maps every time we rest now, even if only for a few moments. Jean Pierre is worried; I can see it in his eyes. He always looks at the part of the map directly south of Seal Lake, the famous "impassable" section. The contour lines crowd black and close on either side of the river at that point, and Jean Pierre shakes his head. He wonders what we'll do if we get stuck up there. I wonder what I'll do when we run out of dried soup. A fatalistic sense has overcome me. I no longer have the energy to worry. What will be will be.

# Part 3

## TICKLING JAYS

# CHAPTER I

When we reach the Wapustan River, which flows into the Naskaupi from the west, we find it to be little more than a broad jumble of rocks and big boulders, bleached and abandoned looking in the sun. Far from the raging torrent Mina saw, the waterway has dwindled to barely a trickle. I am a little disappointed, as I had imagined a more impressive scene, but also greatly relieved. It demonstrates just how much the dam has reduced these waters and it bodes well for our decision to diverge a little from Mina's route here, for the first time.

At the time of Mina's trip, the Naskaupi River was so fast and high that no one had ever made it through the section below Seal Lake. A portage trail was used instead, away from the main river. Gilbert, at sixteen Mina's youngest guide, had travelled up this part of the river some way while trapping, but he reported it to be impassable. Native people had always avoided this section, so Mina had also walked around it, travelling up the Wapustan River and across country to the lake.

Mina benefited from the use of old Innu trails throughout her trip, although the Wapustan trail was likely not to have been one of them. All records show, and Jean Pierre confirms it, that the Innu often took a trail out at Red Wine River overland to Seal Lake and, when travelling within the lower reaches of the Naskaupi, would use the trails

Mina followed when she portaged around the rapids. So the trail Mina used up the Wapustan River was never a well-worn route, and it has now been abandoned for almost half a century. To follow her path here, Jean Pierre and I would need to cut a trail wide enough· for the canoe through thick spruce and birch trees across some of the roughest country in Canada. I have been told, however, that although in parts the Naskaupi has rapids and even waterfalls, there are banks, and they may be a better option than the portage route. It is a gamble. Either way could mean failure, or worse.

Our numbers tip the scales. Mina had the luxury of four strong guides to carry the kit, the supplies, and the two nineteen-foot canoes. With only Jean Pierre and I to carry ours, a long portage across country isn't an appealing prospect—despite his Herculean strength. We decide to take a chance. The existence of the dam is, ironically, a blessing, as it has lowered the water level to such an extent that the exposed banks, though rough and boulder strewn, may give us a path. With some trepidation, Jean Pierre and I turn our backs on the Wapustan and continue forward, up the Naskaupi.

Despite the steep valley, the riverbanks are initially wide and covered in pebbles. Jean Pierre goes on to scout ahead, leaving me alone, drained by the heat rebounding off the rocks and half-blinded by the river, whose myriad waves reflect the hard sun like a smashed mirror. Behind me, I can feel the dense, unknown forest pressing against my senses. I deliberately turn and look at the sweep of the valley away to the south up which we have struggled. The mountains are a faint blue in the distance and have an almost imperial air of contentment. Nothing moves in the harsh light, and the river's hypnotic glare is disorienting. I have a sense of waiting. Our greatest test is somewhere ahead of us, just around a bend somewhere on this never-ending river.

Jean Pierre eventually returns.

"The valley is very steep . . . see?" He holds his hand level against the river, emphasizing the angle. I nod.

"Farther ahead?"

"I cannot see too far—there are so many bends—but this does not last." He indicates the relatively gentle water sliding past us.

For most of the afternoon, we continue our slow progress up the river, lining the canoe along the riverbank, staggering from rock to rock as the kindly pebbles grow in size.

"God knows what we'll do when this oppressive heat breaks. The rain will turn the fine, grey powder on these rocks into slime."

Jean Pierre nods and keeps walking, not mentioning the fact that he walks almost constantly on rocks covered in water and rarely stumbles. Our spirits have lifted after the first few hundred yards, as the rapids have grown weaker and are replaced by a strong current. Deceptive, but not such an impediment to our progress. Then we turn a corner.

The bend in the river to the west and the belt of thick forest had masked the roar of water falling down an increasingly narrow valley. Our eyes are drawn, however, to the riverbank. A wall of sheer rock maybe thirty feet high overhangs the first set of rapids and continues for about forty feet before a deep cleft cuts into the bank. Farther on, higher, steeper sections of rock continue as far as we can see.

I swallow, not entirely sure what this means for us. My eternal optimism bubbles below a surface that knows this is bordering on the impossible. I turn to Jean Pierre, whose skills have bred within me an almost childlike belief in him. He stares at the rock and sucks on a match. I search his face for a clue, watching his sharp eyes dart around our obstacle, weighing it up, considering, measuring, thinking.

I look at the clear water surging past us and across to the opposite bank. It would be pointless to attempt a crossing to the other, less dramatic side. We would be swept away in an instant, our plucky wooden canoe torn and smashed on a rock. I see in my mind's eye our bags and supplies being carried away on the current, the fishing rod snagged on some willows.

"What can we do?" I try not to sound plaintive.

"We can climb." Jean Pierre indicates the first wall with a nod and a flick of his hand, the kind I am now becoming expert at interpreting.

"I'll go first. You hold the canoe." He thrusts the lining rope into my hands. "I'll climb over and around. You stay there and I'll pull her around from the side."

Only half understanding what he means, I know the plan will

become obvious once I follow his lead. Jean Pierre reaches the beginning of the rocks in two strides and starts to climb up a diagonal shelf I had not noticed. Halfway up, it narrows into sheer rock, and Jean Pierre turns and climbs straight up, moving smoothly, like a lynx stalking its prey. At the top, he turns and beckons to me to follow him, then points to where the shelf narrows away, indicating that I am to stay there, before he disappears over the top and into the trees.

Climbing up the shelf isn't very difficult. I thank my lucky stars for giving me arachnophobia, not vertigo. When I reach as far as I can go, I turn, facing out across the water, and wedge myself into the rock, my hiking boots gripping the rough stone in a reassuring way.

I can hear nothing but the sound of the rapids. The sun sears into my hat, but the rope is still cold in my hands, the tension caused by the canoe below wringing water out of it. Directly below me is the start of the rapid, with a small section of smooth but fast water to the right, protected by another rocky overhang farther up.

At first, the canoe bobs harmlessly at the end of the rope. I look over the edge at the water rushing below and the canoe sitting there, innocently. The longer I crouch here, the more the canoe is dragged into the current. She becomes heavier in my hands, pulling like a skittish stallion on a halter lead. I check that the rope isn't wound around my fingers, but I notice it sliding farther to the left, chafing on the rock, the way it always does in a bad thriller.

"Jean Pierre!" My voice isn't loud—as though by not shouting I can negate the fact that the canoe is beginning to pull too strongly, so much so that I know I won't be able to hold her for much longer. Another jerk. My boot slips a little, sending a small puff of gravel over the edge. I hear it rattle on the canoe below.

Leaning forward a little, I look down. Jean Pierre's hands are reaching around the corner of rock, feeling for the bow of the canoe. He's climbed down the cleft in the rock and waded into the protected patch of water above the rapid. The river is up to his chest and only a few degrees above freezing.

I haul on the rope, trying to pull the canoe closer to Jean Pierre's outstretched hands, but the current is too strong. "Come on," I think to myself. "We can't get stuck here. We have to keep going."

It seems almost surreal to me, that this one event could put an end to our entire expedition. Despite the physical and mental barriers I've been fighting every day of this trip, I am not ready to give up.

I can only watch as Jean Pierre gets a fingertip to the break plate, then a hold on the bow. I let go of the rope and close my eyes in relief. Then I look up. All I have to do now is climb the cliff above me.

I twist on the narrow ledge and make the mistake of looking at my feet. I get a view of the rapid below, at a dizzying angle. Although it's not far to the top of the cliff and the rock is sloping slightly, I know that if I slip and lose my footing, the ledge will not be wide enough to prevent me from falling into the water. I try one or two potential toe holds in vain. The lichen comes off in my hands. I fight the panic rising from my stomach, distracted by hearing Jean Pierre calling my name. I have to do this.

Taking a deep breath, I surge up the rock, relying on momentum to take me to the top, not looking down. I scrabble, my eyes fixed on a tree root some feet ahead, kicking and gouging my way through what feels like acres of caribou moss, clawing for the rock beneath.

It works. I reach the top, only to sink up to my calves in the moss, and I discover that the path down into the cleft where Jean Pierre is waiting is no path at all, but a similarly steep drop into thick willows.

Ahead lies the next wall of rock.

In a strange way, the cultural divide between us comes closer to being breached in extreme moments like this. The Innu ability not to express emotions such as fear, anxiety, depression, or anger is, I've found, a great help. Instead of being hysterical, I try to react as Jean Pierre might, and this enables me to focus more on a situation or a task. For his part, Jean Pierre occasionally asks me, more out of curiosity than anything else, if I am nervous or afraid. Maybe this means I am learning the Innu way or perhaps he is not accustomed to reading such emotions. Recently, I have noticed he has made his inquiries with a greater note of concern.

This is one such time. As I reach the top of the cliff, his voice echoes up to me from the unseen depths of the cleft below, containing a tight question. Maybe he is worried that I really did fall off the cliff and was swept away, the sound of the splash disguised by the roar of the river. As I stand on the edge, knee-deep in moss and other springy things I can't identify, I cannot see a path down. Some spruce and a mass of willows block my view. Jean Pierre's footprints have been obscured, as all the vegetation springs back the moment a foot leaves the ground, blocking the path again and hiding all evidence that it is indeed possible to pass through.

"I'm at the top," I call back. "Which way did you get down?"

"The corner. Past the birch. It's not so steep."

This is hard to believe as I look, but knowing there is no other option, I push forward, holding onto the trunk of a young tree as I slide down into the willows. For a moment, all I can see is green and I'm completely disoriented, but Jean Pierre calls out to me, guiding me through, until I step out onto some rocks crammed between the two cliffs. Our canoe is tied up, and she's bobbing on the swell from the rapid, her break plate tapping irregularly on a boulder. Jean Pierre is sitting casually, smoking a cigarette. He's soaked up to his chest.

"You were fantastic. Well done."

He shrugs. "We must portage around the next one. The cliff is too long. We'll go across the back of the rock," he says, waving the ubiquitous cigarette at some dense undergrowth, "and through to the other side. Then we'll camp."

It's another tortuous portage, and this time we have to cut the trail first. Jean Pierre takes his axe and disappears back into the willows behind us while I start to unload the canoe. It's very difficult, as there is no bank—just rocks, then deep water. I balance our kit on the boulders of the little cove, leaving an energized canoe bouncing about crazily. Just as I've finished, leaving the heaviest food sack for Jean Pierre to lift out, I hear the sound of metal on wood.

Snapping an elementary trail toward the sound, I find Jean Pierre hard at work, cutting away willows and smaller saplings from an area about four feet wide. I go past him, pushing through until I step out into the more usual spruce forest. It's dark and still away from the river, the only sound the drone of a billion mosquitoes beyond my all-encompassing mesh.

It takes Jean Pierre less than an hour to open up a short portage trail for us, and we slowly trek back and forth with the kit, sliding, climbing, and getting snagged. The last thing to be carried is the canoe herself. Together, we pull her up onto the rocks, out of the water, to a place where Jean Pierre can stand evenly. Bending down, he grasps her by the thwart and rolls her onto his shoulders in a single, deft movement, the shape of the canoe fitting his form perfectly. Slowly, he rises from the crouched position, like a weightlifter in some bizarre power competition. With his head almost touching the bottom of the canoe, he tips her back a little so he can see, then walks slowly, staggering a little on the rocks, up the trail. "It's nothing," he assures me. "My grandfather could carry the canoe like this for hours, often with a sack of flour on top."

This smacks of machismo to me, but I say nothing. I ceased to be surprised by Jean Pierre's physical capabilities a long time ago.

Our camp is on a nice, flat space about thirty feet back from the top of the second cliff. A series of rocky shelves and a slope provide access to the water, but the power of the river almost pulls me in when I go to fetch some for tea, the big pan filling instantly and snapping my wrist back painfully before I can safely haul it back up.

There are many trees from which I can pick boughs tonight. In place of the sparse, stunted forest of the past days, the valley seems to have pushed the forest in on itself, and the spruce, balsam, and birch grow tall and abundant. It's the best camp we've had since the sandy cove where the jets overflew us and we relax into it. We've already travelled farther than many thought possible and we're still a day ahead of Mina. But it's been a hard day, and the physical work is beginning to take its toll on me.

We desperately need a "day off." Mina ensured that she and her men had one day of rest each week—usually a Sunday, when she wore her good blouse and a hat. One may laugh at this maintenance of city standards in the forest, but I suspect it was as good for morale as for physical recuperation. The one thing that has driven us on, however, has been the good weather. As happened on Grand Lake, we may find ourselves halted by rain and high winds or worse—snow—at any time, so we must make the best of the current warm temperatures and dry days.

Though I have little motivation just now—partly because I'm very tired—I've never questioned my decision to make this trip—not seriously, at least. Whenever we've faced a new hazard, beaten down the flames of another fire, hacked and struggled and hauled our way across a new section of river, I've been cheered on by each tiny victory and have drawn strength from surviving another day. Yet just for now, all that joy has drained away, and I record my despairing thoughts in the video diary.

A minute or two later, as I switch off the camcorder, Jean Pierre snaps a twig with his foot as he approaches. Knowing his ability to cross shingle in silence, I suspect that he has done this on purpose to warn me of his approach. Did he hear what I said into the camera? It was a private moment of self-doubt that I would have felt uncomfortable sharing, but characteristically, Jean Pierre says nothing.

I make the most of our temporary comforts by warming water on the stove and washing all over in the tent before our gear is put inside. The excess water just drains away into the boughs, leaving the top layers as dry and springy as ever. It's a wonderful feeling to be clean again, but unpleasant then to dress once more, pulling on pants that could virtually walk by themselves. The relentless dirt of a trip like this does get to me quite literally—under my fingernails, ingrained into every bit of exposed flesh, made sticky by the fly repellent. At least here the "dirt" is "clean." There are few pollutants and toxins, mostly just good honest dirt. And I've remained remarkably healthy the whole time. Sometimes the body knows when it cannot afford to weaken.

I cook up rice, meat, and dried vegetables for dinner, and we sit chatting. We've stopped early this evening, allowing for a little social time. As ever, Jean Pierre talks about his hopes and fears for the fate of his people, revealing, as always, a deep sense of engagement and responsibility. I can't help but compare his ambitions with those of George Elson, whose wish, effectively, was to become more "white." His diary reveals his desires to further his career with one of the big trapping and trading companies and to marry a white woman. Of course, George was only part Cree and lived in the world of whites. His problems were those associated with people of mixed blood everywhere—of being undeservedly classified as a second-class citizen in a society not of his making.

Jean Pierre is different. He wants little of the white world. I ask him what his plans are when we finish this trip.

"I'll return to work on my ecotourism camp at Kamistastin." I recall him telling me of it when we met for the first time, but now he recounts his plans in detail, his eyes bright with enthusiasm. Jean Pierre established a foundation for this purpose three years ago, named after his great-grandfather, Tshikapisk.

"I want to help build something for the Innu themselves," Jean Pierre continues, waving away a mosquito. "Something that keeps Innu culture—our values and traditions—and teaches them to the young people. This is our big problem. Our young people do not know about their culture, how to live in the country. They do not have the skills that would allow them to make choices."

"Where do the tourists come into this?"

"They will come and stay at a camp in the country and live as we do—hunting and fishing for food, making snowshoes, preparing animal hides. We can protect our land from development and teach our young people at the same time."

The plan is also striking in its contradiction to the "development" Labrador has undergone in recent years. Despite the current land-claims process, every day development reduces the amount of land available to discuss, and the government refuses to suspend these projects while the talks are underway. Big projects like Churchill do not present the only problems. Individual prospector claims put pressure on the environment, but the provincial government has protected their interests, along with those of the larger corporations, throughout the claims talks.

Jean Pierre mutters, "They are stealing the land from beneath our feet." His recent good mood is evaporating. He goes on to explain how he believes that the refusal to suspend development during the claims talks is designed to put pressure on the Innu to settle quickly, for whatever is on offer.

"They want to give us money for our land, the way governments have done elsewhere," he says. "Sure, the people become rich, but they no longer have their land. They are no longer Indian."

The Innu are an intrinsic part of the land and it, in turn, defines them. They see themselves as its custodians, as those who protect the land from flooding, mining, and other "development." I look at our little camp, the tent cozy and warm from the light within, standing alone beneath the stars, held in the palm of the unending forest. I imagine hundreds of these tents all across the Sub-Arctic, a web of occupation and connection to the land stretching back thousands of years.

Here in Labrador, we have witnessed in one generation a process that took three hundred years to unfold in other parts of North America. And somehow, I suspect the result will be no better if the current trends continue. Although the dispossession of the original inhabitants of Labrador began soon after the arrival of Europeans, the pace quickened less than fifty years ago—much less than a human lifetime. Soon, the settlement of the Innu—their slow and painful absorption into white culture—will be almost completed, in physical terms at least.

Where once missionaries and tradesmen tempted and cajoled the Innu to leave the land, now the promises of good housing and compulsory schooling, welfare cheques, military activity, and industrial projects have all but finished the job of settling the Innu. The frame of reference for the land-claims talks indicates how the governments concerned think of the Innu. It is they who are to "claim" rights to Labrador from the government, not the reverse. But as Jean Pierre says, "It is they who should apply to us." He looks up at me quickly, then away again. "We don't object to the settlers here, but they should not take our land, poison it, then make us ask them for it back."

The land-claims process itself seems to be re-educating the Innu on how to view their own land. To all hunter-gatherer peoples, there is no better place than their land, literally nowhere they would rather be, however "wild" or unappealing it may seem to people from outside. It is theirs because they have always lived there, harvested its food, and learned its rhythms. They never dominate it; they understand it and work with it to survive. Knowledge, not control, is important.

In this context, the burden of being able to prove ownership is almost impossible and leads to dances around percentages of land already divided between provinces, just as the Innu themselves are, with some in Labrador and some in Quebec. As Jean Pierre has shown me, theirs is an oral culture. But how to prove ownership based on this? It is not quantifiable in a way Western scientists or administrators understand, yet the stories, the very ones Jean Pierre tells me almost every night, link the past and the present, the people and the land.

As in almost all Indigenous cultures, the stories that tell the history of the land are its title deeds. Not only do they themselves tell of human associations with, knowledge of, and rights to land, but the acts of speaking the words—and of listening to them—confer ownership over long periods of time. Inevitably, such ways of knowing are inadmissible in Western courts of law, dismissed as "hearsay." Time after time, consultations, court hearings, and other processes dealing with industrial activity or any other "development" in Nitassinan receive oral representations from Innu people that appear to have little or no impact on the decisions made.

The Innu and others like them exist at the margins of the "developed" world, just as we are at the margins of theirs. Yet the relationship is not equal, and from the time when I first came to Labrador over a year ago, I have often thought how many Innu appear to be existing on the margins of their own lives, too—ghosts, caught between two ways of being. The trails I've followed since have led not just deep into the country, but, unexpectedly, deep into a place of ideas and myths, language and histories that are the real expedition.

Tiring of politics, Jean Pierre leans back on one elbow, strains forward to light another cigarette, and tells me one of those stories instead.

Some people caught a bird, a jay. They tormented it and plucked it clean—all its feathers were gone and the bird felt cold. It flew away, but called back to the people and they knew something bad was going to happen. A big storm blew up. There was lots of snow and the men could not go out to hunt for food. One man lived apart with his family and when he went to look for caribou, he found that the snow stopped suddenly when he left the camp. He went back to his wife and told her they were leaving, but she must not tell the other people. They left and he killed a caribou. This made him strong again and he went back to the camp of the people. It was still snowing there and all the people were very hungry.

# CHAPTER 2

The next morning sees us back at our usual routine, lining, walking, and portaging. The valley is becoming increasingly narrow, however, and the river faster, the rapids bigger. I can see the concern on Jean Pierre's face. At every rest stop, he looks at the maps again, not to identify our location, but because the river ahead worries him. There are falls marked between us and Seal Lake. They are small ones compared to Maid Marion Falls ahead, which we know will mean a portage—a two-day trip away from the river, at least. These falls, however, do not seem to hold out the promise of a route around them. On the map, both sides are black with contour lines. Our only hope is some kind of bank through what may be a gorge.

Jean Pierre knows as well as I do the reputation of this section of the Naskaupi, and although he agreed wholeheartedly with our decision not to follow the portage route, this is a part of the river he has never seen before, and I know he doubts our ability to survive it. In the quieter sections of this trip, he has said to me that he could paddle where we have walked and lined if he were travelling with another Innu man and without our kit. The words are not accusatory or judgemental; he is just stating the facts.

Here, though, no one could paddle upstream. Even going downstream would be a challenge for experienced canoeists.

At lunchtime, we come across two surprises: one good and one very bad indeed.

The river opens out into a wide, curving bend to the west. We are travelling on the eastern, or right, bank. Ahead, the bank disappears entirely. The side of the mountain cuts straight down into the river, the last twenty feet or so nothing but sheer rock. The trees growing on the mountain seem to be clinging on at crazy angles: as the mountainside is so steep, the tips of their branches can almost touch it. This goes on for as far as we can see, around the bend. It is an insurmountable obstacle.

Jean Pierre and I look at each other, and as one, we draw to a halt, tying up the canoe and sitting on some rocks, baking in the heat. The sun is a deadening thing, clamping down on our heads and shoulders, making the smallest task a test of strength and will.

"What will we do now?"

Jean Pierre rolls out our maps once again, now worn at the edges and smudged with dirt and dead mosquitoes. He traces the path of the river with the end of a twig.

"Hmmm," he says. "We may be able to get past here, but it can only get worse ahead . . . Maybe." He sucks his lip. "We will see." He gets up and walks to the river's edge. I stare at some dried marten dung on a rock next to me, bleached and solid as concrete.

"We will cross the river and use the other bank," Jean Pierre announces, walking back toward me.

I look at the water, remembering all too clearly what happened the last time we tried to cross the river. Yet the river here looks very different. It seems to be running off a small plateau. For a few hundred feet alongside the sheer rock section, the rapids are nonexistent and the water is glassy and smooth.

"Don't be fooled," warns Jean Pierre, nodding at the water. "It looks calm, but it is flowing very fast. There is a strong current." I look more closely and see that he is right. The lack of white water is very deceptive.

"But you think we can cross?"

"Yes, but we must paddle very hard. If the current takes us—

bang." He makes a motion with his hands to signify the canoe being carried away and smashed on the rocks. "See that line there? If we cross that, we will be taken down the rapids." I look at the oddly straight line of a rapid that marks the end of the calm section and the beginning of the white water.

"Okay."

It feels odd being in the canoe again after so many days of lining and portaging. I kneel, taking my foam mat from the seat and placing it on the floor. My hands are cold and the paddle feels far too light and insubstantial in my hands.

"Aim for that rock," Jean Pierre says, pointing out a large boulder farther up the opposite shore. Then he pushes us away from the safety of the shallow water and we are out in the river. Instantly, I feel a strong surge all around, like a dozen ropes pulling us sideways. I dig deep and pull hard on the paddle. The water is as dark and unresponsive as molasses.

"Paddle!"

I can feel Jean Pierre's strong strokes propelling us forward, but they are not quite enough. I paddle with everything I have, adrenalin giving me muscles I never thought I'd feel. For one lingering moment, we hang, seemingly motionless in the middle, poised between success and failure, between knowing the security of dry land and truly experiencing the fury of the river.

Then, without my noticing it, we are nearing the opposite bank. It seems like seconds, or years, since we left the other one.

"Relax! We're okay." Jean Pierre works the canoe over to the bank, broadside, and gets out, holding it steady for me. I must have gone white, as he asks, with disarming surprise, "Were you nervous?"

Now that we've arrived, it becomes apparent that this western side of the river also has little respite to offer. Large boulders disappear into dense forest—not the kind of open spruce on moss we've seen so far, but a tangle of willows and deciduous trees that seems to stretch back endlessly from the river.

"I'll go ahead and see what it's like." Jean Pierre disappears along the boulder-strewn bank, smoothly and quickly.

It's hot, waiting, but somehow I've ceased to notice the temperature. My arms start to burn, but I don't move, as though by staying still I can calm the maelstrom of thoughts and emotions charging through me. I have a strong feeling that this may be our final challenge on the trip, yet every part of my being denies it, refuses to accept it, throws a strop, and walks away from the idea. Nothing moves. I look around the corner. I can't see Jean Pierre, or even his red cap. At the speed he can move across boulders, I judge him to be maybe a half-mile upriver by now.

After a long while, I see him again, a splash of bright colour against the grey rocks. Yet he doesn't come all the way back. Instead, he sits for a long time, looking north, away from me, a speck of determined solitude in an ocean of emptiness. I'm fairly sure the news is bad and even more certain that he is relishing a few last minutes by himself in his beloved "country."

Eventually, he reappears, the grating of his boots on the rocks startling me out of my reverie.

"Well?"

"It's no better. The valley, it's more narrow; the river, it's like this." He brings both hands down vertically, to a point. "There are more big rapids, and I'm worried we could not get past or round. There are big, big boulders straight into the water where it is deep and fast."

I stare upstream. It's true that we've escaped the walls of sheer rock on the opposite side of the river, but this bank is not very promising either. Where previously we saw sandbanks, scree, deadfall, or smaller rocks and sand near the water, we are now sitting among a jumble of large boulders, some the size of cars. They would be difficult to portage over, but not impossible. Jean Pierre sees my doubtful face.

"Look at the water," he says. I look. There are no shallow edges here, and the river powers past, shining pale brown over the rocks. It is a river in full glory, rushing, fighting down the valley, giving no quarter, offering no respite.

For about two hundred yards ahead, though, it certainly seems possible. It's no more difficult than the trail we've already covered.

"Can't we continue up this bank as we have been so far? lining? portaging?"

Jean Pierre shakes his head.

"It's a very difficult position here. Farther ahead, it is even bigger. We could move on for a while, but if we get stuck, we could not get picked up. The valley is too narrow for even a helicopter up there."

I can't say anything. My mind, as ever when presented with seemingly impossible situations, is running through all the potential solutions. Like Sherlock Holmes, I truly believe that "when the impossible has been ruled out, whatever remains must be the answer." Yet I can see the valley becoming narrower. The pasture-like pieces of flat ground that held the mountains at bay for so much of our journey have disappeared.

"Let me see the map." I know it's futile, but we pore over the well-worn page again. I recall the smug counting of pages those first days as we travelled twenty-eight miles, seventeen miles, ten. We paddled across nearly six pages of the large-scale maps in one day, carefully counting those remaining and anticipating beating Mina to Ungava. I look at our location now. The sites of two previous camps are circled on the same page. We've been reduced to covering two, maybe three, miles a day. Now, at the top of the page, my eye is again drawn to the narrow river, where, at its densest point, horizontal lines cross the river. A waterfall. I scan the country on either side for a potential portage route, but the high hills are interspersed with a miasma of low marsh and shallow ponds, of the kind that stole Leonidas' energy as he flailed through them.

Jean Pierre says nothing. He just follows the river with a twig on the map.

"Is this what you saw up there?"

He nods.

"It would be so dangerous to go on. I would be too afraid that you would be swept away, and I can't do it alone. We need more manpower. If we had another guide, we could try it, but even then . . ." He shakes his head. "Anyway, these cliffs"—he points opposite—"continue. It's an extremely difficult position." Jean Pierre looks at the sky, white now in the heat haze. "Also, I don't know when the weather will break, but it will soon. It would not be good to be on these rocks in the rain."

"Are you saying we should come out?"

He avoids the question directly, but I know him well enough to understand what he is saying to me.

I stare at the ground, my mind whirling. We could go back to the Wapustan and attempt the long portage, cutting the trail as we went. Deep down, I know that, too, would be impossible. We made the right decision there. Now I must again make the right decision here.

"Can we canoe back down to North West River?" My heart sinks at the very thought. Coming out is bad enough, but going over old ground would be rubbing salt into the wound.

"I cannot kneel in the canoe to run the rapids," Jean Pierre says. I turn in surprise.

"Why not?"

"I've injured my knee." He holds it ruefully. "I slipped on the rocks at the edge of the water and smacked the front of my knee on a rock. I can't put pressure on it."

"When did this happen?" I say, unable to believe I didn't know, or notice.

"A few days ago."

Really, I should not be surprised that he hasn't mentioned this. Jean Pierre refuses to acknowledge any kind of physical weakness and won't see a doctor, ever. A few years ago, I remember him telling me, he broke his leg—badly. Rather than go to the hospital, he set it himself between a splint of two straight sticks and allowed it to heal at home, with no drugs of any kind, or plaster.

From the corner of my eye, I see him glance quickly at my downcast face. As always, when I look upset, he tries to make it better.

"We've come a long way and achieved so much, just you and I together, I am not disappointed. But I am disappointed that I could not do it for you."

I feel my heart break at the simple kindness of those words, his eyes creased against the sun, flickering away from the emotion.

"I'll make the call."

He looks at me. "You are the boss."

"We have no choice," I reply quietly, numbed by the truth. "Isn't that right?"

*It is possible to change the direction of a bird in flight, if you know how. As you see a jay fly across a river, whistle. When it is halfway across the water, it will waver and wobble, then turn back for the land it knows, tickled by the tune.*

"I'm going fishing, so we can get something to eat."

We make a fire and have tea. I feel physically incapable of calling for help. Not because I don't agree we need to, but because it will start a long, painful process of admitting to and explaining failure. For now, that is how it feels. We have not reached Ungava. We have not even reached the George River. There will be ways of coming to terms with this in the future, and I remember George's words to me as I left North West River: "You've succeeded simply by starting." Right now, though, I don't have the energy. Just a few short weeks ago, I would have agreed with that, but at this moment, all I can feel is the shame of a perceived failure.

Eventually, Jean Pierre agrees to call, a little confused. He doesn't understand my reluctance as I sit motionless on a rock, listening to the water. Slowly, I unzip the case around the satellite telephone, our only way of communicating with the outside world. We've used it periodically to "check in" with the home base in England, to update the website, and to receive messages from well-wishers. Jean Pierre has talked to Katie and I to Stuart. Now, however, we will be using it for the one reason it was brought and the one reason I do not want to use it.

"We're not eligible for emergency help," Jean Pierre says a few minutes later, pushing the aerial back into place and handing the phone to me.

"What?"

"They won't come and get us because we haven't had an accident and we have all our food. They say it's not an emergency."

This was not something I had anticipated. I'd thought only to call for help if the situation was life threatening. Now, although we cannot go forward, we are, thankfully, not in any immediate danger, but no one will come to get us.

"Do they expect us to stay here until our food runs out and then pick us up?"

Jean Pierre shrugs. I turn and look down the valley.

Now, the situation has overcome my original squeamishness and I come to grips with dealing with it. We can't sit here indefinitely.

"Joe? It's Alex here."

"Hi, Alex, what's up?" I tell him, and it's less traumatic than I had anticipated. To their credit, neither he nor Jonathan makes a fuss, and they even introduce a note of calm to the discussions. After a short while, Joe calls me back. He confirms that as I can't get an emergency pick-up, I'll be forced to charter a private helicopter to come and get us.

"But I don't know how soon they'll be able to come," he warns. "You know about the forest fires?"

"*What?* Forest fires?"

Jean Pierre looks up sharply from the campfire, listening. My stomach does a flip and I almost start laughing hysterically. What else could possibly go wrong?

"There are over seventy forest fires to the north of Happy Valley. They've been burning for several days."

Happy Valley is southeast of our current position. There is no wind at the moment, but if that were to change, we could be in real danger.

"How far are they from the Naskaupi Valley?" My fingers are white from gripping the phone so tightly.

"Well, they're all around Grand Lake at the moment. You should be okay. How far up are you?"

"Five miles below Seal Lake."

"You'll be fine. The fires are nowhere near you." For once, his calming tones do little for my nerves.

I report the news to Jean Pierre.

"If we get a wind, those fires could be here in a few hours."

We turn simultaneously and look south down the valley.

"There, just to the left of that hill—that's not just haze, surely? Is it moving?" Suddenly, I feel incredibly vulnerable.

Jean Pierre squints into the distance.

"Maybe smoke. I can't see. Watch it."

Taking the phone from me, he says he'll try to find us a helicopter. What follows are several conversations in rapid fire Innu-aimun. After the first few, Jean Pierre shakes his head and says, "No, they are all booked up—used by the firefighters for several days."

He returns to the phone and makes more calls. I catch the occasional word in English, but mostly I can guess what he's saying, especially when he holds his knee or looks around at the nearest mountain, giving our location. During all this, I can feel the pressure of time ticking past. What if each moment is bringing the fires closer to us?

Eventually, he hands me the phone once again, evidently satisfied.

"The Innu Band Council in Sheshatshiu will send a helicopter to pick us up, but they don't know when. We must wait until one is available to refuel and come out here. It could be days."

"What about the fires?"

"There is nothing we can do. We cannot outrun them. If they come up here, travelling fast . . ."

". . . we won't stand a chance." For the first time on this trip, I really am afraid. Not just nervous, or overwhelmed, or emotional, but plain frightened for my life.

"We will be okay." Jean Pierre, as ever, seeks to reassure me. "There is one thing—if we have no choice."

"Yes?"

"If the fire comes this way, we could go in the water by the bank and let it pass us by. Here, where it's calm."

The fact that this plan gives me some reassurance is an indication of how serious this could be. Life or death. Icy water and fast currents become a refuge in the face of a forest fire.

"Sure, we won't get burned to death; we'll just suffocate. The fire will suck up all the oxygen."

"It would be our only option."

It is now late afternoon and we have much to think about, but none of it is pleasant and the fires make us both a little jumpy. Once, we hear the distant hum of an engine and jump up, but it is far away.

"Fighting fires," says Jean Pierre, and I nod, then realize that means the fires are getting closer to us.

It is an odd kind of limbo; we eat, drink tea, and film the area around, but it's difficult to settle. We discuss the fires and scour the southern horizon for signs of smoke. The weather has turned more hazy (or smoky?) and it is difficult to see. We both try to surreptitiously sniff the air, but I, for one, cannot detect any acrid note in the symphony of the forest. A small breeze—barely a zephyr—cools my face, and I stiffen, but there is nothing more.

A real tension grips the camp now, and Jean Pierre walks away downstream a few hundred yards, where he sits for a long time. Maybe looking for smoke, but I know he'll be thinking about leaving the country and returning to town. I realize he, too, must be disappointed not to have travelled farther, to be forced to return to the monotony of life in the settlement. Is he thinking of Mr. T? Probably. There have been many times on this trip that I've seen Jean Pierre standing alone, looking out across the landscape, perhaps thinking of his last trip with Mr. T and the country.

That thought just makes me feel worse.

From here, the southward slope of the valley is very evident and looks impossible to travel, despite the fact that we were doing just that as recently as this morning.

This morning. It seems like a million years ago.

Looking around, I suddenly realize that the place where we are right now has seen very little human traffic. We are probably part of only a handful of people ever to have been here. The landscape is pristine. How many people in the world have ever been in truly untouched terrain? I wonder. Even the top of Everest is full of trash; previously unknown desert islands are covered in candy-bar wrappings and used detergent bottles discarded from passing ships. Yet here, the water tastes sweet, ours are rare footprints in the sand, and the trees may never have seen an axe until now.

"We must put the canoe up high, away from the river," says Jean Pierre, making me jump as he appears suddenly at my shoulder (how does he *do* that?). I realize with a lurch that our canoe will be left here, almost as pristine as the landscape. It's true that she was built to be abandoned, but not this early. She's still a beautiful craft, and apart from a few scratches and the hole in her canvas, she is perfect. Jean Pierre sees my face.

"Maybe we can strap her to the helicopter, but for now, we must put her away."

We unload the canoe completely and pull her right up, across the shore and into a thicket of willows. Turning her over, Jean Pierre lifts her high, resting her snugly in the centre. We take the paddles back to the camp.

"What will you do with her?" Jean Pierre asks.

"I don't know." I'm still coming to terms with the idea of defeat; I cannot formulate far-reaching plans just yet. The idea of going back to Happy Valley seems strange and unwelcome.

"I could come and get her in the winter, at the first snows," says Jean Pierre.

"How?" I ask, thinking of this trip on foot in the winter. Too far, surely, even for Jean Pierre, for the sake of a canoe alone?

"Snowmobile, or maybe helicopter."

I'm reminded of George Elson's return trips to the place where he and Dillon left Leonidas Hubbard, and his ability to locate the valuable possessions that were left scattered under eight feet of snow.

As the light starts to fade, we know that for today, at least, there will be no helicopter to come and rescue us. For maybe the last time on this trip, I follow Jean Pierre through the thick strip of willows, struggling to keep my balance on the rocks underfoot as the springing boughs push and whip at me. They are one thing I won't miss. We camp just beyond their limit—at the edge of the forest proper. It's a fairly decent site, but the coming night and forest cover mean it's almost pitch black as we finally climb into our sleeping bags. I've almost become accustomed to the thought of being in the bush during a forest fire.

It's probably our last night out here, and I think of the thousand things I never asked Jean Pierre, things I know he'll never talk about willingly once we leave the country. Despite the short time Jean Pierre and I have been together, I realize it is soon to come to an end, which is a strange thought. I dare not think I know him well at all, even after all our trials together, yet I shall miss him. It has been an unusual and emotional experience—to be thrown together with someone I barely know in such extreme circumstances, someone upon whom my life has depended every day, then to lose him again, equally abruptly. In such circumstances, people often form very close bonds, and a large part of me is reluctant to leave the country and this remarkable man who continues to intrigue me.

Mina also felt regret at the thought of saying goodbye to her guides. She already misses them when, on arrival at the George River post at Ungava, she lives with Mr. and Mrs. Ford, the Hudson's Bay Company factor and his wife, while her men pitch their tents outside. Mina's diary, which she continued to keep during the long weeks they spent waiting for the *Pelican* supply ship to arrive at the post, tells us a great deal about her feelings regarding the expedition, her time in the North, and her guides.

Despite her pleasure at once more enjoying the company of other women, particularly that of Mrs. Ford, Mina finds herself drawn again and again to the Inuit women at the post and to the mountains themselves, where she goes one day alone, walking and running in unexpected good weather. There is a sense of joy, careless perhaps, that is evident as she relishes what could be her last moments of soli-tude in the Labrador wilderness: *"Moon just coming up over the mountains, very fine. For first time had taken revolver out of holster and left it behind. Thought of wolf. Decided to wave my red cap at him and then watch him run."*

It is her impending farewell to her long-time companions, however, that preoccupies Mina much of the time while she is at the post. Each of them has his own unique qualities, which she recalls fondly in her diary: Gilbert's artistic ability, Job's character and impressive capabilities. Yet most of all, it is George Elson whose fate concerns her the most. At this point, while writing the first drafts of her book, she christens him "Great Heart." There is almost a sense of fretting in her words as she writes her thoughts about his future. There is also a feeling of impending loss, an understanding that very soon, she will no longer be part of that future. In the meantime, Mina helps George as best she can through conversations, the details of which remain a mystery. Shortly before their return to Newfoundland on board the *Pelican*, she writes, "*Had a pretty good talk with Geo tonight and feel encouraged about him more than I have ever done before. How I hope he may work up to his possibilities. They are great.*"

George did go on to fulfill some of his potential when he returned to James Bay, becoming a manager with a French fur-trading company. Mina never forgot her friend, however, and shared with him the royalties from her book about their expedition. Thirty years later, when Mina was sixty-six years old, she returned to Canada for one last trip. Together, she and George canoed the Moose River, reliving, it can be certain, old memories from their by then famous Labrador expedition. It was to be the last time the two old comrades would ever meet.

I roll over, facing where I sense Jean Pierre is in the palpable darkness.

"Tell me one more story."

"Which one?"

"Any."

The only light in the tent is the glow of the machine recording Jean Pierre's voice for the last time. We could be in any shelter at any time during the past thousand years, but for that light. The story would be largely the same, except for the language he is using.

Jean Pierre is an eloquent man, but the dynamics of Innu-aimun shape the stories he tells me in English. I can hear it, behind the words that somehow don't quite fit the images. The rhythms are entirely different. The spoken word has immense value in hunter-gatherer societies: it defines knowledge, which is vital for survival. Each word is weighed and used with care. The complexities and information specific to this section of Labrador—the ground, the hunting conditions, the animals—are only truly expressible in Innu-aimun or, farther north, Inuktitut. English is the language of the law courts, the welfare offices, and the police. Its use speaks of the dominance and significance of that world—the world of the majority.

When I first met Jean Pierre, I was surprised that English was his second language. Now I understand that when these stories can be told only in English, there will have been another shift, another loss, another step toward a life the Innu did not choose for themselves.

White Canadians and non-Indigenous peoples the world over express a certain inevitability when they think about the future of people like Jean Pierre. It's unavoidable, isn't it, that they "progress" into the "modern" world? Learn our languages, eat our food, and live in houses like ours? Anything else, surely, would be unrealistic?

It is not difficult to understand that attitude, but while the clock cannot be turned back, it is not for non-Indigenous people to decide how Indigenous people should live. It is for the Innu, for Indigenous peoples all over the world, to decide their own future. It is not idealism to say this; it is recognition of human dignity.

The idea that Native peoples are somehow stuck in a Stone Age time warp—survivors from prehistory—is a theme that has run throughout all literature since the first contact between Natives and Europeans. In 1898, Randle Holme wrote: *"This interesting race* [the Innu] *is therefore, I believe, found in Labrador in a state far more primitive than in any other part of the continent of North America."* This account is revealing, as it both tells us of the relative lack of contact the Innu had with white settlers as late as the end of the nineteenth century and also speaks volumes about the historical European view of "Indians." They are perceived as existing somewhere farther down the ladder of human progress, not as a group of humans who have lived for centuries in environments that many Europeans would not survive in, and who have complex social structures and economic practices that are merely different from those of Western society.

I hope Jean Pierre's Kamistastin project will prove to be a way forward here in Labrador, and I ask him, as the story comes to an end, "What is important for the future of the Innu?"

He thinks for a moment, then replies, "Knowledge, choices, Innu values, traditions, culture, most of all identity. And a good heart. Without that, I would be nothing."

# CHAPTER 3

We wake early the following morning to the sound of a helicopter nearby. In the quiet of the dawn, it sounds monstrously loud, and I can't judge whether or not it's overhead. We look at each other in panic. Could it be them? this early? Maybe. Half-dressed, we stagger out of the tent and push our way through the willows onto the small beach where we had our fire the previous night.

"No, not for us." Jean Pierre points to a black speck moving south, fast. "Maybe checking for fires."

The wake-up call has spurred us into action, and we realize there is a lot to do before we can be picked up. I re-pack parts of our kit and Jean Pierre clears a flat section of the riverbank here for the helicopter to land on, moving all the larger rocks and throwing them into the bush.

After this burst of activity, we return to waiting and the hours pass. No helicopter comes. The heat shows no sign of breaking and there seem to be few mosquitoes. It must be well over ninety-five degrees Fahrenheit, I realize, for that to happen. A sense of anticipation sits between us. We will be rescued, but when? Will it be in time?

We both constantly scour the southern horizon for smoke. My heart does a quick two-step when Jean Pierre, whose eyes are far keener than mine, shouts, "Smoke! Is that smoke? There! Between the fold in the hills to the southeast?"

I look. The heat haze makes it almost impossible to distinguish anything else, but there certainly does seem to be a thickening—the ridge is a little less perceptible, perhaps?

Jean Pierre makes another call. We cannot have the phone turned on all the time, as it uses our finite battery power, so we can only make calls, or receive them, at designated times. When he hands me the phone, Jean Pierre looks grim.

"There are no helicopters right now. Maybe not for a while. We may have to use a seaplane."

"But where would it land?"

Jean Pierre takes out the maps and rolls them onto the ground, weighing each corner down with a stone. He points to the east of the river.

"On the other side of the mountain, there is a small lake. It's big enough for the plane to land."

I look at him, mouth open, my head spinning. Although it is only about two miles away, to reach it we would have to cross the river again, scale the cliff, climb the hill above, and cut a trail to the lake across whatever lay beyond it. The trek would take at least a day.

"How would we get the kit up there?"

"We couldn't. Just one small pack each."

I look at the equipment piled on the ground, my heart sinking at the thought of this desperate measure, the kit I would need to leave behind, the cameras. Worth thousands of dollars. I think of the months it took to accumulate all that gear, of the hours I worked—and will need to work still—to pay for it.

"I'll start re-packing."

I start to pull essentials out of bags, my fingers bungling simple clasps, one eye on the steep sides of the hill above the river on the opposite bank.

"Is this a definite plan?"

"No, I need to call back in a couple of hours to check. There are now over eighty fires around Happy Valley. It depends if they come under control, but we need to be ready."

"We can wait."

"Not if the fires spread this way."

By mid-day, the tension is unbearable. We make a final call before we refloat the canoe to cross the river. It brings good news. Unexpectedly, a helicopter will be available for a short window of time to fly out and retrieve us.

Relief at last. Once the decision was made, I wanted to come out as quickly and easily as possible. The struggle is all internal now. Yet I also share some of Mina's feelings about coming out. Her reluctance to leave the "Far North" of the George River post was, for her, eased by the two months she spent living there—canoeing for pleasure, getting to know the Inuit population, learning something of the hardships of the frontier settler's life.

At this point, our experiences diverge widely, of course, but a part of me is also reluctant to return to the complicated, high-pressure life of the rest of the world as I know it. Not just because of the daunting task of explaining events out here, but also because there is a rhythm, a simplicity to travelling in the country. Alien and disorienting though much of this trip was when I first left North West River, it all seems natural and automatic now. How will I sleep, I wonder, without the scent of crushed spruce needles and waking to see the sun making patterns through the trees on the walls of our bright new tent?

I'll be leaving the clean waters and fresh green forest for the prefabricated sprawl of Happy Valley, then later the smog and rush of crowded European cities, where the sun only reflects pointlessly off a million automobiles standing nose to bumper between tall, shaded buildings. The blare of horns and shouts of street vendors will replace the roar of the river and the high keening cry of the eagles into the silent emptiness beyond.

I think of all the things Mina saw that I will never see: the wild glory of Maid Marion Falls; the "strange wild beauty" of Seal Lake that "buries itself in the deep parts of one's being," just a few short miles north of us; the open tundra around the George River; and the polar bears of Ungava. All are now lost to me.

As I sit and write these words in my diary, I think of one of Mina's last entries on her journey ninety-five years before:

*It was such a beautiful evening too and all hearts glad that we had come so far in safety. We are now north 55 degrees in latitude and yet has never seemed to me and the men say the same, as if we were far from the world. Just far enough to be nice. I wish I need never go back. I suppose I shall never again be taken care of in the gentle careful way I have been since leaving North West River. I came away expecting to have all sorts of hardships to endure and have had none.*

I could have written those very words but for the difference in latitude.

The helicopter's engine note is at first no more than a resonance of the river itself, a guttural growl. But then the vibration separates out to something different and unnatural. Suddenly it is there, directly above us, a glare of sun on glass and a strong, hot wind.

"Get out of the way!" Jean Pierre shouts. I realize I must be standing staring, right in the landing place, although it seems only a moment, less than a second, since the helicopter appeared. Long enough for the world to change.

The pilots are cheerful and friendly. Their stocky legs are brown below the line of informal shorts. Aviator glasses are pulled off, hands shaken. They are, to my eyes, very typically Canadian, and I like them instantly. They are unable to take the canoe as well as us, however, and no amount of persuasive argument on the part of Jean Pierre can apparently change their minds. I try not to think about it. Reluctance, exhaustion, despair, relief, embarrassment are all jostling behind my cold eyes.

Fortunately, the rest of the equipment is stowed with no problem and we take off, encased in our bubble of glass and technology, leaving the land so lightly, I barely notice the connection being broken.

I look over at Jean Pierre, a little excited despite himself—maybe from the flight, maybe because of the prospect of seeing his family again. He points down below us at the unending opening up of valleys below our feet. Just a strip of metal separates us from the landscape, but it might as well be an entire galaxy now. Civilization has us. Labrador has reverted to being no more than a landscape again. Something to be looked at, considered from a distance, talked about, but not touched, experienced, loved.

"Naskaupi!" Jean Pierre's voice is faint and crackling in the headset of the helicopter. I look down again. From up here, it seems like any other of the innumerable river valleys that cross Labrador. It has sunk back into anonymity from the startling and commanding presence it had little more than thirty-six hours ago.

What is Jean Pierre feeling as he looks out across the land? I can't pretend I will ever know. At this moment, he seems animated. Perhaps his interest in seeing Labrador from the air again is overriding other thoughts or regrets. Certainly, he sees with different eyes than I. It was my dream that was abandoned by the side of that river.

The journey seems to take minutes, though in reality it is much longer. How much longer, I cannot say. What my eyes see, my mind does not register. Eventually, the helicopter banks to the left and we see the shacks of the heliport standing on the plain below. We're home again, on the shores of Lake Melville. Mountains and river have ceded to delta and the twisting insistence of roads.

We're almost landed now, the engines powering down, seatbelts clicking open. Normalcy reigns. We've been transported between worlds. When we finally touch lightly down, I can see a collection of cars parked behind a wire fence, and I strain to see if one belongs to Joe or Jonathan. I can't remember if they even knew when we would be arriving. I don't care anymore. The fewer people I see, the better. I need yet to reconcile myself to the end of the adventure.

There is a strange lack of activity, an unsettling silence as the blades of the helicopter slow to a stop. A gate opens and a pick-up I don't recognize crawls toward us, stopping close enough to unload our kit. It's a friend of Jean Pierre, and as the cab door opens, his family all tumble out. Jean Pierre moves forward to hold them, saying words I don't understand and smiling, the youngest girl holding onto his leg. I stand apart, awkward and unnoticed. It seems appropriate.

Eventually, Jean Pierre introduces me and everyone looks at me a little shyly. I try to smile back.

"You must be Mary," I say to the child with big brown eyes, who has been picked up and is holding tightly onto Daddy. She turns away and buries her face in his arms. The men unload everything into the back of the pick-up and everyone climbs in. At the last moment:

"You need a ride?"

"Thanks."

It is an ignominious return, particularly when compared to Mina's triumph. Her extended stay at the George River post was a useful decompression chamber before she boarded the *Pelican* and sailed south. Travelling on connecting ferries, she eventually arrived home in New York, where she wrote the account of her expedition.

Shortly after her return, Mina also embarked on a series of lectures concerning both her trip and the work she did while travelling in Labrador. Some commentators had been skeptical about her plans but audiences loved her, one writing in a letter, "[Mrs Hubbard] *was so delightful, casual and in places humorous. She spoke so naturally and unhurriedly that one caught every word. Her charm of manner, grace of movement and beautiful choice of gown were as delightful as her lecture.*"

Engagements such as these took Mina to England, where she met the man who, in 1909, was to become her second husband. Harold Ellis was the son of the wealthy Quaker industrialist John Edward Ellis, who later became the British under-secretary to India.

The couple were married in Ontario, the place of Mina's birth, but they returned to live in England. Despite being almost forty years old when she married Harold, Mina managed to give birth to three children, and her surviving descendants all now live in England and Ireland, bringing the family back, full circle, to its origins.

This brief period of conventionality ended in the 1920s, when Mina and Harold were divorced—a relatively rare occurrence eighty years ago. Although she returned occasionally to America and Canada, Mina continued to live in Hampstead, London, taking care of injured

Canadian servicemen in her home during World War II, donating her speaking fees to a hostel for Canadian music students, and later bequeathing part of her estate for the establishment of a college.

Mina died in England in 1956 at Coulston, Surrey, at the age of eighty-six. In a moment of confusion, she walked onto the railway tracks there and was hit by a train. My image of her in those later years, however, is of the Mina in one of those photographs filed away in the archives at Memorial University in Newfoundland: a self-assured but kindly woman striding down Oxford Street in sensible shoes, wearing a cape and carrying a walking cane. Would she be proud of what Jean Pierre and I attempted to do? Maybe. I could imagine her raising an eyebrow at our story. Would she be pleased that her journey—and perhaps, more important, the last journey of her husband Leonidas—had not been forgotten? Yes, I feel sure of that.

# CHAPTER 4

During my last days in Happy Valley, I stay once more at Joe's house. I spend my time ploughing through a list of people who need to be informed, cancelling our flights back from Ungava, and booking new ones to take me home. I eat everything I can get my hands on (I lost about fourteen pounds on the trip), and I give an interview on local radio.

Yet nothing makes an impression on my low mood. As I lie on Joe's sofa one night, watching TV (ever notice how you don't miss it when you're away, but when you are there, it is almost impossible to turn off?), he arrives home from attending a formal dinner.

"Come out, Alex, and look at these stars."

Reluctantly, I join him on the deck outside. It is surprisingly warm, and we stand for a while, just looking at the Milky Way, scattered like spilt glitter across the sky.

"Everyone was talking about you tonight."

"Oh, wonderful. Did you deny all knowledge?"

"They said only good things, Alex. None of them have ever done what you did."

I see everyone else in turn. Jonathan and Annette invite me over for dinner, their friend Guy Playfair pays me a visit, and everyone is kind. Walking along the street one afternoon, I see a car pull up next to me.

"Alex! I heard you were back! Jump in, I'll give you a ride."

It's George, the firefighter. I tell him all about the trip and he relishes every detail.

"Did you know about the fires? We've been busy as hell for days."

As Jean Pierre predicted, the weather has indeed broken and I stay inside, watching the rain drip disconsolately onto the deck and slowly coming to terms with my time on the trail. Despite the depression, the overwhelming sense of failure, a small but persistent voice inside me continues to call out that nothing was in vain, that the battle started the day I decided to go to Labrador, and that I won through. Reaching out and touching life here, in a place so unlike any I have ever known, was the prize.

Yet this leaves just one question unanswered. Is it true? I ask myself. Is Labrador really the land God gave to Cain?

God gave Cain a wilderness. It was a place beyond knowledge, beyond control, beyond the frontier, beyond civilization. Wilderness is a term used by settled peoples for land that is unproductive and therefore available, ripe to be tamed and waiting for its fate, a tabula rasa. It is the great unknown on the periphery of "civilization."

For five hundred years the great landscapes of the Americas *have* been tamed. Forests have been felled, prairies have been sown with crops. But not Labrador, not yet. Despite being one of the first places to be seen by Europeans, it is one of the last pieces of "wilderness" on the continent. Too wild, too dangerous, it has been left largely alone—a "blank space" on the maps of people such as the Hubbards.

Now, as the twenty-first century begins, Labrador is wanted—needed, some say—for industrial use. The rich heritage of its natural resources means that Newfoundland and Labrador is expected to become the province with the fastest growing economy in Canada over the next ten years. The mighty rivers and deep valleys can be used to make more hydroelectric power; the bountiful mineral reserves can drive factories all over the world. It is also needed for the practice of war, far away from the dense populations of Europe and the rest of the Americas.

Labrador is, therefore, one of the last frontiers, a line between the factories and farms of one people and the hunting grounds of another. But even the notion of a "frontier" derives not from hunting peoples but from the shared genetic memory of those who have descended from settled peoples. In this line of thinking, nomads and hunters are "savages" who are doomed, like Cain, to wander through wild lands. The very words "doomed to wander" tell of a cultural hostility to nomadic lifestyles.

Yet to the Innu and to Indigenous peoples all over the world, the place in which they wander *is* home. It is not a wilderness at all. The Innu (meaning "the people") inhabit *nutshimit* ("the country"). Indigenous groups, from the Huaorani of Ecuador to the Xhosa of Africa, often translate their words in this way. It speaks of a symbiotic relationship with the land that is central to their existence and identity; the land provides everything they need to live and it is as much their territory as is a house to a city dweller. These "wild lands" do not lie beyond *their* knowledge, or use. Every hill, every river was named long before Mina, Leonidas, or any other European explorers came and named them for themselves.

The situation in Labrador is an ancient, almost biblical encounter between peoples. This may be one of the last times it will happen in North America, so an important stage in history is unfolding before our eyes. Of all the great First Nations, the Innu are one of the few who have still signed no treaty giving up their land. But displacement and absorption have shifted and wrenched them away from their traditional hunting grounds. The settlement of the Innu and the use of their land for resource development are killing their culture. Jean Pierre is sadly no longer typical of the Innu and a new generation has already emerged, one that knows more about life in the settlements than life in the country.

With tragic irony, therefore, as the Innu leave for a more settled life and the modern world intrudes more into *nutshimit*, the country becomes more like the uninhabited wilderness Europeans originally considered it to be. Labrador, as it begins its twenty-first century and for the first time since the Ice Age, has become a true uninhabited wilderness, thanks to white cultures.

The country I saw as I travelled up the Naskaupi was full of overgrown trails and empty, unused camps. The bears, moose, wolves, and lynx now have the land more or less to themselves. Where even fifty years ago, bands of Innu travelled regularly from inland lakes to the coast and back, where trappers moved slowly along their lines, there is now only emptiness.

Today, it takes the appropriately modern innovations of the helicopter and snowmobile to travel into the country, where once it took canoes and well-worn trails. An artificial lake far bigger than any in nature has swallowed the known corners of Lake Michikamau and created a miasma of drowned forests. Rivers run too shallow for canoeists to travel. Jets frighten animals and humans alike, and many pieces of ground with promising minerals have someone else's name pinned to them on maps hundreds of miles away. These things have made Labrador the wilderness Jacques Cartier believed he saw in 1534, but it took half a millennium for his judgement to become true.

It seems appropriate that the last person I see when I leave Labrador is Jean Pierre. I say goodbye to Joe at home in his workshop, and Jonathan drives me to the bleak, rainwashed airport on the military base at Goose Bay. The anticlimax leaves me feeling empty and sad. I dislike drawn-out goodbyes, so Jonathan and I say them on the steps. Slowly, I walk into the terminal alone and check in. I have not seen Jean Pierre for several days, and already parts of our trip are assuming a dream-like quality in my memory.

"What time is your flight?"

As quietly as though we were still in the forest, Jean Pierre appears at my side. For the first time in days, I break into a real smile.

"Not for a while yet."

So we sit on the hard plastic chairs of the airport waiting room. In the eyes of anyone passing, Jean Pierre would appear to be the same silent man who walked into Joe's living room that day in July, but I know better. We talk a little about inconsequential things, and slowly the world turns once again, the disappointment fades, and my heart lightens.

The intercom distorts a voice announcing my flight and we get up, moving a little awkwardly toward the gate.

"Well, goodbye, Alex."

We have never really touched each other, but I put my arms around his neck anyway, and for a moment he holds me.

"Thanks, for everything," I whisper. Then I walk through the doorway and onto the runway. A smatter of cold rain strikes my face as I move in line toward the plane. As I climb the steps into the cabin, the caribou bone in my pocket is pressed hard into my leg.

The animal master has taken care of me after all.

# EPILOGUE

When this story began, back in the archive in Newfoundland—or was it earlier than that? Back, I suppose, when I read that article in *National Geographic* and decided to see this place for myself, I thought it would be about quite different things: my adventures, Mina's experiences. Yet it has turned out to be more than that. Labrador has taken this narrative over and given me something other than what I expected. It has taken my words and used them to tell a story I didn't know myself two months ago.

In every adventurer's tale ever recorded, there are faceless people who appear only to carry heavy bags, cook food, or translate, when in fact it was they who embodied the real stories. Whether or not Mina realized it, she was travelling not only into a physically unmapped landscape, but also into a cultural and racial unknown. Her written records gave the "faceless" people names, personalities, and desires—making George Elson a hero and famous in his own right. Maybe she was one of the first to do so and maybe not, yet her writings differ strikingly in terms of attitude from those of Erlandson, written less than seventy years earlier. Whether or not this was intentional, her work was as much about her response to her guides as fellow humans and the worlds they inhabited as it was about rivers and mountains and "uncharted territory."

Where male explorers had seen only a "wilderness" to be conquered, Mina experienced it as a home—hers, her guides', and that of the Native people she met. Her less aggressive attitude toward the land—one which she sought to understand, know, and be a part of—had more in common with the approach of Native people themselves than of her fellow white explorers.

As I sit here, writing these final words at home in my study above the harbour, where a seagull sits on my roof and tap, tap, taps for food, I look back on those days in Labrador with a mixture of pleasure and regret. Do I regret taking my canoe and pushing her out onto the water at North West River that grey, misty day in July, with a long trail and a hundred unknown dangers in front of me? No, I don't regret that moment. Because it is the most significant, enriching, and exciting thing I have ever done. It opened my eyes to realities that had previously been nothing more than remote statistics and taught me the true value of qualities such as friendship, honour, and dedication.

I do regret that we did not reach Ungava Bay, but as time passes, I dwell less on this and more on the things we did accomplish. Against all odds, I found a way to those shores of Labrador and a path into the hills. I no longer feel I need to justify the wish to do that. The almost daily setbacks I experienced on the way now serve only to sweeten the hard-won memory of those hills. To follow Mina into Labrador, to breathe the same clear air, to paddle the same waters, to hear the eagles cry and the rivers roar—those were my goals. In reaching them, I am satisfied. Yet by the time I left Labrador, those aims stood second to the desire to understand the place Labrador is today, and that is the experience I recall with the most pleasure.

Certain images of that place will stay forever in my mind. The sun breaking through and shining on Grand Lake, the first light touching the walls of the tent, the rainbow that fell into the dark forest after a thunderstorm, the perfect stillness of a Labrador sunset, and the boom of rapids softened by mile upon mile of fir, alder, and spruce. These were the moments when I felt the insignificance of our presence there and the pure thrill of existence, running away through my fingers like sand.

But the images associated with Jean Pierre are the ones that will likely stay with me the longest: the night he told me about Mr. T, the rambling myths that cradled me to sleep, and the tactful care he showed for me at every step along the way. Neither Mina nor I would have a story to tell if it had not been for our guides. Our stories are their stories. Our hopes, our adventures, our achievements are theirs, too. So the regrets are mine and the pleasures I owe to Jean Pierre.

I hope I have told the real story of this trip, this place called Labrador. I found it not in the rivers, achingly cold and clear, or the ancient valleys, or the endless hills. I found it instead in the hearts and minds of the people who live there, Innu and Canadian alike. It was they who made this expedition successful and worthwhile—a true journey, irrespective of our final destination.

# NOTES

This trip would not have been possible if not for the generous and enthusiastic help of several companies, charities and grant-making bodies, both in the UK and in North America.

SPONSORS
Trading Places, Helston, UK (outdoor clothing and equipment)
GlobalStar, Canada (satellite phone)
Labrador Specialty Services, Happy Valley, Labrador, Canada (airtime and a GPS)
Northwoods Canoe Company, Maine, USA (a classic wooden canoe)
SprayWay, UK (outdoor clothing)
Toby Jones (website and communications)
The Hypatia Trust, UK (electronic equipment)
Innu Band Council of Sheshatshiu, Canada

GRANTS
Captain Scott Society "Spirit of Adventure" Award (UK)
Himalayan Kingdom's Wilderness Award (UK)
Foundation 211 for Space Technology (USA/UK)

SOURCES AND FURTHER READING

The most significant source for this book were the people of Labrador. I have tried to reproduce their words and our conversations as closely as possible. The words and opinions expressed by Jean Pierre are, of course, his own and are not intended to represent those of the Innu community as a whole.

The second most important source were the writings of Mina Hubbard. I am most grateful to the staff of Memorial University of Newfoundland archive, holders of her original diary, photographs, the diaries of Leonidas and George Elson and other artefacts, as well as the National Archives of Canada in Ottawa, which holds copies of Mina's work.

Other writings by or about Mina include M. Hubbard, "Unknown Labrador" in the *Journal of the Manchester Geographical Society*, 1907, vol 23 (4); M. Hubbard, *A Woman's Way Through Unknown Labrador*, McLure, 1908; R. Buchanan, "Is Landscape Gendered?" a MUN paper, 2001; C. Iwata and J. Niemi, "Women's Ways in Labrador," *Woodswomen News*, 1983, vol 2, an account of a trip down the George River by a group of women canoeists from Minnesota; C. Porsild, "Coming in from the Cold," *Atlantis*, 2000, vol 25.1, a useful overview of writings about frontierswomen in Canada; J.G. Millais, *Nature*, February 4, 1904; J. Niemi and B. Wiesner, *Rivers Running Free*, Seal Press, 1984; J. Graham, *Women's Sphere*, September 31, 1908; L.N. La Framboise, *Travellers in Skirts*, University of Alberta, 1997.

Much of my information about Happy Valley-Goose Bay and Northwest River came from the Goudie family, one way or another. Horace Goudie's book, *Trails to Remember*, Jesperson Press, 1991, is a very readable insight into the life of a trapper, and Elizabeth Goudie's *Woman of Labrador*, Nimbus Classics, 1996, offers the female perspective. Other interesting works relating to the area include Bernie Howgate's *Journey Through Labrador* and *Newfie or Bust*, published by Travelling Man Enterprises; E. Plaice, *The Native Game*, ISER, MUN, 1990; J. Wilson, "Lured by a Wintry Paradise," *The Express*, September 19, 1997; R. Hanbury-Tenison, "Back to

Nature," *Geographical*, October 1997. A fascinating historical account of the area can be found in Erland Erlandson's diary as an HBC clerk in 1843, in *Northern Quebec and Labrador Journals and Correspondence*, Davies and Johnson (Eds), The Hudson's Bay Company Record Society, 1963 (Public Record Office, London). Similarly interesting are: W. Cabot, *Labrador*, Boston: Small Maynard & Co, 1920; W.T. Grenfell, *Labrador, The Country and the People*, New York: Macmillan, 1909; A.C. Twomey, *Needle to the North*, Canada: Oberon Press, 1942; R.F. Holme, "Journey into the Interior of Labrador," *Royal Geographical Society Proceedings* 10, 1887; photographs and artefacts of Dillon Wallace in Labrador 1903/5, private collection, Happy Valley-Goose Bay.

Most of my knowledge about the Innu and their history came from Jean Pierre and the report he publicized in 1999, *Canada's Tibet: The Killing of the Innu*, published by Survival for Tribal Peoples, London, www.survival.org.uk. There are many other excellent publications relating political and social issues currently affecting the Innu, their history and their traditional practices and beliefs. A good overall insight can be found on the Innu Nation website at www.innu.ca. Otherwise, Peter Armitage's *The Innu*, New York: Chelsea House, 1991, introduces some basic facts. Marie Wadden's *Nitassinan: The Innu Struggle to Reclaim Their Homeland*, Vancouver: Douglas & McIntyre, 1991, offers very good first hand accounts of life for the Innu today, as does the BBC video *The Two Worlds of the Innu*. Peter Desbarats' *What They Used to Tell About*, McClelland & Stewart, Toronto, 1969, records a selection of traditional Innu stories. Also worthy of consideration are E. Leacock and R. Lee, *Politics and History in Band Societies*, Cambridge University Press, 1982, and F. Speck and L. Eiseley, "Montagnais-Naskapi Bands," *Proceedings of the American Philosophical Society* 85(2). Many newspaper articles appeared at the same time as the report by Survival. They included "Innu Suicide Plight," BBC News, November 8, 1999; "Speaker on Innu Deaths Learns of Son's Suicide," *Toronto Star*, November 8, 1999; "Cry For The Innu," *The Globe and Mail*, November 11, 1999. Other sources of information included: H. Brody, *The Other Side of Eden,* London: Faber and Faber, 2001, an impressive and gripping analysis of the historical, cultural and anthropological differences between hunter-gatherers and farming peoples; "An Up Close and Personal Look at Voisey's Bay," *The Labradorian,* July 2, 2001; "Mikak: Inuit Ambassador," *The Kingston Whig Standard,* January 9, 1999; "Portrait of Micoc . . . ," *Sotheby's Catalogue,* September 23, 1997; Newfoundland *&* Labrador Provincial Government website www.gov.nf.ca, for mining, land claims, archaeology and other statistics; J.C. Thomson, *&* J.S. Thomson, "Archaeology in Newfoundland and Labrador," *Annual Report,* Newfoundland Museum, 1986; *Report on the Proposed Voisey's Bay Mine and Mill Project,* Environmental Assessment Panel, March 1999; *The Government of Canada Responds to Voisey's Bay Environmental Panel Report,* press release, August 3, 1999; Voisey's Bay Mine/Mill Project *Environmental Impact Statement,* 1997; E. May, *At the Cutting Edge: The Crisis in Canada's Forests,* Toronto: Key Porter, 1998; www.nunavut.com; D. Wallace, *The Lure of the Labrador Wild,* Fleming H. Revell, 1905; D. Wallace, *The Long Labrador Trail,* London: Hodder *&* Stoughton, 1907.

Readers can visit the expedition web site at www.labrador2000. org.uk.

# ACKNOWLEDGEMENTS

Thanks are due to many people without whose help and support there would have been no story to write. In Labrador and Newfoundland they are: Jean Pierre "Napes" Ashini whose story this is as much as it is mine; Joe Goudie for helping me believe in my own dreams; Jonathan and Annette Cumming for tireless research above and beyond; Horace Goudie; Guy Playfair; Dave and Ann Raeburn for taking me in; the Innu Band Council of Sheshatshiu; George Way; Bernie Howgate; Anthony Jenkinson; George Saunders of Labrador Specialty Services; GlobalStar; Jeff Gilhooley at CBC; Roberta Buchanan and Bryan Greene for the advice and information. At home in the UK and Ireland: Toby Jones for sterling work on the website and communications; The Hypatia Trust; Richard Lemmon at Trading Places; Helston and SprayWay UK for the great kit; James Wilson; Survival International; John Davies for the map and the other members of the Captain Scott Society for their support (and excellent dinner!); Michelle Smith and Joanna Tomasso for their sharp eyes; Ben Russell; Judy Stevens and Betty Ellis; Dick and Steve at the Himalayan Kingdom's Wilderness Award; Chameleon TV; Foundation 211. In the USA: Rollin Thurlow of the wonderful Northwoods Canoe Company, Maine, and everyone else along the way. Finally, thanks go to my long suffering parents, Chris and Graham Pratt, and my partner, Stuart Seear, with apologies for all the sleepless nights!